Psychotherapy and Religion in Japan

Can merely changing one's perspective on one's past lead to the alleviation of mental and physical suffering? Are our personal pasts an inviolable terrain, or are they capable of reinterpretation and revision? This book explores the Japanese practice of Naikan, a psychotherapeutic method which combines meditation-like body engagement with the recovery of memory and the reconstruction of one's autobiography in order to bring about healing and a changed notion of the self. Although it arose out of a Shin Buddhist self-cultivation practice, Naikan has achieved success in Japan, in both hospitals and dedicated centres, as a therapy for addiction and physical and mental illnesses, and has spread abroad to both Europe and the USA. The Naikan method operates along the borders of religion and therapy, inviting an investigation into the distinctiveness and interpenetration of these two domains. Drawing upon the author's personal experiences of participation in Naikan, this book situates an ethnography of Naikan, its setting, practices, and the roles played by practitioners and clients, within the context of both Japanese society and the Buddhist tradition. It is an important resource for those interested in the roles of memory, autobiography and narrative in health and recovery, the dialogue between Western psychotherapies and Buddhist thought, and the practice of Naikan and its place in Japanese culture and society.

Chikako Ozawa-de Silva is Assistant Professor of Anthropology at Emory University. Her work focuses on cross-cultural understandings of health and illness, mind and body, religious healing practices, medicine and therapy in the fields of medical anthropology, psychological anthropology and the anthropology of religion by bringing together Western and Asian (particularly Japanese and Tibetan) methodologies and epistemologies.

Japan Anthropology Workshop series
Series Editor: Joy Hendry
Oxford Brookes University

Psychotherapy and Religion in Japan

The Japanese introspection practice of Naikan

Chikako Ozawa-de Silva

Routledge
Taylor & Francis Group

LONDON AND NEW YORK

First published 2006
by Routledge
2 Park Square, Milton Park, Abingdon, Oxon, OX14 4RN

Simultaneously published in the USA and Canada
by Routledge
270 Madison Ave, New York NY 10016

Routledge is an imprint of the Taylor & Francis Group, an informa business

Transferred to Digital Printing 2009

Typeset in Times New Roman by
Book Now Ltd

British Library Cataloguing in Publication Data
A catalogue record for this book is available from the British Library

Library of Congress Cataloging in Publication Data
Ozawa-de Silva, Chikako, 1970–
Psychotherapy and religion in Japan: the japanese introspection practice
of naikan/Chikako Ozawa-de Silva.
    p. cm.–(Japan anthropology workshop series)
Includes bibliographical references and index.
1. Naikan psychotherapy–Japan. 2. Meditation–Zen Buddhism. 3. Meditation–
Japan. 4. Introspection–Japan. I. Title. II. Series.

RC489.M43O93 2006
616.89′166–dc22   2006005563

ISBN10: 0–415–33675–9 (hbk)
ISBN10: 0–415–54568–4 (pbk)
ISBN10: 0–203–42234–1 (ebk)

ISBN13: 978–0–415–33675–8 (hbk)
ISBN13: 978–0–415–54568–6 (pbk)
ISBN13: 978–0–203–42234–2 (ebk)

Contents

Illustrations

Series editor's preface

It is a pleasure, as always, to write an introductory preface to the latest book in the Japan Anthropology Workshop series, which can boast a steadily increasing number of high-quality examples of work in the field. The present volume is no exception; indeed it brings many of the qualities of earlier books into a single edition, and adds some important new features to a subject that is already quite well known in the literature. As with the first in our series, this one is authored by a Japanese scholar, but this time trained and quite tested in Europe and the United States. It is, like the volumes of Nakano and Wu, based on detailed ethnographic study, set in a sound base of contemporary theory, and following the collection of Mathews and White, it brings into print important work from another up-and-coming new anthropologist. At the same time, and a little like its predecessor in the series by Røkkum, it brings the Japanese material into a global comparative dimension.

Ozawa-de Silva has chosen for her topic a Japanese practice of introspection, known as Naikan therapy. Developed in Japan, and based on very Japanese ways of constraining the body, the practice encourages individuals critically to search their memories as a form of healing that is at the same time quite comparable with methods found elsewhere. In true ethnographic fashion, the author has tried out the practice and engaged with many others who have done the same, and her clear and vivid descriptions of the experience bring the reader into as close a contact with the situation as any good novelist might. This is important for the continuing impact of the book, for the comparative dimension calls on aspects of religion and psychotherapy that are much more widely known and therefore likely to be recognizable to, and create common ground with, readers from a wide range of backgrounds. By Chapter 3, where some individual characters are introduced, one can almost engage with them on a personal level.

Having drawn in her audience completely, Ozawa-de Silva then leads us through a series of interesting analyses that touch on perspectives ranging from the role of the body in reconstructing memory to the mystical aspects of defining the self. On the one hand, the arguments are culturally specific and deepen our understanding of Japan and some powerful elements of

Buddhist thinking there. The history and development of Naikan therapy is traced within this context, and brings into sharp focus its basic social organization, built around the ideas of its founder, Yoshimoto, but carried forward and developed through his followers. On the other hand, it also becomes clear that the practice has been successfully transported into other social milieux, and responds to wider needs. Indeed, the last chapter shows how it has even become part of 'new age' global thinking about the importance for healing of a broader spiritual awareness. In thus proposing ways of 'reconciling East and West', and breaking down divisions of their cultural relativity, the book (unknowingly) lays a path towards the next volume in the series, entitled *Dismantling the East West Dichotomy*.

Joy Hendry

Acknowledgements

This book comes from ethnographic research I conducted in Japan and Austria from 1997 to 2003. The research was made possible by generous grants from the Matsushita Foundation, the Okamoto Mental Health Foundation, the Oxford-Kobe Scholarship, the Japan Foundation Endowment, the Sasakawa Fund and the Toyota Foundation. It was initially undertaken whilst I was a postgraduate at the Institute of Social and Cultural Anthropology at Oxford University. I would like express my deep gratitude to David Parkin. I appreciate his supportive, open-minded and flexible attitude in guiding me. I also thank my friend, Eyal Ben-Ari, for offering to read my manuscript and providing valuable feedback throughout the writing stage.

Further writing was done whilst a Visiting Research Scholar at the Department of Social Medicine, Harvard University, and I thank Mary-Jo and Byron Good for their kindness in inviting and supporting me there. I enjoyed one of the most intellectually stimulating years I have had, due to their presence and that of many other enthusiastic faculty members and graduate students in the field of medical anthropology. Thanks to the Goods, I was introduced to numerous medical anthropologists with interests in psychiatry and Japan. At the Reischauer Institute, I was able to have valuable conversations with Galen Amstutz on Shin Buddhism, whose expert knowledge proved very valuable. I appreciate his kindness, interest and time in reading my entire manuscript.

Robert Desjarlais taught me a great deal about bottom-up ethnography and the importance of a humane attitude, and while at Harvard together our conversations always proved stimulating. His genuine enthusiasm for his research and genuine concern for Nepal's Yolmo Buddhist people eventually led me to my latest interest in Tibetan Buddhism and Tibetan medicine. Moreover, he helped me to appreciate the discipline of anthropology more by presenting a way of being a truly ethical researcher without being bound up in the hierarchy of observer and observed, such as when he brought one of his 'informants', really a friend, to a talk to answer questions from the audience.

My time as a Postdoctoral Fellow at the University of Chicago was also invaluable for me, and I am grateful to Jim Ketelaar, Director of the Center for Japanese Studies, whose support and conversations with me on Japanese religions benefited me greatly. I would also like to thank Jean Comaroff at the Department of Anthropology, who first welcomed me, and whom I remember fondly for an excited conversation on critical medical anthropology. I owe more than gratitude to Tanya Luhrmann at the Department of Comparative Human Development, who took the initiative to advise me during my time there, and whose insightful comments on my manuscript helped me to restructure several parts of the book.

I am grateful to many members of the Emory community, my new home, and particularly to Robert and Leslee Paul, who have been a source of intellectual stimulation as well as warm and friendly support. I would also like to thank my colleagues at the Department of Anthropology, especially Bradd Shore, Peter Brown, Carla Freeman and Carol Worthman, for their friendship and advice. I am happy to have such supportive and encouraging colleagues.

I also thank Geshe Lobsang Tenzin, Director of the Drepung Loseling Institute, for kindly allowing the inclusion of his talk in Chapter 6 of this work, and more generally for a great number of important insights regarding Buddhist thought and practice. I would also like to thank my friend, Christine Holmberg, who has been my long-time dialogue partner since our meeting at Harvard, for her honest and insightful comments on my work, and my husband, Brendan Ozawa-de Silva, who read all the revisions I wrote and gave me advice, comments and editorial support.

Lastly, I would like to thank the many people in the Naikan community in Japan and Austria who are the very reason this book is possible. My gratitude goes out to Dr Ishii Akira, who opened many doors for me and introduced me to many Naikan practitioners, scholars and *Naikan-sha*, and who spent a great a deal of time being interviewed by me; to the Shimizu family, who became like a second family to me; to Franz Ritter for his kind hospitality in Austria; and to Yanagita-sensei, Dr Takemoto, Yoshimoto Kinuko-sensei and Yoshimoto Masanobu, the people I always think about whenever I think about Naikan, who helped me and always encouraged me to publish a book on Naikan in English. This book is only possible because of their enthusiasm and tireless efforts, and thus it is dedicated to them.

1   Introduction

Memory, healing and the body, though often treated independently, are clearly interrelated subjects. The task for the anthropologist is to study them in a specific cultural context and thereby provide an ethnographic basis for theoretical arguments. The more these subjects are viewed differently in the chosen context from standard Western approaches, the more insightful such a study may prove to be. Such is the case with Naikan, a Japanese method involving meditation-like body engagement with memory recovery and the reconstruction of autobiography to bring about healing and a changed notion of the self.

Naikan is unusual in that it lies on the borderline between psychotherapy and religion. Therefore, I believe the ethnography of Naikan and the theoretical exploration of this practice will shed new light on issues concerning both these areas. Intentionally, I do not start this book with a comprehensive study of psychotherapy and religion in Japan, but rather challenge certain norms in the study of these subjects by demonstrating how Naikan views suffering, successful therapy, healing and selfhood.

During Naikan, clients, most of whom have come for the sake of healing or treatment of some kind, reflect back on their lives since birth, remembering what they have received from others, what they gave back in return, and what trouble they caused others. All the while, they are confined to a three-foot by three-foot square area in a room, separated by a paper screen from others, where they must sit for one week, fifteen hours a day. During this time, except for meals, baths, using the restrooms and sleeping, they are interrupted only by the Naikan practitioner, who comes at set intervals to listen to them, whereupon they relate in 'confessional' style what memories they have recovered and how they feel about them. Naikan therefore displays a clear intersection of body practices, recovery of memory and healing.

Yet Naikan is not a practice done by individuals on their own; it has a social presence, is loosely organized and reflects cultural conditions in Japan. Clients come to Naikan centres run by Naikan practitioners who disagree in their assessments of to what extent Naikan is 'religious', 'scientific', 'psychotherapeutic' or 'spiritual'. They meet for Naikan annual conferences, debate on the future of Naikan, write books and seek to promote Naikan abroad. Furthermore, the most prominent Naikan practitioners today are all personal students of the founder of Naikan, Yoshimoto Ishin. Thus, Naikan practice is best understood within the broader social, cultural and religious contexts in which it emerged and now develops.

In this book, therefore, I proceed along two trajectories. The first is an internal investigation of Naikan, ethnographic and theoretical, asking how Naikan operates, why it proves effective and what light it sheds on the connections between the body, memory and healing. Here I draw on my own ethnographic work, most particularly my field work experience of Naikan as a client and a practitioner, my integration into the Naikan community, my conversations with Naikan practitioners and clients, and tapes of Naikan confessions provided to me. The second trajectory involves looking outward from Naikan to the broader context in which it finds itself, asking how Naikan is organized socially and whether it is a 'movement'; how Naikan relates back to its Shin Buddhist heritage and forward to healing-driven phenomena like New Age; and to what extent Naikan can be said to be 'religious', 'psychotherapeutic', 'scientific' or 'spiritual', or whether these are stages through which Naikan has been developing.

While an ethnography of Naikan constitutes the core of this book, a sub-theme running throughout is my contention that it may be insufficient and even misleading at times to adopt solely Western approaches to issues such as memory and the body and apply them to practices such as Naikan. I am aware that the 'East–West' dichotomy can be overly simplistic and oriental-izing; in this book, I use the term 'West' not to discriminate the geographical boundaries between Japan, on the one hand, and Europe and North America, on the other, but rather as an unavoidable short-hand to indicate as 'Western' a dominant view in current social science which is deeply rooted in the biomedical framework as well as a specific philosophical tradition of development. Therefore, it is to be understood that the Japanese also share and are deeply rooted within 'Western' perspectives as well as maintaining 'non-Western' ideas which come from alternative sources, including non-biomedical ones.

Thus, for example, contemporary discussions on body and mind, and how they relate to one another or interconnect, already proceed based upon certain assumptions that the complexity of human existence can be reduced to these two separate entities. In some cultural systems of thought, the human entity is divided into five categories rather than the two categories of body and mind. Oftentimes, it is not acknowledged that body–mind is not a fact (as the current body–body discussion in neurology suggests), but rather one way of making sense about the complexity of human existence. To this end, I will delve into the works of Japanese scholars not yet widely known in Britain and North America, and use their approaches to critique contem-porary discourse in the fields of anthropology, sociology and psychology on memory and the body. I will develop this into an examination of the nature of the body, of 'body–mind' and of memory, and the organization of autobiography.

The book is organized into chapters as follows. In this Introduction, I aim to make clear my reasons for choosing Naikan in terms of theoretical interest and ethnographic value. I then devote a section to providing the necessary background information on the Naikan practice: a detailed description of the practice itself, its history and development, and its philosophy. Following that, I turn to the concept of 'mental illness' in the Japanese context, since it differs markedly from Western understandings. I then describe my field-work and research methodology, and what difficulties I had gaining entry into the Naikan community. I conclude with a detailed account of my personal experience of Naikan as a client.

Chapter 2 continues from my personal experience of Naikan as a client to develop an ethnographic description of the characteristics of Naikan settings, examining in particular how the Naikan environment is carefully constructed around certain themes. This provides background information on actual Naikan practice, setting the scene for subsequent theoretical analysis. I focus especially on the distinctive nature of Naikan's internal framework regarding meditative body practice and the practitioner–client relationship in the confession-style sessions.

Chapters 3 and 4 can be read as two parts of one theme, namely the process of the recovery of memory and the reconstruction of autobiography that takes place in Naikan, and how this might effect healing. In Chapter 3, which is primarily ethnographic, I present the confessional narratives of five Naikan clients to show varieties of Naikan experience and to illustrate the important role of the practitioner. In analysing clients' narration over time of their life stories, I draw out specifically the significant change in their views of themselves, significant others and their illnesses, and how clients connect this change with healing and self-transformation. This raises the question of why Naikan would lead to such transformative and healing experiences.

In Chapter 4 I seek to provide an answer to this question by developing theoretically a host of important and interrelated issues including narrative, memory, autobiography and self. Drawing on literature in medical anthro-pology on illness narratives (Sansom 1982; Kleinman 1988, 1991; Good 1995), in psychology and neurology on the nature of memory and imagery, and in anthropology and sociology on social memory, metaphor and the self, I set forth my own understanding of how the recovery of memory and reconstruction of autobiography in the specific Naikan setting and along its prescribed themes can effect such significant transformations among clients, with some experiences even bordering on the religious or mystical.

In Chapter 5 I discuss the three interrelated topics of studies of the self, Naikan's Buddhist religious heritage and the role of 'mother' in Naikan. I propose that much of Naikan's efficacy depends upon an understanding of interdependent selfhood that in turn derives from classical Buddhist teachings, and the focus on the mother is an especially effective means used in Naikan to bring about insight into these topics in clients. Although publicly Naikan is portrayed as not being religious, there remain many religious elements in Naikan inherited from its origins in Shin Buddhist (*Jōdo Shinshū*) self-cultivation practices. Therefore I compare and contrast Naikan's world view to that of Shin Buddhism, and examine how Yoshimoto modified the Shin Buddhist practice *mishirabe* to found the secular Naikan method.

Having spent the first two-thirds of the book dealing with the individual's experience of Naikan and the theoretical issues involved, in Chapter 6 I turn outward to study the social and ideological organization of Naikan centres. Here I describe the loose organizational structure of Naikan and its various national and international associations, and I provide data on Naikan's scale and development within Japan and internationally. I explore trends in the legitimation, theorization and representation of Naikan, and as well as issues of current distribution and staffing, conflict within the Naikan communities and the social position of Naikan in Japan. I also look at the issue of Naikan 'variants', and the pressure within the Naikan community to keep Naikan true to the ideals and methods of its founder in the absence of formalized regulations.

Naikan also has elements that seem 'radical' or 'anti-traditional', and I explore these in Chapter 7. In recent years the portrayal of Naikan has been shifting towards a language of self-healing and the achievement of happiness and self-realization that is reminiscent of New Age beliefs. Therefore I examine Naikan's relationship to broader phenomena such as New Age, New Religious Movements and the recent 'Healing Boom' in Japan, and question whether this represents a real change in Naikan, or merely one of image, ending with my own theory of how Naikan has evolved over the decades and where it is now heading.

Until now, very little of this material has been studied in such a manner. Most of the research done on Naikan has been in Japanese, and this has been mainly from a medical perspective. Very little scholarship exists in English thus far. A significant, yet brief, anthropological treatment is a single chapter by Takie Lebra (1982) in her book on Japanese behaviour. The only figure I am aware of who has conducted in-depth research on Naikan is David Reynolds (1980, 1983, 1989), an American anthropologist and practising therapist, who has written and edited a series of accounts on Naikan. *Naikan Psychotherapy* (1983) is an especially excellent monograph, wherein he presents a clear and thorough explanation of the practice and depictions of various Naikan centres in Japan. A few anthropologists, such as Lock (1980), Ohnuki-Tierney (1984), Kleinman (1991) and Dale (1991), refer to Naikan, but invariably rely upon Reynolds.

For readers who might be familiar with Reynolds' book, let me clarify a couple of points I have made in this book which come from a different interpretation of Naikan than that found in his work. First, Reynolds' title, *Naikan Psychotherapy*, gives the impression that Naikan was established and is practised primarily as a psychotherapy. I was also convinced that Naikan was only a psychotherapy until I entered the field and realized the multi-dimensional aspect of Naikan, seeing that psychotherapy may be one aspect of Naikan but one that cannot represent it in its entirety. Although Naikan is applied as a form of psychotherapy at various hospitals and is widely known for its effectiveness for drug addiction and alcoholism, many Naikan practitioners view Naikan as a way of life, and more than a psychotherapy. For example, throughout my participant observation of Naikan, I kept noticing the religious aspects of Naikan in its worldview, which might not be explicitly expressed verbally, but which nevertheless play a central role throughout the Naikan process. Therefore, I chose to use the terms 'Naikan' or 'Naikan Method'.

Reynolds also does not touch upon the issue of 'preparation for death', which I find to be at the core of Naikan's worldview. Additionally, the situation of Naikan has changed since the time of Reynolds' study, especially following the death of Naikan's founder, Yoshimoto. Thus, in exploring the religious dimension in greater depth, especially the connection with Buddhist thought and tradition, and in connecting this with other questions of theoretical interest in the fields of psychology and anthropology, this work goes beyond what has been covered in other studies.

My own book aims to remedy a gap in the literature, and furthermore to incorporate an ethnography of Naikan into broader theoretical debates. In the style of my ethnography, I have allowed distinct and sometimes opposed voices to be heard in their own words in order to retain some of the polyvocality of the perspectives of various practitioners, clients and researchers, as well as the complexity in the issues discussed. The importance of this has been stressed by recent experimental and literary ethnographies of Japan (Ben-Ari 1990). Thus I provide verbatim transcripts of actual Naikan confessions, include first-hand accounts of Naikan clients and practitioners of their experiences (such as a poem written by one client to describe his mystical experience during Naikan), and highlight a few of the most important Naikan practitioners. It should also be noted that the Japanese convention is to place family names before given names, and so I provide them in that order.

Naikan practice

The Japanese word *nai* can be translated as 'inner' and *kan* as 'looking'. Thus, Naikan literally translates as 'inner-looking' or 'introspection'. Those who engage in Naikan are called *Naikan-sha*, which simply means 'a person who does Naikan'. Unlike the term 'client', there is no connotation of the *Naikan-sha* being ill, a patient or someone paying for a service from a therapist. The practitioner is called a *Mensetsu-sha*, or 'the person who interviews', yet since they also engage in Naikan themselves, they are also *Naikan-sha*. Although in this book I will retain the convention of using the words 'client' and 'practitioner' for clarity, these terms can be misleading if they are not understood in light of the Japanese.

As the word Naikan implies, clients are required to examine themselves by recalling their past deeds in relation to significant others. This encourages clients to review their deeds from a perspective other than their own. The subjective self-history of the client, created to make sense of one's existence and past experiences (e.g. through self-victimization), thereby comes under critique. If it is recognized as being false or distorted, a new life narrative can be reconstructed. In Naikan, this process of memory recovery and reconstruction of autobiography is seen as central for healing.

Clients rise at 5.00 a.m. or 6.00 a.m., depending on the Naikan centre. They fold up their futons and set up their individual paper screens in the corners of the room. Until 9.00 p.m. they will sit behind their screens in the small square space formed by the two sides of the screen and the two walls of the corner of the room. The time frame is strict and clients are only permitted to leave for the toilet and bathing (twenty minutes is allowed for the latter). Male clients and female clients are taken to separate rooms. They take their meals in the same room, still sitting behind their screens, and at the end of the day they lean their screens against the wall, lay out their futons and sleep.

Clients are asked to recall their past, year by year, from early childhood to the present, and are visited every two hours by the practitioner for a *mensetsu* (interview), during which clients report on their self-examination thus far. Furthermore, this recollection must take place along prescribed lines. Clients choose a significant person in their life, usually starting with their mother, then they recall their past in relation to that person along Naikan's 'three themes': what the client received from that person, what he or she returned to that person, and what trouble he or she caused that person. In addition, two other themes can be used if the practitioner feels the need: that of 'lying and stealing', and that of calculating the amount of money the client's parents spent for his or her upbringing.

This goes on for seven consecutive days, which comprise one Naikan session. The physical engagement of sitting for over 100 hours in a single week is a very distinctive element of Naikan, even though there is no fixed sitting posture like Zen meditation. During this whole time the client is confined to a half-mat space, three feet by three feet square, enclosed by a paper screen. Although this cell-like space provides sensory deprivation for the client to concentrate on memory recall, it does not create total isolation. There are usually two to four clients in a room, and the fact that they are separated only by a thin screen means that clients are aware of each other's presence, though they are not permitted to speak. This space, therefore, does not 'leave the client totally alone [but] allows the client to be by him/herself in a protected environment' (Nagayama 1998: 90). Except in hospitals, the practitioner shares his house with his clients, making the setting of Naikan very family-oriented.

Highly ritualistic patterns are repeated every day by client and practitioner.

Before *mensetsu* (the confessional interview), the practitioner kneels before the client's paper screen, presses his hands together and bows. Only then does he part the screen, whereupon he repeats the gesture, and the client responds in kind. After *mensetsu*, the practitioner and client again press their hands together and bow. Then the practitioner closes the client's screen and, for the fourth time, presses his hands together and bows. Considering that one *mensetsu* only lasts for three to five minutes, the four bows by the practitioner (and two by the client) represent an important part of each interview.

A client sits upright on his or her knees in the *seiza* posture during *mensetsu*. The practitioner's speech is also couched in ritual. He always repeats the same phrase to initiate the interview: 'What have you examined about yourself, at what age, and in relation to whom?' (*Tadaima no jikan wa donata ni taisuru itsugoro no gojishin wo shirabete kudasaimashita ka?*) When a client makes a confession, the practitioner usually listens in silence, and then thanks the client and concludes the interview by prompting further self-examination: 'What are you going to examine next, at what age and in relation to whom?' (*Tsugi no jikan wa donatani taisuru gojishin wo shirabete kudasaimasu ka?*). In Chapters 2–4 I will discuss the significance of such ritualistic patterns. Their origin lies in the beliefs of the founder of Naikan, Yoshimoto Ishin.

Naikan origins

Yoshimoto Ishin was born in 1916 to parents who were Shin Buddhists by religion and fertilizer merchants by occupation. At age nine, Yoshimoto's two-year-old sister died of a cold, an event that spurred his mother to seek after truth in Buddhism. At a young age, therefore, Yoshimoto mastered complicated Buddhist teachings, and at age twenty-one, he attempted the very demanding Shin Buddhist self-cultivation practice *mishirabe* ('self-search' or 'self-examination'), aimed at achieving enlightenment. At the time when he tried it, *mishirabe* was seen as a 'pagan activity' by many other Shin Buddhists (Yoshimoto 1997), since orthodox Shin Buddhism relies solely on *nembutsu*, the prayer to Amida Buddha, for salvation.[1] *Mishirabe*, on the other hand, requires going for several days without food, water or sleep, until one either achieves enlightenment or gives up. The practice is so intense that those engaging in it, called *byōnin* or 'sick men',[2] often write out a will before initiating it, and any belts or chains they might be wearing are removed to prevent them from committing suicide.

Unsurprisingly, then, Yoshimoto failed at his first attempt, giving up after the third day. His master told him he had no chance of achieving enlightenment, because he was too 'big-headed', that is, intellectually or conceptually inclined rather than having actual experiential understanding. Indeed, it was thought that Yoshimoto's intellectual understanding of Buddhism through its religious literature worked negatively to prevent him from achieving enlightenment. Another two attempts at *mishirabe* also failed. Meanwhile, his fiancée Kinuko (who later became his wife) underwent *mishirabe* and succeeded, achieving enlightenment. After their marriage, Yoshimoto attempted a fourth time in 1937, and this time succeeded in achieving enlightenment.

According to Yoshimoto, the moment he achieved enlightenment he felt a strong urge to spread this method and to let everyone experience this. Indeed, he felt this was to be his life-long commitment. However, being realistic, he realized he would need funds for this, and he also realized that *mishirabe* in its current form would be too intense and difficult for most people. To handle the financial problem, he started up a leather company; for the latter problem, he created Naikan. He simplified *mishirabe* by removing the obligation to do without food, water and sleep, yet he retained the idea that the guide would ask the 'sick man' questions, such as where he might go after death (meaning the Pure Land or hell). By 1941 he had begun to use the term 'Naikan Method' to describe his modified *mishirabe*, although it was not until 1968 that he established Naikan's 'Three Themes' to guide reflection:

1   what one received from another person;
2   what one returned to that person;
3   what trouble one caused that person.

In 1953 he retired from his business, at the age of 38, and started a *Naikan Dōjō*, or Naikan Training Hall, providing free Naikan at his own expense.

In 1954 Yoshimoto was appointed as a prison chaplain at Nara juvenile prison. Yoshimoto initially started to spread the Naikan Method at the prison because he found the environment, with its confined spaces and isolation, was ideal for Naikan, but also because his Shin Buddhist belief was that 'even the good man can attain salvation, let alone the sinner'. In introducing Naikan to prisons, Yoshimoto had to prove that it was non-religious, and he modified Naikan accordingly. In 1957 he changed the name of the Naikan Training Hall to the 'Naikan Educational Institute' (*Naikan Kyōiku Kenshūsho*). During the early 1960s Naikan successfully spread among reformatories and institutions for juvenile delinquents, and in 1965 Yoshimoto started charging a small fee for Naikan, taking others' advice that free Naikan might actually dissuade people from doing it, since Naikan might then be mistaken for an obscure new religion.

Also in the 1960s, Yoshimoto's vigorous promotion of Naikan began to reach academic circles. Tapes Yoshimoto had made of Naikan clients' confessions reached universities, high schools and other institutes, attracting the attention of, among others, psychologist Dr Takeuchi. Naikan began to be recognized more widely in medicine, psychology, education and even the training sections of companies. In 1971 Yoshimoto again changed the name of his Naikan Educational Institute to simply 'Naikan Centre' (*Naikan*

Kenshūsho). This remains the name of his Naikan centre, and most practitioners use this name to refer to their own practices as well. Around the same time, he gave several lectures at universities and the National Defence Agency. Between 1978 and 1982 he was invited five times by NHK, the Japan Broadcasting Corporation, to appear on their documentary programmes. The number of Naikan clients increased steeply after 1975 and the Naikan centre in Nara attracted over 1,000 clients per year until Yoshimoto's death in 1987.

By that time other Naikan centres had opened in Japan. One of the most ardent Naikan followers, a Zen Buddhist monk by the name of Usami Shūhō, opened a Naikan centre in 1970; that same year another Naikan centre was started in Tokyo. Soon thereafter, a number of medically-oriented books were published by psychologists, including *Naikan Therapy* (*Naikan Ryōhō*, 1972) by Okumura, Yamamoto and Sato, and *Zen-like Therapy: Naikan Method* (*Zen-teki Ryōhō: Naikan hō*, 1972) edited by Sato. Takemoto, a psychiatrist who had himself experienced Naikan, started a Naikan centre within his hospital, specializing in the treatment of alcoholics in Kagoshima. Psychologists presented papers on Naikan at medical conferences such as the International Medical Symposium on Alcoholism and Drug Addiction, and the International Psychosomatic Medical Association.

In 1978 Naikan practitioners and others founded the Japan Naikan Association (*Nihon Naikan Gakkai*), with the purpose of establishing and securing the Naikan Method, so that it would survive Yoshimoto's death. This association decided to hold an annual conference for elucidating the method and theory of Naikan. During the first few years these conferences contained a mixture of religious, educational and reform training, as well as medical and psychological approaches to Naikan Method, but the trend gradually shifted towards medical and psychological approaches, treating Naikan as 'psychotherapy'. More recently, another trend has been moving Naikan away from medicalization towards 'spirituality' and 'happiness'. Later in the book, we will explore these shifts in detail, and what they say about Naikan.

Naikan's philosophy

A practice such as Naikan, arising as it did out of a specific religious method for enlightenment and self-cultivation, naturally has its own philosophy, serving to answer questions such as: What is the fundamental nature of human beings? What is mental illness and how can it be treated? What is the nature of our relationships with each other, and with nature? In examining such issues, we must keep in mind that any therapeutic method is fundamentally supported by its epistemological presuppositions.

As a pious Shin Buddhist, Yoshimoto's world view was in line with that of his religion. Shinran, the founder of Shin Buddhism, always bore in mind the inevitability of death. One of Shinran's well-known maxims is that 'Even criminals can achieve salvation', by which he meant that people who do not realize the evil in their minds are worse than criminals who are at least aware of their sins. According to Shinran, everyone in this world is alive through dependence on other people, and it is inevitable that we all create trouble for other people and for nature. For example, to live we must take the life of animals or plants. By nature, human beings have 'inevitable sin', and need to be aware of this and grateful for life, which is in this sense a gift from others, and consists of processes beyond our control and knowledge. In this regard, many scholars have noted that the beliefs of Shin Buddhism seem to parallel those of Christianity (Amstutz 1997), especially Protestant forms of Christianity that see 'sin' as more of a metaphysical state than individual wrong deeds.

In common with other Buddhists, Yoshimoto also believed in reincarnation. In Socratic fashion, he used to say: 'Your present situation and how you are is the outcome of your deeds in the past and is the causation of the future. So knowing yourself in the present is the short-cut to knowing about your future'. To remind himself of the fleetingness of life, Yoshimoto hung on his wall a piece of calligraphy that said simply 'death'. He related this preoccupation with death in everyday life to *mujōkan*, roughly translated as 'a sense of uncertainty', which he explained is 'to hold on to death and think of what will happen and where you will go if you die now'. His view was that to be able to achieve this, it is crucial to recognize one's own guilt. Naikan was the ideal method to achieve such a purpose; doing Naikan was, for him, to work on the discovery of the true self.

The relation between Naikan and religion has been a controversial issue, and one that will be investigated in detail in Chapter 5. While the Buddhist origin of Naikan is taken for granted within the Naikan community, differences exist between those who see its religious elements as beneficial and those who seek to establish it on a 'scientific' basis. The former tend to be those who run Naikan centres and wish to maintain Yoshimoto's original spirit, while the latter tend to be medical practitioners working in hospital settings. Some Naikan researchers, such as Ishii (1979: 27–8), Kusunoki (1979: 23) and Murata (1991: 4–5), say it is natural that Naikan has a fundamental association with religion, since Naikan is a method for gazing into oneself and religion also serves this function. At the same time, Ishii (1979: 27–8), Miyazaki (1989: 2–3) and Kusunoki (1979: 23–4)[3] also stress that religion is often attached to an image of superstition, and Naikan should avoid using obviously religious terms to prevent such potentially distorting views. Others, such as Yanagita (1980: 73, 1997: 111) say that Naikan is a pre-religious experience, and since Naikan contains the essence of all religions without being limited any one religion, it is somehow above them all.

Though the current trend in Naikan is to avoid obvious Buddhist terminology, many clients have an almost religious experience when they achieve sudden realization of themselves and life. Many clients start to use passive expressions such as *ikasareteiru* ('being lived'), *aisareteiru* ('being loved') and *kizukasetemorau* ('being led to sudden insight'). People come to feel that they are not living alone, but have been supported by all the other people around them. Some clients even feel that they are supported by nature and are part of it. The sense of 'being connected' is often a significant realization in Naikan experience. Clients become grateful of everything around them and grateful for their own body. This seems to happen especially to people who have been suffering from chronic health problems. Things they used to take for granted or things they used to hate they now feel grateful for after they realize how egoistic and selfish they have been. They often see light or see things in a golden light, and report that trees and nature and other people suddenly look beautiful. These experiences, notions and imagery are very similar to religious experiences (James 1999), and it is interesting that people who do not have any religion nevertheless often have such experiences during Naikan.

It is of note that Yoshimoto emphasized experience over theory. This seems to have its origin in his own struggles, since, as we have seen, his *mishirabe* guide told him his extensive learning was an obstacle to his achieving enlightenment. He was also in a sense a Japanese Weberian who recognized that charisma always rapidly becomes routinized, and this led him to an anti-organizational stance. Many of the structural problems of the contemporary Naikan communities stem from the resulting tension between the desire to remain true to Yoshimoto's original vision and the inevitable pressures for formalization in a movement that soon began to spread nation-wide. This parallels the processes of institutionalization noted by Victor Turner (1969) in his discussion of the Franciscan movement in medieval Europe and other examples of routinization.

Mental illness in Japan

It is interesting to note that psychoanalysis, or for that matter other schools of psychotherapy deriving from Freud (including that of Jung), have had very little direct impact on therapy or medicine in Japan. This is not because they have not been studied, or are unknown to medical practitioners and psychotherapists. On the contrary, psychoanalysis is known, but it is not widely accepted. Almost all the scholars who deal with Japan mention this lack of interest. Ohnuki-Tierney comments that 'it has been pointed out that Freudian psychoanalysis has never been widely accepted, despite the fact that the Japanese have eagerly adopted many Western technological and intellectual innovations' (1984: 84). Some have pointed out that there are no psychological training institutes in Japan (Roland 1991: 75).

As is recognized in the field of medical anthropology, mental illness is a form of illness most widely open to interpretation and to the influence of cultural factors, as shown by Kleinman, Good and Littlewood, among others. Kleinman's studies of depression and neurasthenia in China (Kleinman 1986, 1991; Kleinman and Good 1985) are classics regarding somatization and mental illness in Asian cultures. By showing the absence of the concept of depression among Chinese at that time, despite the fact that many Chinese suffered from symptoms which would have been diagnosed as depression under the diagnosis system in the United States, he exposed the medical myth that depression is universal. His research demonstrated the distinction between 'disease' and 'illness': whereas disease is a biological malfunction, illness is the cultural and personal understanding of disease. He thereby also revealed the fallacy of seeing Western diagnostic categories as 'culture-free' universal models.

Littlewood's work on mental illness and health, with consideration for the role of religion and symbolic classification (Littlewood 1980; Littlewood and Dein 1995; Littlewood and Lipsedge 1997), shows that what seems to be 'socially abnormal behaviour' may in fact derive from different sets of culturally shared public symbols among minority groups. He thereby demonstrates the inappropriateness of relying in an undifferentiated way on rigid, inflexible and Euro-centric systems of classification. He also discusses the idea of normality and abnormality in different cultures and societies and how abnormality is received and understood. These are themes I will return to in Chapter 4 in discussing metaphor, symbol and illness.

When it comes to Japan, if there is one central concept in understanding Japanese concepts of illness, whether mental or physical, it is the idea of *ki* (Chinese *chi* or *qi*). The word *ki* can be roughly translated as 'vital energy', not in the sense of an energy acquired by an individual through the consumption of foods and vitamins, but in the sense of a cosmic force localized in the individual. *Ki* can be seen as a kind of wind-like energy that is both physical and connected to the mind. *Ki* pervades nature, and essentially illness is understood to be caused by an imbalance in one's *ki*, brought about by bad habits, a wrong diet, failure in relationships or moral deficiencies. Accordingly, the regaining of one's health is a matter of rebalancing one's *ki* (Yuasa 1993).

Indigenous Japanese thought (i.e. that not influenced by ideas coming from Western biomedicine or psychiatry) does not strictly speaking have the concepts of mental illness, psychological problems or even of 'psychodynamics' as understood in Western usage. Rather, health and illness are understood as a matter of balancing the *ki* energy. Thus, mental illness is understood as an imbalance of *ki*, as is physical illness. *Ki* is not just a Japanese and Chinese concept, but is observed elsewhere; it is called *rLung* in Tibetan medical studies and *prana* in Ayurvedic medicine. Tibetan medicine is unique here, as it provides the most detailed explanation in regard to *rLung* as wind energy, noting that it accompanies, and is required for, any mobility, both physical and mental.

With the introduction of Western biomedicine after the Meiji restoration in 1868, indigenous systems came under pressure for being 'pre-modern' or unscientific, but they have never been driven out and are indeed probably undergoing revival at the present time (Lock 1980). In Japanese practice the body is often not treated separately from the mind (Ikemi 1963, 1973), so health itself is approached, at least ideally, in an integrated way, as a spiritual as well as a physical condition.

It is worth noting at least in passing that Japanese concepts of illness, whether mental or physical, are rooted in distinctive understandings of the relationship between body and mind, so that the two are essentially seen as a single interactive entity (the 'bodymind'). This complex point will be developed further in the course of this book, but some salient points can be abstracted briefly here. First, the mind and body constitute a single indivisible entity, so pathological conditions in one will produce pathological symptoms in the other, its mirror and partner. Furthermore, intuition rather than reason is the path to understanding the subtle interactions within the mind–body complex. Second, it is not a 'fact' but rather a convention that we call certain aspects of our experience 'physical' and others 'mental'. What we consider physical can often, from another perspective, be seen as mental, and vice versa. Third, not only therapy, but everyday life, religious practices and the arts (especially traditional ones such as the tea ceremony, archery and calligraphy) are aimed at *shugyō*, originally a Buddhist term meaning 'self-cultivation' or 'enhancement of the personality and training of the spirit by means of the body' (Yuasa 1987: 85), not in the sense of expanding the ego, but in overcoming it. Fourth, meditation, not psychotherapy, is the main basis for this process (1987: 207–16). Fifth, the purpose of Japanese psychotherapy is essentially to focus and positively direct one's *ki*, the universal energy that flows through everything, including (especially) human individuals (Yuasa 1993).

The Japanese psychoanalyst Doi (1981: 109) points out that the notion of *ki* implies that human emotions are in a constant state of flux. Expressions of emotion and temperament in Japanese idiom illustrate this. To say one's '*ki* dances' means one is excited, whereas '*ki* sinks' means being depressed. To say of something that 'it rubs my *ki*' is to say that it is annoying. If someone has 'small *ki*' he is timid, if he has 'long *ki*' he is patient, but if he 'loses *ki*' he has fainted. Thus, a change in one's *ki* balance affects one's condition, both physically and emotionally. Illness as disharmony is referred to in Japanese as *yamai wa ki kara*, or 'illness from the mind (*ki*)'. Madness is *kichigai* which means '*ki* has changed'.

Lock (1980: 85) explains that illnesses of *ki* symptoms include depression, obsession, neurosis and hypochondria. This may sound very much like psychology until one recognizes that *ki* as 'mind' should be understood in a primarily Buddhist sense and not in the sense of some emanation from the physical brain. Any Buddhist meditation master might warn against the dangers of psychologizing meditation. Meditation properly understood in the Buddhist tradition is not a set of psychological techniques, but a cessation of gross psychological processes, without which the true self cannot surface. Psychology in this context means the perpetuation of the false mind, not its overcoming.

In the past, the dominant perception of *ki* was to assume that *ki* was merely a part of the cultural beliefs of Japan and other parts of East Asia. In the last decade or so, however, Chi Gong, Tai chi and hatha yoga have been becoming increasingly popular in Europe and the USA. At present, there are no scientific instruments capable of measuring *ki* (although it is considered relatively easy for individuals to feel it for themselves), so this remains a spot that biomedicine currently cannot reach; but if an instrument were to be discovered, practitioners of medical systems that employ *ki* believe, this might lead to a significant paradigm shift in the field of biomedicine.

The average Japanese would most likely pass through life without any contact with Western psychotherapeutic practices. Except for severe cases, visiting a psychiatric hospital or receiving psychotherapeutic treatment would not be an obvious choice for most Japanese, even though the stigma attached to such choices has been decreasing over the years, in particular since the tragic Kobe earthquake and the sarin gas attack by the AUM Shinrikyō cult. Instead, the place of first resort for many would be religion.

While many Japanese claim not to be particularly religious, the so-called 'New Religions', like *Sōka Gakkai*, have attracted millions, often through their involvement in healing activities (Hardacre 1986); the connection between these 'new religions', healing and Naikan will be explored later in this book.

Fieldwork

My basic ethnographic method used during fieldwork was participant observation, conversations and informal interviews with Naikan-related people. In addition, I was given recorded confessions, made for the guidance of other clients, which provide a large archive of primary data chronicling individuals' process of self-reconstruction. I have also used the available written texts and literature on Naikan, internal Naikan publications and the proceedings of the annual Naikan conferences. Such sources present each practitioner's understanding of the nature of Naikan which naturally reveals intriguing issues such as conflicts, power struggles and theories of the ideal Naikan client and the ideal practitioner.

The main part of my fieldwork was carried out over fourteen months from August 1997 to September 1998, followed by a brief visit to the *Neue Welt* centre and other Naikan centres in Austria in July 2001, and a subsequent visit to the *Meisō no Mori* (Meditation Forest) Naikan centre in Japan in October 2003. In my field research and post-field research, I examined Naikan from various perspectives. First, I underwent Naikan as a client, doing a full one-week session at *Meisō no Mori* in 1997 (and another week-long session at that same centre in 2003). After that first session, I was trained as a practitioner, and I also worked as a female assistant supporting Naikan practitioners by preparing meals and serving food to clients, tasks often performed by the practitioner's wife. Through these experiences, I saw aspects of Naikan which would have remained hidden from me, and was able to make valuable contacts and obtain information, including recorded confessional-interview tapes of others' Naikan sessions.

I also attended regularly held but widely dispersed post-Naikan meetings, Naikan workshops, the annual Naikan conference, two-day workshops and informal as well as public Naikan-related meetings. I conducted formal and conversational interviews with several Naikan practitioners, Yoshimoto's wife, clinical psychologists who work on Naikan, practitioners' wives who help in the preparation of meals and the care of clients, and people who experienced Naikan, including regular clients who have experienced Naikan as often as ten times or more. I stayed several times at the Naikan centres in Nara and Tochigi for periods of up to two weeks.

Thus, at *Meisō no Mori* Naikan centre in Tochigi, I spent one week as a client and later returned a few times as an assistant in one-week sessions. At Yoshimoto's Naikan Centre in Nara, which is the original Naikan centre, I spent between one and two weeks on each of some seven visits as a trainee practitioner. Since there is no certification established or required to be a Naikan practitioner other than having oneself been through the process, my request to be a trainee practitioner was accepted by both *Meisō no Mori* and Yoshimoto's Naikan Centre. My experience of Naikan as a client and being a researcher were considered positively.

I started my Naikan practice at Yoshimoto's centre, and for the first couple of days followed Kurata's Naikan interview sessions, each time sitting beside him to observe the interview. Since each Naikan client's space is surrounded by a tall screen, my sitting behind the screen did not disturb the interview. Naikan confessional interviews are conducted about eight times a day every two hours. They are not like counselling in which practitioners give advice and suggestions. I was told by Kurata that I should remind myself to be humble and listen to the clients quietly, and that giving opinions or advice was the last thing practitioners should do.

I also made short visits to five other Naikan centres. Two are hospitals in the southern (Kagoshima) and western (Tottori) parts of Japan, which apply Naikan as a part of medical treatment. The Takemoto Hospital in Kagoshima uses Naikan mainly for treating alcoholism. The Tottori University Hospital applies Naikan as a therapy for various symptoms, including neurosis, psychosomatic illnesses such as eating disorders, alcohol and drug dependence, depression and schizophrenia. In Wakayama I visited a Naikan centre located within a Shin Buddhist temple, and I also visited a Naikan centre near Yoshimoto's centre in Nara, run by Professor Miki, a psychologist who teaches at Osaka University, and his wife. In Tokyo I visited a newly-founded Naikan centre located on the top floor of a business hotel. The president of this chain of business hotels is a committed *Naikan-sha* (person who does Naikan). He has experienced Naikan more than thirty times and his future ambition is to open Naikan centres in all his hotels. In my interview with him, he told me that a week of Naikan was as refreshing as taking a nice long bath at a hot spring. He said, 'I feel so good. A week of Naikan is even better than a week-long trip to Hawaii and much less expensive.'

Entering the Naikan community

Entry and access to the Naikan community were initiated by an exchange of letters with Professor Murase, who was the leading figure in the academic research of Naikan and former president of the Japan Naikan Association. He was trained as a psychologist and published several books on Naikan, both in Japanese and English (1982, 1996), but passed away in the spring of 1998. He was already quite ill when I first wrote to him in the spring of 1997 after reading his books on Naikan, but he kindly introduced me to a couple of key individuals in the Naikan community.

The second person I contacted was Dr Takemoto, a psychiatrist and the director of the hospital that uses Naikan to treat alcoholism, who was subsequently elected president of the Japan Naikan Association after Murase's death. I found my discussion with him very helpful, and he also provided me with dozens of articles and Naikan-related information as well as introducing me to my next contacts. He was very positive about researchers working on Naikan and introducing it abroad, as he thought that the Japanese tend to accept that which is recognized and recommended in the West. He hoped that my research could introduce Naikan to Europe and that its reputation there could then be re-imported into Japan.

Professor Ishii was the third person I met. He then became a close informant throughout my fieldwork and introduced me to the Tochigi Naikan centre to experience Naikan. On the whole, doctors, academic researchers and intellectuals were happy to speak with me and told me of the necessity of academics theorizing Naikan, which could help to legitimize it and increase its popularity. Interviewing Naikan practitioners also proved invaluable, as they taught me many things, sometimes verbally, but oftentimes non-verbally or between the lines. Initially, I felt more nervous talking to the Naikan practitioners than to the doctors or researchers, as I was not sure what they thought about the idea of being analysed by a scholar. What I sensed was that while most Naikan practitioners were aware of the possible benefits of academic research on Naikan, they were also anxious that a researcher without a deep understanding of Naikan might represent it in a false, misleading or overly theoretical manner. As much as I wanted to learn about Naikan from them, they seemed to be just as interested in learning who I was, and what my understanding of Naikan seemed to be.

One *Naikan-sha* told me that Naikan is a phenomenon to be continuously experienced and therefore it would take many years to have any understanding of it. Naikan, according to her, should not be understood through research, but through experience. By respecting such comments and taking into consideration that Naikan is a complex subject on the borderline between psychotherapy and religion, I made a conscious decision not to engage in interviews with a set group of questions, but rather to be a good listener by being as flexible and open-minded as I could. Oftentimes, sharing my personal Naikan experience was a good way to have engaging interviews in which other people could also share their experiences.

One interesting description I kept hearing was that many people referred to Naikan as 'sitting', which is a popular way of describing Buddhist meditation, especially in the Zen tradition (*zazen*, or 'seated meditation', is frequently called simply 'sitting'). They told me, 'Naikan cannot be understood by the head, but only through the skin and body by sitting.' It is certainly true that my experience of Naikan as a client helped a great deal. At the conclusion of the interview, many practitioners often encouraged me to introduce and theorize Naikan for its own future survival.

Being a female researcher turned out to be very fortunate as I was able to see the role of women at Naikan centres by participating in the preparation of meals for Naikan clients. As I describe later, women are less visible at Naikan centres. If I had not been able to join them in the kitchen, I might not have realized how valuable the work of these women is to the Naikan centres, and how demanding as well. Naikan's basis in Shin Buddhism is reflected in the fact that it is formally committed to an ideal of sexual equality. Practitioners can be of either sex and participation is open to all regardless of gender. In practice, however, the majority of practitioners are male and their wives tend to assist by dealing with the domestic responsibilities of running a Naikan centre.

The medical anthropology of Japan has been characterized by a concern with biomedicine in its Western form or with the adaptation of traditional Chinese medicine to Japanese practice (Lock 1980; Ohnuki-Tierney 1984). Very little work has been devoted to other forms of medical practice, except for some work on the social organization of mental asylums, on 'new' neuroses especially among Japanese women (Lock 1980), and on one other major form of indigenous psychotherapy, Morita Therapy (Reynolds 1976). Some of the most interesting work has been on peripheral areas, for example William LaFleur's (1992) work on abortion and its connection with Buddhist practice and cosmology, or Lock's (2001) and Ohnuki-Tierney's (1994) work on brain death as the indicator of the cessation of life where potential organ transplants are concerned. In addition to its ethnographic contribution, this book also intends to relate more systematically the question of psychotherapeutic practices to wider issues in the medical anthropology of Japan and to the conceptual clarification of the language used to talk about psychotherapeutic procedures in a society where the lines between neurosis/normality and therapy/religion are drawn rather differently than they are in the West.

Doing Naikan

Throughout the book, I will draw on my ethnographic research, including my experiences as a Naikan client, practitioner and assistant. However, for a clear presentation of Naikan as it is experienced by clients, I think it is best to provide a detailed account of my own week-long session as a client undergoing Naikan for the first time. As will be shown in subsequent chapters, I think my experiences, despite being a researcher, are not untypical of Naikan clients.

After being introduced to a few Naikan centres in Japan by Professor Ishii, I decided to visit *Meisō no Mori*, a popular Naikan centre in Tochigi prefecture, just a few hours' train distance from Tokyo. I rang and told them that I would like to have Naikan treatment. The only question I was asked was how I knew about their Naikan centre and who recommended me. I explained I was an anthropologist interested in researching the Naikan Method. Fortunately, Mr Yanagita, the founder and former director of *Meisō no Mori*, did not have any problem with this and welcomed me.

I was quite nervous on the way to the centre. After the religious group AUM's gas attack in 1995, there was a general uneasiness in Japan regarding new religions and meditation practices that required travelling out to a secluded place for a week. Upon my arrival at *Meisō no Mori*, I was taken to a small room and asked to write in a notebook my name, age and the name of the person who introduced me to the centre, yet interestingly I was not asked the purpose of my visit. Along with another new client who had just arrived, I then received a twenty-minute long informational talk by the director, Mr Shimizu Yasuhiro. This consisted primarily of practical issues, such as how I would receive my meals, bathe and sleep, since we would not be allowed to talk for the entire week upon starting Naikan. I would have to wake up by 6.00 a.m. and fold my futon, change clothes, wash my face and start the morning cleaning, which involved sweeping the garden, wiping the floor and cleaning the bathroom. I would be allowed twenty minutes' bath time, and a practitioner would bring us a card saying which time slot I had been allocated for that day. Some days, I would have to bathe in the early afternoon, other days in the evening. Meals would be served three times a day, and I would eat the meal while remaining behind my screen. At 9.00 p.m. I would fold the screen and prepare my bed for sleep. I would not be permitted to talk to any of the other clients for the whole week.

Mr Shimizu then proceeded to explain the Naikan method itself, including certain ritualistic forms. When coming for *mensetsu*, or confessional interview, the practitioner says to the client behind the screen 'Excuse me', and then opens the screen enough so that client and practitioner are face to face. The client is supposed to kneel and sit upright. The practitioner bows, and the client bows in return. The practitioner then asks 'What have you examined this time?' and the client must respond according to Naikan's three themes in order, i.e. 'I have examined such-and-such a period in my life in relation to so-and-so'. The client then explains, in strict order, what the client received from that person, what the client returned to that person and what trouble the client caused that person. After this report, the practitioner asks what the client will examine next, and the client answers. This is the format of *mensetsu*.

Mr Shimizu also told us to relax and not be bothered too much about the sitting posture. I was also warned that the first few days might be tiring, but that my body would adjust and I would be more comfortable after the fourth day. Interestingly, I was told not to try hard to remember the past. Mr Shimuzu explained that this would not help; rather, past memories would start to flow gradually by the third or fourth day. I was not quite sure what that would be like, and also felt dubious about how 'natural' the flow of memories would be, as it seemed to me that the highly structured nature of the Naikan environment would induce a flow of memories in clients that might seem natural, but would actually be highly artificial. In any case, never having experienced anything like this before, I felt a mixture of excitement and doubt. I was relieved to hear that I would not have to say anything I didn't want to during the *mensetsu*. (Later, when I did experience a sudden flow of past memories, it was like the well-known saying about a taste of food, a scent or some other sensory experience suddenly triggering a vivid past memory associated with that experience. So it was a natural flow induced by recalling certain specific aspects of the past.)

For the first day, I did not feel comfortable sitting in my small space behind the paper screen. I couldn't help noticing all sorts of sounds, such as the coughs, snores and voices (during their *mensetsu*) of the other clients. I became acutely aware of the kitchen sounds, bathroom sounds and even the bathtub being filled with hot water. I eagerly awaited the mealtime, thinking that was the best part of the day. During our meal, former clients' *mensetsu* tapes were broadcast. I found this interesting, but also uncomfortable due to the occasional sobbing and vivid emotions captured on tape. I felt that I did not want to show my emotions like that.

At 9.00 p.m. I returned to my room, which I was sharing with another woman, who seemed to be already in her second or third day. When we prepared for sleep, she helped me with the bedding. When I thanked her verbally, she did not reply, and it suddenly struck me how strange it was not to talk to anyone.

I could not sleep well that night. I was missing my flat in Tokyo and I kept noticing the sounds of people going to the bathroom now and again. Even though my sleep was shallow, I had a dream in which I escaped from a dormitory and met up with my friends, then returned to the dormitory and pondered how I might excuse my absence. Later, I wondered if this dream reflected my desire to escape from the centre, since I was not yet comfortable being in this new environment.[4]

My second day started with a headache. I was nervous trying to follow the ritualistic format of the *mensetsu*, and could not concentrate on my own Naikan. I felt irritation and discomfort the whole day. Typically, clients are told to start Naikan by recalling their early childhood in relation to their mother: what you have received from your mother, what you returned to your mother (obviously not much) and what trouble you caused your mother. Yet my attempt to remember my childhood in relation to my mother was not very successful; I could think of nothing up to age three or four. My first memory was of the night before I started kindergarten: I was very nervous and unhappy that I had to leave home and spend such a long time with people I didn't know. I felt, however, that this memory had nothing to do with my mother, or what I received from her, gave to her or what trouble I caused her.

Fortunately I had read several books about Naikan before my visit, so I knew most people cannot remember anything in detail for the first three days, and that clients find it difficult to settle in to the new environment. Therefore, I was relatively relaxed about the fact that I could not remember much. Indeed, even though the space I was given was not comfortable, I was relieved that I did not find it as intolerable as it had been described in my readings. I was content in the fact that I was able to give at least some report each time Mr Shimizu visited me for *mensetsu*. I also became aware that Mr Shimizu was not the only practitioner at *Meisō no Mori*; his mother, too, was a practitioner. I found that I was more comfortable when Mrs Shimizu came to visit me for *mensetsu*, as I found her motherly and therefore warm compared to her young son. I occasionally felt self-conscious in front of Mr Shimizu, because it seemed embarrassing to narrate intimate issues to a man of my age. Mrs Shimizu told me later that many clients had said similar things (about feeling more comfortable with one practitioner than with another), and it was good to have more than one practitioner for that reason.

On the third day, I woke up fresh and my headache was finally gone. Since the books I had read had said some people start remembering their past vividly from the third day, I thought that this might happen to me. Some Naikan clients, now in their fourth or fifth day, were sobbing during their *mensetsu*. I, on the contrary, was still having streaks of shallow memories without emotional involvement. I realized that I was paying too much attention to how I ought to behave in the Naikan centre, i.e. how to act and what to say during the *mensetsu*, and not losing myself in the process of the recovery of memory. I tried not to think about anything else except the Naikan themes, but this typically only lasted for a few minutes before my mind began to wander. While sitting quiet and closing my eyes, present concerns and thoughts occupied my mind, keeping me from focusing on recalling memories from certain periods of my life.

The day finished without any remarkable change in me, but compared with the second day, it had been much more comfortable. One thing I noticed was that I did not feel isolated at all, despite being confined to a small space behind a screen. There were always the daily household sounds of someone coughing, the cooking in the kitchen, the laundry machine and so on, to remind me that I was not alone.

The fourth day went quite smoothly, and held a significant realization for me. At the beginning, I was a little sleepy and noticed the sound of the rain outside. Then, while recalling one incident, I came to see that Naikan's first theme ('What did you receive from this person?') and third theme ('What kind of trouble did you cause this person?') could be seen as two sides of the same coin. It really depended on how one interpreted the event and occasion. The specific incident I was recalling was in regard to my father while I was a Master's student in the UK. I had wanted a copy of Merleau-Ponty's *Phenomenology of Perception* in Japanese, since I wished to read it through quickly and my reading speed was much faster in Japanese. I rang my father and asked him to search for the book and airmail it to me as soon as possible. Since the book was not available where he was, he eventually asked my brother to find it and ship it to me. My father must have looked for the book in five or more bookstores in vain, and after that my brother had to search for it. Even worse, the book had cost over £70.

Initially, I had been recalling this incident under the first theme of 'What did I receive from this person [my father]', but as I did so it became clear to me that this was also a source of trouble I had caused him (the third theme), since after all I could have simply borrowed the book from the library and read it in English. Instead, I had wasted his time and money, just in order to save some time and effort on my part. That was the moment when it struck me how complex and penetrating Naikan's three themes really are. Although they appear simple and self-evident, I realized suddenly that there is nothing self-evident about them at all. It all depends, I felt, on the level of one's understanding and interpretation of the situation. Depending on one's perspective, the same situation could be seen as something one received from another or some trouble one caused another. When I came to this realization, I felt how dependent I was, how often I had troubled other people, and how supportive they were regardless of my selfishness, and how they went to great lengths to help me. I was stunned by the fact that I could not live without relying on other people.

Despite this key realization, I was still frustrated by my slow progress. I was distressed by not being able to remember incidents as vividly as other clients. Each time I listened to the confession tapes during meals, I was inspired by their clarity and sincerity in recalling the past. In contrast, I felt like I was still scratching the surface. I comforted myself in thinking that at least I was more concentrated than in the first few days, and that this was why it felt that time was passing more quickly.

The morning of the fifth day was very chilly. I wrapped myself with the provided blanket. By then, my tendency to overanalyse myself and constant questioning of how my mind was working (second guessing my thoughts, wondering how I was being influenced by the confessional tapes being broadcast at meals, etc.) was beginning to cease, and I hoped I could simply concentrate on doing Naikan. While recalling memories in relation to my younger brother, I realized how selfish I was and the next thing I knew, a tear fell from my face. Even more surprisingly, I cried during the *mensetsu* in front of Mr Shimizu. Instead of feeling embarrassed, it was cathartic. Breaking the notion that crying was equivalent to being ashamed made me feel free, as if I had removed one layer of a mask I wore in front of others. I realized how people can develop so many masks as they grow, even forgetting how to remove them, since the masks become such a natural part of their identities.

Everyone who was on their fifth day of Naikan was asked for an individual session with Mr Shimizu that evening. When my turn came, I went to Mr Shimizu's office. There, he advised me to try making short reports without any interpretation. For example, instead of justifying my misbehaviour as warranted by others' misbehaviour towards me, I should just acknowledge my own part and leave out the rest. Excuses, self-justification and explanation should be left out, since Naikan involves only concentrating on the three themes. Mr Shimizu used the example of a baseball commentary: 'The pitcher throws the ball, the catcher misses the catch, and the batter runs'. The addition of explanation or justification only dilutes the purpose of Naikan and prevents the client from facing the 'mere facts'.

I found this interesting, since I hadn't been aware that I was doing that. I had merely assumed that I had to make my narrative intelligible to the listener. The desire to control the narration and have it 'make sense' to the listener was so natural that it was difficult to stop. Yet I realized self-justification blocks the process of Naikan, because even when we realize the trouble we caused others, we immediately try to make sense of why we did it, and end up justifying our behaviour instead of acknowledging it. Thus, we might say 'I was late in meeting him, *but* this was because the train was not running on schedule'. What Naikan seeks to effect in the client is the ability to see what it is like to wait for someone else and not know the reason why that person is late. Even if it was not our intention to cause trouble, we still need to recognize that trouble was in fact caused for that person. I started realizing how difficult it is to see the same situation from another person's perspective.

I woke up in the middle of my dream on the sixth day, a sign that I was starting to feel very comfortable sleeping at the Naikan centre. I started doing Naikan in relation to my mother for the second time. It is often recommended by the practitioner to repeat the same theme in relation to the same person, especially as the first two days of Naikan are usually lacking in depth and concentration. The day went uneventfully, but in the evening a sense of gratitude towards my mother started to overwhelm me, and my body began to feel very warm. As if re-experiencing my childhood with my mother in an enjoyable way, memories of my past were like a nostalgic film, in which I could taste my mother's cooking, feel the warmth of her palm. My whole way of recalling the past changed, from a passive and detached view to an active engagement in which I re-experienced the past and felt my mother's existence.

I also had a new realization, namely that I had used to think of my mother as a superwoman who could do everything: cook, sing, arrange flowers, write calligraphy, teach. Somehow I had lost that respect for her and begun to look down on all the things she did. I became a person who could not cook, wrote calligraphy badly, and had no interest in flower arrangement or singing. I was shocked by what I had been doing unconsciously all these years, without even thinking I had a problem with my mother. Later that day, I started remembering all the great food my mother had cooked for us and again I realized how ungrateful I was to her. It had all been tasty, but I never appreciated it. I was disturbed by my new discovery, but it was time to go to sleep.

The final morning began. I woke early after having several dreams. In one of them, my parents were reading books in small and uncomfortable chairs. When I suggested that they buy better chairs, or a sofa, they replied that it was their sofa I was sleeping on as a bed. I felt embarrassed that I had been happily using their sofa as a bed without even noticing; at the same time, I was angry at them for never having told me.

While continuing Naikan in relation to my mother, I realized that it had been about the time I had started high school when I started showing less respect to my mother. When I was small, my mother was like a hero, but by the time I started high school, I started to feel that my knowledge exceeded that of my mother, and I stopped respecting her. I thought she was boring, moralistic and unphilosophical. I then remembered that she started private tuition as a side job when I started high school in order to save up money for university fees for me and my brother and sister. Every day she taught in the evening and at night, and she still cooked for us every day. I, on the other hand, never cooked dinner, not even once.

I then recalled that after dinner, whenever I had tried to chat with my mother, she used to say 'Go upstairs and study', which I had always taken as a sign of rejection. It became clear to me that my feelings of rejection had convinced me that she was an uninteresting person to talk with. I was stunned by my childishness and also shocked that I had not noticed the simple fact that she must have been tired after all that teaching and cooking. The end of dinner did not yet represent the end of the day for her, for she had still to mark more than fifty students' quizzes and prepare for the next day's teaching, activities that would keep her up until midnight. I had thought I was a child who loved her parents, but although I was thankful to my mother, I had failed to recognize her as an interesting, wonderful person. I realized that my refusal to do so was a response to my feelings about her not recognizing and accepting me. This was a major realization that came to me during Naikan, and it only started on the final day.

My Naikan continued until lunch time, after which I was asked to write my comments on my Naikan experience, including what I appreciated and what I might suggest changing. After this, I met with Mr Shimizu for *zadankai*, a discussion. Later, I would learn that during *zadankai*, clients completing Naikan sit in a circle with the practitioner(s) and exchange their opinions and feelings after Naikan. The practitioner never asks the name of clients or refers to them by name when asking questions. After a week of total silence (except for the brief *mensetsu* sessions), people are usually very happy to express their feelings. In my case, however, since there was only one other person who finished Naikan on that day, I had a personal interview with Shimizu. He asked me how I felt after my week of Naikan, and what I thought about Naikan. I told him that the biggest turning point during my Naikan was when I realized my lack of respect and gratitude toward my mother. The *zadankai* took about fifteen minutes, and that was the completion of my Naikan session.

This concludes the description of my experience as a Naikan client. With this description in mind, and keeping in mind the theoretical issues outlined above, we can now turn to a deeper examination of the Naikan client's experience by investigating the unique features of the Naikan setting.

Plate 1.1 Ishin Yoshimoto, the founder of Naikan. Taken from Yoshimoto's Naikan centre in Nara. The inscription reads Nai Kan from right to left.

Plate 1.2 The entrance gate to Yoshimoto's Naikan centre in Nara. The inscription on the right reads Shin-shū Naikan Ji (Shin Buddhist Naikan Temple). The left reads Naikan Kenshūsho (Naikan Centre).

2   Enclosed silence, sacred space

Death, meditation and confession in the Naikan environment

The setting of Naikan is one of its central and most important aspects. Carefully constructed and regulated in almost every regard, its particular environment of highly structured freedom creates the Naikan experience for the client. There is the restriction of speech, the restriction of space, the restriction of choice with regard to where and when one eats, sleeps or bathes. There is sensory deprivation, a carefully structured time schedule, prescribed rituals involving body practice, prescribed ways of remembering the past. There are the inputs of soothing music played in the morning, and at some centres recorded Naikan confessional tapes during meal times. This is a highly controlled environment, an environment of enclosed silence and sacred space.

In this chapter I will explore how this takes place. I begin with the theme of death and rebirth, symbolized in Naikan through its small enclosed areas for clients and the silence they are required to maintain. Although death has never been discussed before with regard to Naikan, it lies at the core of Naikan practice, a fact evidenced by the striking parallels between the experiences of Naikan clients and those of near-death survivors. I then turn to the issues of meditation and the body. Naikan practice necessitates a demanding bodily engagement, and this calls for an enquiry into similarities with meditation practices, as well as into the issues of the body, embodiment and the mind–body relationship in both Western and Japanese philosophical traditions. Following this, I will examine the client–practitioner relationship. It is the practitioner who creates the Naikan environment for the client, but the practitioner's role is not quite the idealized depiction given by practitioners themselves. Lastly I will examine the *mensetsu* interview between client and practitioner, comparing it with Catholic confession and psycho-analysis. I will conclude by compiling the ways in which all these aspects of the Naikan environment help shape the process of narrative self-disclosure and reconstruction of autobiography.

Death as the essence of Naikan

There is a well-known saying of Yoshimoto: 'Do Naikan as an engagement with death' (*Shi wo toritsumete Naikan seyo*). When conducting Naikan,

Yoshimoto used to ask questions such as 'If you died now, where would you go?' and 'For what purpose were human beings born?' Initially, I held such phrases to be merely a reflection of his religious beliefs.

I took Yoshimoto's saying to mean that one must do Naikan 'as if one were dead', a favoured concept among Japanese indicating one's strong commitment in dealing with something. Since I was not asked questions like Yoshimoto's at the *Meisō no Mori* Naikan centre, I assumed they were simply statements of his personal values, and not to be taken too seriously. Indeed, few Naikan clients told me that they were asked any question which had anything to do with death (I know of only one person who encountered such a question during her week of Naikan). However, once I began interviewing Naikan practitioners and medical doctors who conduct Naikan at their hospitals, I realized that the death aspect of Naikan, though hidden for the most part, is still of great importance. The thought first came to me when I saw the calligraphy of the single word *shi*, or 'death', hanging on the wall of Yoshimoto's living room at the Naikan centre in Nara. When I asked his wife Kinuko about it, she said that death is what Naikan is about.

For some reason, this element of death has not been studied, or even mentioned, up to now – neither in Reynolds's work, nor in other academic writing on Naikan. It is not emphasized at Naikan centres, and practitioners no longer directly ask questions like Yoshimoto's. Nevertheless, so many clients report a 'rebirth experience' during or after Naikan that it is evident that the notion of death lies at the core of Naikan. In fact, as I will show, it is integrated into the whole setting of Naikan, and may be seen as the essence of Naikan.

Takemoto Takahiro (1978), a medical doctor and the leading figure in introducing Naikan to hospitals, explains the purpose of Naikan from his experience of seeing many clients on their deathbed. When patients realize they are about to die, Takemoto says, they often reflect on their life and whether they had been kind to other people or had hurt them. For many of them, their final words are 'Thank you very much' or 'Please look after those who will be left behind'. Such a life-review enables one to reflect on what kind of person one was in life, and what one should have or could have done in the past; it is a serious self-examination, which most people will have at one point in their life. Yet it is also rather late to have this experience in the final moments before death. Rather, it should be done in the midst of life, and this is where Takemoto sees the purpose of Naikan (Takemoto 1978: 104–5). Naikan is thus a preliminary facing of death, and, if done deeply enough, actually eventuates an experience of fundamental renewal, described by clients and practitioners alike as 'rebirth'.

Tomb and womb

Naikan's function as a 'preparation for death' is centred around its carefully constructed environment. There are several interesting opinions about the tiny space created by the screen, which is in fact called 'sacred space' (*hōza*). Two Naikan practitioners, Dr Takemoto and Professor Ishii, have described it to me as a 'womb environment'. Later, a woman told me about an experience she had when doing Naikan for the third time. Upon sitting down behind the screen on the first day, she felt so relaxed, warm and happy that she could return to that space that she began to cry. When I told her of the 'womb environment' idea, she thought it described her situation. Ishii told me that he realized that the recovery of very early memories often deepens Naikan, and so he conducts 'womb Naikan' occasionally as a part of the standard Naikan practice. He has clients wrap themselves up in a blanket and lie on the floor until 'they are born', a process that takes about three hours.

At the same time, the Naikan setting is constructed so as to create a death-bed or tomb-like environment. Clients are isolated from daily reality and activities for seven days in a tiny space in which one must sit still – a situation that resembles that of lying in a death bed. One practitioner even describes the situation in Naikan by saying, 'Your consciousness is dead even though your body is still alive'. Other practitioners say that during Naikan one's 'ego' dies, whereupon one can achieve unexpected awareness. (Here, it is to be noted that 'ego' or *ga* in this context refers to a self-centred sense of oneself, rather than the more general term 'ego' employed in Western psychology. Although self-centredness can certainly be found across cultures, there may be more consensus in Japan that a self-cherishing mental attitude is not to be viewed positively.) Of course, people dying or having near-death experiences supposedly become free from the so-called 'ego', but in a Western context it might not be considered that one's 'ego' is dead, or expressed in such language.

The opposing symbols in Naikan of 'womb' and 'tomb', birth and death, synthesize to form a new symbol – that of rebirth. The pattern of passing through death to achieve new life has obvious parallels in religious traditions – resurrection, rebirth, reincarnation or enlightenment – but also in Jungian psychology and various forms of psychotherapy. It also no doubt reflects Naikan's development out of *mishirabe*, in which deprivation of food, sleep and personal contact was extremely severe, much more so than in Naikan, and could even lead to suicide. Yet what is interesting in the case of Naikan is how this theme is symbolized and constructed in a specific space, and that it continues to be experienced even after practitioners have stopped directing clients to view Naikan in this way by using 'death' language.

This 'tomb and womb' environment recalls Van Gennep's (1960) concept of 'liminality' as an intermediary stage in a rite of passage consisting of separation, liminality and reintegration. Liminality is therefore a borderline state, after separation but before reintegration, and Van Gennep explains that in some African tribal groups boys in this second stage are indeed seen as 'dead'. Later, Turner (1969) extended Van Gennep's notion of liminality further in his discussion of communitas, arguing that liminality itself tends to become religious or semi-religious in complex industrial societies. In Naikan, clients undergo a week-long separation from wider society and even from each other during which they seek, and sometimes experience, transformation before being reintegrated back into society.

Naikan's confined space also brings to mind Japanese mourning rituals. This is a point developed and argued by the psychologist and Naikan scholar Takino Isao (1980). When people are in mourning, they confine themselves in the house and spend time thinking about the dead. However, they are not only feeling sorrow, but also a strong need to unify themselves with the deceased by reflecting on their past relationship with that person. By requiring clients to undergo a sustained examination of relationships with significant others, Naikan recreates this aspect of the mourning ritual. Both Kawahara (1996: 60) and Takino (1980: 58) describe life as a succession of losses from birth to death, and Takino argues that whether or not such losses continue to create anxiety and pain for us depends on how we accept such experiences and whether they make our hearts richer or poorer. What is necessary, he argues, is knowing *mujō*, uncertainty or transience. Therefore, accepting one's mortality and approaching death is the ultimate essence of Naikan for him.

In taking this route, Takino is following a course set out by Yoshimoto, who emphasized the importance of *mujōkan*, which he interpreted to mean feeling the transience of this life and this world and having an earnest anxiety about what will happen to us if we die at this moment (Yoshimoto 1978b: 32). Nowadays, Yoshimoto's sayings are not overtly expressed in contemporary Naikan practice, yet as shown in Takino's thought the attitudes still exist underneath.

This approach to death must be understood, however, in its Japanese context, in which it connects with a host of other self-cultivation practices regarding the 'loss of self'. Such practices include fasting, Zen meditation, the way (*michi*) and others. The Buddha taught 'Of all footprints, those of the elephant are supreme. Of all meditations, meditation on impermanence is supreme.' Rather than a state of being dead, then, it is a dynamic process of losing one's 'self'. Clients are separated from daily life and exist in this tomb-like environment as if facing death or engaging in a mourning ritual, so that they experience, in the psychologist Wakayama's (1982: 22) words, 'a life of dying', whereafter they return to daily life as persons reborn.

Clients who achieve 'deep' Naikan may reach a state of feeling ready to die at any moment. This was viewed positively by Yoshimoto, who used to say, 'Concentrate on Naikan each second, since we never know when we are going to die'. Most clients, however, cannot bring themselves to this state of consciousness or maintain it permanently. The result is a more temporary experience that has some interesting parallels in studies of near-death experiences.

Naikan and near-death experiences

Near-death experiences are usually the result of clinical death during surgery or in the course of an accident, despite which the person survives.[1] While Naikan does not include any extreme physical states in its clients, there is a striking similarity in the language used by near-death survivors and Naikan clients to describe the 'outer limits' of their respective experiences.

For example, many Naikan clients report that they see a bright light during Naikan, one of the most recognized phenomena in near-death experiences. Kübler-Ross (1997: 141) explains that once the person having a near-death experience passes some symbol of shifting (such as a tunnel, gate or bridge), they see a light which is utterly bright and whiter than white. As they approach this light, they are wrapped in an unconditional love, and during this time they do not fear death and have a feeling of omniscience.

What is interesting is that in front of this light the person is questioned about what he or she has done. The person recognizes the wrong decisions and mistakes made during life, how others suffered so much because of such choices and that what is of utmost importance is love (Kübler-Ross 1997: 142). Such realizations are very similar to those made by Naikan clients. Furthermore, research on the flashback experience of near-death survivors reveals many cases in which a whole life-review takes place from early life up to the time of the experience. People experiencing this may also become aware of what they should have done in past situations and what troubles they caused others. For that one moment, they are able to review their life from a non-egocentric perspective. The nature and context of such flashback experiences shares a remarkable amount with the recovery of memory triggered by Naikan practice. Naikan seems to be a method which brings clients to the point of being able to look back upon their life as people may naturally do when they know they are dying soon.

This may not be surprising when we remember that Naikan's roots lie in an ascetic, self-enlightenment practice of Shin Buddhism. In the context of the belief in reincarnation, one wants to achieve a better life before this life ends, since if one does not 'purify' one's karma, one would have an even harder time in the next life. However, a full exploration of Naikan's heritage in Shin Buddhism will be reserved for Chapter 5.

Later in this book I will link this phenomenon of death and rebirth to the discovery of one's autobiographical memory. I expect Naikan's special environment has a great effect on the way one's memory is recalled. First, however, it remains to continue our examination of the Naikan setting by turning to the issue of meditation and bodily engagement.

Meditation and the body

Naikan has many similarities to forms of meditation in that it requires bodily engagement for long periods of time and aims at achieving a state of altered consciousness and self-awareness. These similarities have been noted by both scholars writing on Naikan (Ishida 1984) and Naikan practitioners (Usami 1978: 176, 1980: 84). Like Japanese forms of meditation, Naikan uses a method of 'starting with the form (*kata*)'. This means that one's activities, physical mobility and posture, and environment are all determined in advance, and this 'form' must be followed in order to begin the practice.

Of course, the word 'meditation' does not refer to a single practice or purpose, but encompasses a range of activities. Meditation is often equated with religion, especially with Buddhism, but it is also increasingly being used in secular contexts and in medical settings for its health benefits (Benson 1975; Kabat-Zinn 1990). For some, meditation means specific self-cultivation methods such as Zen or yoga; for others, a gateway to escape a hectic and busy daily life or a way of quiet reflection. Forms of meditation can also be seen as kinds of psychotherapy or health practice. Meditation, then, includes numerous kinds of methods, and the 'form' itself varies in each meditation. Some forms take moving postures (such as Theravada Buddhist 'walking meditation') and others take sitting silently in a certain posture as the norm (Ando 1995: 20). For many Japanese, however, meditation tends to mean Zen-style meditation, which requires sitting in silence for a period of time. All these forms of meditation, however, centre on the practice of working on both body and mind together, asserting explicitly or implicitly their unity. This is especially true in Asian forms of meditative practice in which a combination of techniques – typically involving breathing, silence, posture and sensory deprivation – are employed to gain direct insight into the nature of the self.

Such restrictive forms may not sound appealing, but the idea of being confined in a remote place is not unfamiliar to many Japanese. Japan has traditions of self-cultivation such as Zen and *misogi*, or ritual ablutions (Takeuchi 1997: 3; Horii 1982: 19) that involve leaving one's daily life, confining oneself and sitting still for a period of time. Such practice is reported as involving an initial period of physical and psychic discomfort, succeeded by a gradual settling that eventually ushers in a meditative state. However, for many it is not so easy to do this. Yokoyama (1978: 105–6) has reported that more than 50 per cent of Naikan clients experience difficulty in settling, and teenagers find it more difficult than elderly people. Ishida writes:

> The first two or three days of Naikan is the time where clients reveal several resistances of the 'ego', such as difficulty in recalling memories, a difficulty in self-reproachful thinking and a defiant attitude toward the practitioner ... For two or three days, clients unconsciously strongly resist self-reproachful thinking. However, after the first three days self-reproachful thinking becomes easy and memory recall becomes active. Furthermore, the state of deep Naikan is very similar to the state of a hypnotic trance, namely the state where all resistance has been overcome.
>
> (Ishida 1984: 123)

A similar type of experiential cycle is also reported in Morita therapy (Reynolds 1976) in which enforced bed rest of seven days is the initial method of breaking the normal patterns of the patient's life and enforcing a solitude (usually in a hospital setting) undisturbed by any form of exercise, reading, watching television or other distractions.

Here, too, Naikan maintains a connection to its past in the Shin Buddhist practice of *mishirabe*. *Mishirabe* literally means 'self-examination'; the first word *mi* can mean 'self', 'body' or 'mind and body'. Naikan's interesting characteristic (especially when it is applied as a 'therapy') is that sitting in the same space is considered the appropriate approach to the physical body and, as the word *mishirabe* suggests, it deals with the whole human existence including body, mind and spirit (Miki and Kuroki 1998: 284). The element of 'body practice' in Naikan, then, concerns itself not only with the physical body, but with a concept of body that goes beyond the physical. To explore this issue, we will have to turn to both Western and Eastern philosophical traditions dealing with the issue of the body.

Understanding the body and mind in Naikan

The body has always been a mystery for human beings. In the Western philosophical tradition, it has long been viewed negatively in comparison to concepts such as the 'mind' or 'soul'. For Plato the etymology of the word suggests a view that the body (Greek *soma*) is the tomb (*sema*) of the soul, which was placed there for its punishment.[2] Later, the dualism of body and soul, whereby the body is seen as gross matter and even as evil, preventing the purification of the soul until its liberation by death, was inherited by traditions in Neoplatonism, gnosticism and Christianity. Yet the concept of a disembodied mind without extension in space was firmly established by René Descartes, who regarded the body as a machine, and the mind as utterly superior to it. As such Descartes' philosophy marks a radical break with the world view of the European Middle Ages with its essentially organic view of the universe and its theological conception of man in which it is the existence of the soul, not the presence of the mind, which is the fundamental attribute of humanness.[3]

In the last century a host of critics of the Cartesian mind–body dichotomy have arisen. Nietzsche, for example, reversed the inherent hierarchy in Descartes' dualism, saying 'Behind your thoughts and feelings, my brother, stands a mighty commander, an unknown sage – he is called Self. He lives in your body, he is your body' (Nietzsche 1883 in Synnott 1993: 25). According to Synnott, Nietzsche opposed 'Christianity and the ideology of the body which he identified with Christianity, namely asceticism and negativism' (1993: 25). Freud, too, sought to overcome this dichotomy. According to Murphy, for Freud: 'The human mind also uses its symbolic capacity to reach out and encompass the body, making it just as much a part of the mind as the mind is of the body' (1987: 84). In *Studies on Hysteria* (Breuer and Freud 1957), Freud formulates the theory that the body and mind are one.

Existentialism, phenomenology and post-structuralism further highlighted the inadequacy of Descartes' views and problematized the body. In *Being and Nothingness* (1964), Sartre re-envisioned the Self as body, as opposed to the Self as mind. He writes: 'I *live* my body ... The body is what I immediately am ... I *am* my body to the extent that I *am*' (1964: 428–60). Merleau-Ponty, in his *Phenomenology of Perception* (1978), suggests the further original sense of space which seeks the ground of space in existence and the existence of the body itself which exists under the objective sense of space. His notion of the relation between the self and the body is clearly represented in his phrase 'I am not in front of my body, I am in it, or rather I am it' (1978: 150). Like Husserl before him, he grapples with the idea of the body being both *seeing* and *seen* (Merleau-Ponty 1964). As Turner summarizes:

> In trying to understand human perception, Merleau-Ponty argued that perception is always undertaken from a particular place or perspectives. It is not possible to talk about human perception of the world without a theory of embodiment as the perspective from which observation occurs.
>
> (Turner 1992: 43)

We observe that the body has been either treated as a second-class citizen to the mind, or else privileged above the mind in these philosophical debates. In Buddhism, the mind, until tamed by meditation, is often described as a wild monkey or elephant. The week of sitting in Naikan is remarkably similar to the use of meditation in various forms of Buddhism. At the same time, the Naikan environment resembles a prison cell, which is understandable when one considers that the first place Yoshimoto thought about spreading Naikan to was prison as a reform treatment for inmates. Although Naikan nowadays is used mainly as a psychotherapeutic tool in Japan, rather than in prisons, Naikan is still understood widely as a re-socialization therapy with the corresponding connotations of being rather suppressive and conformist, rather than promoting the independence of clients.

Rethinking Foucault's disciplined body

Whenever I read Foucault, I think that he would have been fascinated by Naikan. He might have been quick to judge that Naikan fits perfectly into his notion of the confinement and discipline of the body (Foucault 1991), as this notion seems very appropriate to the Naikan setting. What is most powerful about Foucault's treatment of the body is that the body is seen as a vehicle to ultimately discipline the mind, but in quite a pessimistic way. My interpretation of Foucault is that the mind is *conditioned* through regulating, controlling and disciplining the body by social institutions such as school, barracks, hospitals and factories. He uses the case of the 'enclosure' and monastic cell to argue that 'the disciplinary space is always, basically, cellular' (1991: 143). The timetable is also a mechanism of control, with its three methods to 'establish rhythms, impose particular occupations, regulate the cycle of repetition' (1991: 149).

At first glance, Naikan seems to fit perfectly the conditions of the prison cell that Foucault discusses. Naikan clients are confined to a cell-like space where they must remain silent; when interaction is initiated by the practitioner, the body movements of pressing one's hands together and bowing are prescribed. There is a strict timetable for getting up in the morning, sweeping, *mensetsu*, taking meals and going to bed. Hence, one might say from Foucault's perspective that the disobedient, 'abnormal' body is being disciplined and trained in a social institution. Indeed, prior to my first Naikan session, I must admit that I was rather anxious, anticipating that my 'self' might be disciplined and tamed after one week of intense Naikan, and I was quite hesitant to accept that idea.

The contribution of these Western thinkers helps to explain the centrality of bodily engagement in Naikan's approach to dealing with clients, many of whom come with problems such as depression, eating disorders or relationship problems. Yet it does not bring us far enough in our study of Naikan. The nature of bodily engagement in Naikan is quite the opposite of what we might expect. Rather than dance therapy, play therapy or exercise, it is a cessation of physical activity for long periods of time. When troubled or depressed by something, a natural tendency might be to do something active, talk out one's problems or seek companionship. In Naikan, however, instead of escaping the problem through activity, sitting forces the person to stay where the problem is. One cannot go anywhere; there is nowhere to go. One must confront the issue.

Yet 'sitting', or doing Naikan, is an uncomfortable process, as we have seen above. In fact, one becomes increasingly aware of one's body through a sense of heaviness and uncomfortable sensations. This is an aspect that Foucault neglects; or, one could say that Foucault's extensive discussion of the body still leaves the 'body' as a rather abstract entity rather than focusing more closely on specific aspects of embodied experience. The Naikan environment and method, therefore, force the client to recognize a present disharmony between mind and body. To better understand this process, we need to supplement our overview with the thought of Japanese philosophers.

Although the Cartesian notion of a total body–mind separation was absent in Japanese history, the Japanese, of course, also have the sense of disharmony between body and mind. What is absent in Japanese thought is the notion of seeing our physical body as a tomb of the soul.

In keeping more in line with Asian traditions, Yuasa (1987) begins from the starting point of seeing no clear ontological distinction between body and mind; the boundary between the two is a fluid one. His contribution, however, is to move beyond this by postulating that mind–body unity is not a natural state, but rather something to be achieved. To illustrate this, he examines body practices existing in Japanese traditional religious practice and art, such as Zen meditation. Another Japanese philosopher, Ichikawa, explains:

> When the degree of unity is high and we are emancipated from environmental control and can make the possible world our own world, we are conscious of the spirit. However, such an intentional structure unifies the orientational structure in itself. On the other hand, when the degree of unity is low and we are controlled by the environment and have less freedom, we feel the body. The ultimate example of this situation is that of a corpse.
>
> (Ichikawa 1991: 117)

The notion of 'unity' is Ichikawa's major concern in defining the body as spirit. This unity has various levels: when we are sleeping or being sick (especially when we have a mental disorder), we experience bodily existence since the level of unity is low, while when the level of unity is high, we experience spiritual existence and feel ourselves as the centre of freedom (1991: 117). In short, actual human beings get close to or far from the spirit and the body as abstract objects. Ichikawa illustrates how what we call or believe to be spiritual things cannot exist without their physical aspects, and vice versa, and he claims that our existence itself unifies the spiritual and physical level. He concludes that the body is spirit: spirit and mind are nothing but two names given to the same reality (1991: 118). When we achieve a certain level of unity 'the body truly becomes the human body' (1991: 119), and the distinction between spirit and mind disappears.[4]

The philosophies of Yuasa and Ichikawa may help to explain what is happening to the body and mind in Naikan. Through rigorous bodily engagement (long periods of immobility) that creates discomfort, Naikan clients are forced to recognize the very disharmony between mind and body of which Ichikawa and Yuasa write. If these philosophers are right, breakthroughs should occur when a higher degree of mind–body unity has been achieved. Indeed, clients concur that deep realizations and insights come to them only after the stage of intense bodily discomfort has been overcome. By the end of the week-long Naikan session, many clients feel well rested and that their body has become lighter. If they have made progress, then, it has been on both physical and mental levels.

This sense of feeling lighter and even achieving the unity of body and mind seems to challenge and contradict Foucault's notion. If Foucault were correct, what happens through Naikan should be the conditioning of the mind (e.g. re-socialization back into a conformist Japanese society) through the conditioning of the body. As I demonstrate, the aspect of conditioning the mind is explicitly apparent in Naikan practice, but what is interesting here is that conditioning the body does not lead to conditioning the mind; rather, the union of body and mind is the result of the *de-conditioning* of one's body and mind. As Naikan is often described as a culturally conservative practice with an aim of re-socializing its clients, this is an important distinction, and one that I elucidate in further detail in Chapters 4 and 5.

A mere facilitator?

Of paramount importance in speaking of the environment of the Naikan centre is the role of the practitioner. It is in the practitioner's house that Naikan is conducted (for typically the Naikan centre is the house of the practitioner); it is the practitioner who instructs the new client as to how to conduct Naikan; it is only the practitioner with whom clients interact while conducting Naikan. Yet despite the obvious importance of their role, practitioners claim that they are mere 'facilitators' or actually 'servants' of the clients. In this section I will problematize the role of the practitioner and question its idealized description by Naikan practitioners, offering up a host of alternative images alongside 'facilitator' and 'servant'. I will then turn to a comparison of the practitioner's role with that of the priest in Catholic confession and the therapist in psychoanalysis.

Ideally, as Yoshimoto repeatedly insisted, the practitioner should not give any advice or comments during the client's confession. Rather than an advisor or counsellor, the practitioner should be a mere facilitator. Takemoto (1981b: 13) discusses that a practitioner's attitude toward a client is one of acceptance; however, if a client's confessional report during *mensetsu* keeps diverting from Naikan's three themes, the practitioner corrects such diversion with a 'stern attitude'. According to Kawahara (1996: 55) the practitioner's attitude should be polite and modest; at the same time, he maintains a 'resolute attitude'.

The practitioner should not enter into the client's private or 'sacred' space; both physically and emotionally, the distance must be maintained. It is hardly surprising, then, that many clients tend to find the practitioner cold and distant, especially at the beginning. I experienced this personally when, while working as a trainee practitioner, a young girl who was a client started to become friendly and relaxed with me. Occasionally, she tried to chat with me and thereby diverge from the required three themes of Naikan. Yet as a practitioner, I could not engage in such conversation; I had to maintain distance in order to help her conduct serious and deep Naikan.

In an environment of isolation, the practitioner functions as the client's mirror: the practitioner's solemn attitude reflects back whatever the client confesses, whereas if the practitioner becomes personally involved or attempts practical advice, the mirror becomes clouded. During *mensetsu* the practitioner listens in silence, sitting very still, so that clients often feel that what they are saying is being reflected back on them, intensifying the experience. This metaphor may be especially appropriate in light of the importance of the mirror as a symbol in Shinto, Buddhism and Japanese folk culture, where the sacred and the human meet in its reflection (Ide 1999: 77).

This connects in an interesting way with Linde's observation that 'stories one tells about oneself are closely tied to the relation one has with one's addressee' (1993: 36). She writes:

> Indeed, the extent to which one knows another person's life story can be viewed as offering one measure of the intimacy of the relationship. Therefore, the exchange of components of life stories is particularly frequent at points in a relationship when intimacy increases.
>
> (Linde 1993: 36)

What is interesting in Naikan is that this 'intimacy' is not created in ways that might be expected, such as through the warmth of the practitioner, or the practitioner sharing his own stories with the client, etc. On the contrary, the practitioner goes out of his way to maintain a stern and almost cold expression throughout the *mensetsu*. The practitioner's linguistic behaviour of maintaining absolute silence for long periods while the client makes a report is particularly unusual in the Japanese context, since in Japanese continual replies of 'I see' and 'Yes' are the norm when listening to a person speak, a linguistic behaviour called 'back-channelling'. Typically there is a conspicuous absence of such back-channelling in Naikan (although Yoshimoto himself was an exception to this rule, as we shall see in Chapter 3). Instead, the feeling of intimacy is environmentally constructed through the client being housed in the practitioner's home, cooked for, cared for and listened to. As I mentioned earlier, from my own experience, clients will often hear household noises such as a baby crying, the sound of a laundry machine and cooking sounds from the kitchen. Such sounds contribute to the feeling that one has become a child again, at home with one's mother; it is the intimacy of the 'womb'.

This raises the issue of the architectural characteristics of Naikan centres. Yoshimoto converted his own house into a Naikan centre, which he called a Naikan *Dōjō* (Naikan Training Hall).[5] He and his family shared the space with clients. Because of the intensity of Naikan, Yoshimoto thought he should be within reach of his clients, and that he and his wife should be close enough to sense when some clients had problems, or did not stay within their screen, or started chatting with other clients.

There are also obvious practical reasons for clients and practitioners sharing one common living space, such as the issue of time. If there are ten clients, one session of *mensetsu* could take over an hour, since some clients might not finish their report within five minutes. That would mean that not long after one session, the practitioner would have to begin the next session, since *mensetsu* is to occur every two hours. Thus, most Naikan centres operate in a similar environment.

Interestingly, this family-style environment is not rare in Japan. Traditionally, Japanese aesthetic culture tends to provide a similar concept about the space between the *sensei* (master) and his disciples. The disciples live in the *sensei's* house and learn their art or skill not only during lesson times but also from the *sensei's* daily way of life. Even though Naikan is a sensory deprivation therapy, this sensory deprivation is conducted within a family-oriented, warm and cosy environment which makes clients feel protected, cared for and even nostalgic. It is this mixture of partial isolation and a home-like family environment that creates the unique space of the Naikan environment.

The model of 'teacher–student' or '*sensei*–disciple' relationship is in fact how Naikan has been viewed in much of the English literature. It is natural to draw this conclusion and recall Foucault's (1967) analysis of power relations between doctors and patients. This is how I myself viewed the situation initially; the practitioner exercised power due to his authority as a father or judge-like figure.

Ultimately, however, the *sensei*/teacher image is unsatisfying, and it is clearly rejected by practitioners themselves. Before conducting my first *mensetsu* as a trainee practitioner, I was told by an experienced Naikan practitioner that I should never assume that I 'guide' or 'teach' clients; rather, I should be aware that each client has a Buddha nature and that the client was allowing me to listen in on his or her confession. Practitioners, I was told, should be humble and never lose the attitude that Naikan clients can teach them many things. Yoshimoto used to say that the presence of clients at his centre to do Naikan was itself a thing of grace, and that there must have been some karma which brought them to Naikan; therefore practitioners should just listen to them and wait for their progress. Later, when I conducted Naikan as a practitioner, I was indeed overwhelmed by especially deep and sincere confessions, and sometimes felt as if I were doing Naikan myself.

In light of the above discussion, claims by Naikan practitioners that they are mere 'facilitators' in the process of Naikan can be only partially true. By carefully constructing such an environment and controlling his behaviour in a specified manner, the practitioner is more than a facilitator. By housing his clients and instructing them in Naikan, he invites comparisons to the role of the *sensei*, or a teacher; at the same time the temporary nature of a client's stay (one week) and the care provided invite comparisons to an inn-keeper. While practitioners describe themselves as 'servants' of their clients, they also appear to be parental figures, caring for, providing for, yet also controlling the behaviour of the client as a receiving and obedient child. Yet these images, too, must be tempered. The practitioner cannot discipline his clients like a parent, nor can he treat them like inferior disciples. In the following sections we will continue to explore the practitioner–client relationship and nuance our understanding of the practitioner's role by looking to Catholic confession and Freudian psychoanalysis.

Mensetsu and Catholic confession

Confession is intrinsic to Naikan. During the *mensetsu*, the report given by the client is often referred to as *zange* ('confession' or 'repentance'). Many Naikan practitioners say Naikan is a 'deep confession'. Confession is a narrative form, and in Naikan it is in fact the only time when a client is able to talk at all. Though it is in the enclosed silence of the client's sacred space where deep reflection and the recovery of memory take place, it is only through the narrative of confession that the client is able to reconstruct discursively in language a new autobiography.

Although Naikan confession seems to share many similarities with Catholic confession, certain significant differences are often pointed out. First, there is no equivalent to God in Naikan to grant forgiveness. Due to this, some have gone so far as to make the remarkable claim that Naikan is too harsh for Americans or Europeans, who would get depressed, whereas it is all right for Japanese, who are somewhat masochistic. Second, Naikan confession is much less private than Catholic confession, as there are other Naikan clients in the shared space. According to one interpretation, this lack of privacy is acceptable for Japanese, who value collectivism over individualism, but would be rejected by Americans and Europeans who would feel their privacy is being violated and therefore find Naikan unethical as a therapy.

However, I would argue that Naikan and Catholic confession are not as different as they might appear by referring to Corinne Kratz's (1991) insightful paper on Catholic confession, which demystifies some aspects of the practice. One of the main purposes of Naikan confession is a reformulation of the self, including values, identity and autobiography; one could say that clients dismantle the pre-existing self-image that they have built up over the years. Yet deconstruction is only half of the process; a new self-image must be constructed, and using language in speech is essential for the solidifying of thoughts and beliefs necessary in this reconstruction of identity. This aspect of Naikan seems in alignment with Catholic confession. As Kratz writes: 'Confession is a definitive process, specifying and unifying notions of personhood and morality and negotiations' (1991: 826).

Kratz's insight into the *definitive process* of confession highlights why many Naikan clients often report that there is a great difference between remembering their past deeds in their head (i.e. conceptual recognition) and reporting them verbally in front of the practitioner. Clients often told me that the act of confession made them feel an *embodied* sense of responsibility for the wrong they committed that was quite different from their more abstract intellectual recognition. Many clients later recalled that their confession felt cathartic. However, there is no easy 'forgiveness' given by the practitioner, who merely remains silent until the client has completed his or her confession. Without a clear response (of forgiveness or otherwise) from the practitioner, one might think that there would be a contradiction between the feeling of responsibility (feeling quite bad about a past misdeed) and a cathartic feeling after confession.

In popular understanding, Catholic confession is an action between a person and God, and upon confessing his or her sin, the person is forgiven (subsequent to further acts of contrition in certain cases). Thus, the priest is, as Kratz writes, a 'mere conduit in the relation between sinner and God and sinner and him- or herself' (1991: 836). In theory at least, Naikan lacks the concept of 'the person and someone else' (such as God); thus, there is only the second of these two relations: the relation between the 'sinner and him- or herself'. The ideal in Naikan is that the client is merely reflected as if in a mirror, which is done through the practitioner. As the practitioner's role is to reflect, not to forgive, clients sometimes find the practitioner rather stern. In this respect, Naikan confession might have a more severe nature than Catholic confession.

Furthermore, there is the purpose of emphasizing the sinfulness of the penitent, present in both Naikan and Catholic confession. Although confession in Naikan does not lead immediately to forgiveness, neither does it do so unambiguously in Catholic confession. Yet the trajectory is the same in both: achieving a recognition of one's salvation or forgiveness through first recognizing one's sinfulness. Kratz writes that in Catholic confession the sinner bears responsibility for his or her sins even after performing the act of penance, and 'penance and punishment for sin are only just, trials to be accepted gladly and gratefully as a sign of God's forgiving kindness' (1991: 831). This bears some similarity to the Buddhist notion of karma, in which negative situations are the result of one's own past actions, such that if faced with a courageous attitude, negative incidents can even be seen as fortunate occasions for exhausting negative karma.

In Naikan, one goal is for the client to awaken to the fact that we all live under the support and love of our parents, friends and all things (Sato 1973: 3). 'All things' may include animistic spirituality and elements of a highly religious nature. By spending a week thinking of all the good things one has received from people throughout one's life, how little one has given in return and how much trouble one has caused, strong twin senses of sinfulness and dependency are developed. Yet the result is not despondency, but a feeling of acceptance or salvation: despite one's faults and failings, one has been supported, loved, forgiven. When Yoshimoto achieved enlightenment through *mishirabe*, he was overwhelmed by realizing that he was already saved by the Great Buddha (Yoshimoto 1997: 93–101).

Catholic confession and Naikan share similarities with regard to what we have called a sacred space of enclosed silence, into which a client or Christian goes by his or her own free choice, and which must not be violated by the practitioner or priest. Yet in this sacred space we also find remarkable differences. While Catholic confession protects the anonymity of the penitent through a curtain, Naikan uses a paper screen that is moved aside slightly for *mensetsu*, so that the practitioner and client can sit face to face. Even more remarkably, clients' confessions are sometimes recorded and may be broadcast at Naikan centres with the permission of the client or handed over to a researcher such as myself (I was able to obtain a large number of such tapes without difficulty). This would be unthinkable in the case of Catholic confession (or psychoanalysis).

With Naikan, however, it is often the case that clients will be stimulated by overhearing other clients' confessions. In fact, this may be part of the reason for having several clients in the same room, rather than totally isolating them from each other. An interesting dialectic is set up between the meditations of the client in the privacy of his or her sacred space and the semi-public expression given to them during *mensetsu*. This is furthered by the fact that each client will be following the same three themes with regard to similar key figures in their lives (mother, father, siblings, teachers, etc.), ensuring a significant degree of overlap.

It is also to be noted that the notion that confession must be private may be a later development in its history. Kratz notes that the privacy involved in Christian confession may have its origins as late as the twelfth century, and that earlier confession might have been more public (Bossy 1985: 48–9, Asad 1983 in Kratz 1991: 830–1). She also points out that 'as the Catholic sacrament of penance, confession is far from an individual matter alone' (1991: 830).

Naikan and psychoanalysis

As Naikan is often viewed as an indigenous Japanese psychotherapy, comparisons with Western forms of psychotherapy naturally arise. Such comparisons are particularly interesting because Naikan is often suggested for cases of mental illness and several hospitals in Japan use Naikan as part of their treatment. However, Naikan is also recommended for those who do not suffer from 'mental illness', and, as has been discussed, this term itself must be understood differently in the Japanese context. We will now see how the *mensetsu* set-up of Naikan resembles psychoanalysis in some ways, but with significant differences.

In Naikan, the practitioner is instructed to remain silent for the most part and, unless the practitioner wishes to bring the client back to Naikan's three themes, he or she may say only the few prescribed set phrases (e.g. 'What are you going to examine next?'). In other words, it is not a dialogue: the practitioner is not delving into the client; rather, the client is divulging as he or she sees fit. Because the client first sits in silence for two hours before talking for five minutes during *mensetsu*, the client can choose not to talk about certain subjects; nor does the client relate experiences freely, but rather in a way structured by Naikan's three themes. Kawahara (1996: 55) explains that in this process of selection by clients, what is important is not recounting to the practitioner everything that the client recalled (which given the short duration of the *mensetsu* would be impossible anyway), but rather examining oneself from the other person's perspective, i.e. the significant other on whom the client was focusing during that session. Takemoto argues that Naikan is highly restrictive in how it directs a client's mode of thinking, yet it allows freedom when it comes to the content of what is recalled and the selection of topics to be reported to the practitioner, who never pursues with additional questions or presses the client to talk about everything (1984b: 83).

The framework of time is also quite different from psychoanalysis. In Naikan, a client is not allowed to skip a period of time in recalling the past. Regardless of the problem or problems the client has, he or she must examine past events in the prescribed order, i.e. year by year, and according to Naikan's three themes. Murase calls this method of recollection 'directed association' (1981b: 23). Takino (1981: 17–19; 1994: 97) writes that of indigenous Japanese psychotherapies, Naikan is the closest to psychoanalysis, since it is a form of self-analysis. Kawahara also describes Naikan as one of the 'self-analysis therapies' (1996: 52). Takino, however, goes on to argue that although both psychoanalysis and Naikan aim at 'self-exploration', the methods differ, and Naikan alone has 'concentration within a framework' (1994: 98). According to Takemoto (1984b: 83–4), the practitioner's attitude encourages the Naikan client to explore themselves independently and autonomously: since a practitioner's attitude is polite and modest with neither criticism nor advice, clients experience a freedom they never experienced before, and it is in this 'free environment' that the client examines past experiences.

Naikan relies therefore on an atmosphere of silence. Reflection and memory recall is conducted in silence by the client. Then, during *mensetsu*, the practitioner listens in silence. Even the practitioner's speech is governed by set statements that are repeated each time and couched in ritual. The client's emotions are almost entirely disregarded, and there is a complete absence of searching for psychological explanations for the client's disorder. Even though there are seven to eight confession times a day, the client is supposed to report what they have recalled strictly by following the three themes within three to five minutes. Naikan therefore does not actively work on a client's emotions; in fact, practitioners believe that being trapped by emotions will only disturb the client's self-discovery. The treatment of emotions in Naikan seems to be aligned with the general Buddhist approach, whereby emotions are seen as arising from ignorance and an untamed mind; therefore, rather than being addressed directly, they are to be dealt with by going to their root by taming the mind and bringing insight to dispel the ignorance.

Although Naikan distinguishes itself in these ways from psychoanalysis, it does share several characteristics with Japanese psychotherapies. Ihara, for example, explains Naikan as a form of psychotherapy, pointing to its sensory deprivation aspect and its emphasis on the autonomy of the client.[6] Like other Japanese psychotherapies, Naikan aims at transformative change of the personality at a deep level through inner experience, rather than at treating individual symptoms. Effects such as quitting smoking or drinking, or the cure of a physical illness, are seen by Ihara as secondary to, and resulting from, this transformative change.

Reynolds has also viewed Naikan as a Japanese form of psychotherapy in line with Morita, Shadan, Seiza and Zen. He lists their characteristics as follows (Reynolds 1983: 111):

1   family-like structure
2   re-socialization
3   experiential guidance by an authority figure
4   Buddhist-based philosophy
5   de-emphasis of intellectual rational knowledge
6   immersion in a group in tandem with isolation
7   the goal of symptom transcendence rather than symptom removal
8   key experiences reported on the fourth or fifth day of treatment
9   humanistic enforcement of severe rules.

This list of characteristics is quite helpful. It is important to point out, however, that a few of the items could be slightly misleading. For example, it is limiting to view Naikan as a psychotherapy alone, since this only reveals one aspect of Naikan practice. Ohnuki-Tierney recognizes this when she writes of Naikan, Morita therapy and Shinryō Naika,[7] 'There are indigenous therapies, but to refer to them as "psychotherapy," as some scholars do, is quite misleading' (1984: 81). As we shall see, those who seriously practice or engage in Naikan do not treat it as a mere therapy, but much more as a fundamental way of life and seeing the world. This attitude affects not only the individual experience of Naikan, as we shall see in Chapters 3 and 4, but also Naikan's social organization, which I will describe in Chapter 6. Furthermore, regarding 're-socialization', I think this word can have connotations that are not appropriate to Naikan, but this requires a more fundamental rethinking of issues of individuality and socialization, which I provide in Chapter 5 in the section on selfhood.

Conclusion

We have examined in this chapter the characteristics of the Naikan environment, which I have described as one of 'sacred space' and 'enclosed silence', and the client–practitioner confessional interview called *mensetsu*. We have also considered the crucial element of death: Naikan as a 'mourning ritual', 'preparation for death' and 'life of dying', and the Naikan environment as a 'tomb'. Yet closely connected with this are concepts of birth and rebirth. The sacred space of Naikan is also the sacred space of the womb; the enclosed silence of Naikan is the enclosed silence of the womb. The practitioner is like a mother or father figure; the first figure a client does Naikan on is the client's mother; the client is like a child in the practitioner's home; and the destination at the end of Naikan is the state of rebirth, salvation and forgiveness.

This atmosphere is created by Naikan's rigid framework, involving reflection and bodily engagement, and one that can be compared and contrasted with Catholic confession and psychoanalysis. While this framework is clearly the core of Naikan's success, it has also been seen as an obstacle in introducing Naikan for general use (Takemoto 1984a, 1984b; Murase 1996). The rigidity of Naikan's confessional style aims not at forcing ideas onto the client, but rather at releasing the autonomous power within the client. It serves as a heuristic method for people to discover themselves; as Kratz says, 'confession is also one mode of self-monitoring' (1991: 830). Confession is a discursive practice of life-narrative that brings together concepts of selfhood and morality, and as such it is the crucial element of Naikan. In the next chapter, we will take a cross-section of Naikan clients and examine their confessions to explore the issue of autobiographical memory and the deconstruction and reconstruction of the self.

Plate 2.1 Foyer of Yoshimoto's house. This view welcomes new Naikan clients: a traditional Japanese wooden house with a traditional garden, evoking feelings of nostalgia.

Plate 2.2 Women in the kitchen preparing meals for Naikan clients.

Plate 2.3 'Death' (*shi*) written in calligraphy by Yoshimoto and hanging in the living room of his Naikan centre in Nara.

Plate 2.4 A typical room for clients to do Naikan, showing the enclosed space for each client, while still in an open room shared by others. (Taken from Yoshimoto's Naikan centre in Nara.)

3   Naikan confessions

Yanagita explained the Naikan experience as the 'rearrangement of self-history' (1997: 149). He saw it as a process of 'reviewing one's life history from new perspectives and reconstructing it from a dark and unfortunate life-history to a bright and joyful one' (1979: 30). In a similar vein, Ishii explains Naikan as 'a way to happiness'.[1] To a large extent, however, this rearrangement takes place discursively through the narration of the client during the *mensetsu* confession and in his or her interaction with the practitioner. The 'way to happiness' is through narration and confession. Having examined in the last chapter the Naikan environment and the effects it creates, we will now turn to look at the confession itself in detail.

I present here transcripts I have made of actual Naikan confessions from recordings given to me at Yoshimoto's Naikan centre in Nara, and at Yanagita and Shimizu's *Meisō no Mori* Naikan centre in Tochigi. Recordings are made when the practitioner feels that the client is making good progress, or the recording will be useful later for playing back to other clients. These recordings are broadcast during meal times at many Naikan centres and are intended to help clients in their own progress. The permission of the client is always requested at the end of the Naikan session before using that tape later for broadcasting, and the client can also purchase the recording of his or her session.

Some clients say that they would like to continue daily Naikan by themselves after they return home and the tapes would be good motivation to remind them about Naikan. Others say that they were so moved by some confessions that they want to listen to them again and again after returning home. In one case, a client who had confessed during the Naikan session to cheating on his wife and never having loved her resolved to be honest with her and went home and gave her his Naikan tapes to listen to.

At *Meisō no Mori* and possibly other Naikan centres, following the actual Naikan session clients are invited to make comments on their experiences, which are also recorded and may be included on the edited tapes. Usually a client's tape is edited so that it will fit onto a 60- or 90-minute tape (or more rarely onto two tapes, which would contain almost the full length of the recording), and it is these edited tapes which are broadcast, whereas the originals may be given back to the client. For example, when I left *Meisō no Mori*, I received two 90-minute tapes containing my full confessions and a 60-minute tape with my post-Naikan comments. In the edited tapes that are played at the centres, often the first three or four days, which are considered less interesting or less deep, are cut more heavily, whereas the final two days are left in greater detail. Favourite recordings are broadcast more often than others, and at some centres recordings are even selected and played individually to clients on headphones, depending upon what issues the practitioner feels the client needs help with.

These transcripts are revealing in many ways. They illustrate the Naikan process and the experience of the clients, yet they also show that the practitioner's actual function in Naikan differs significantly from the idealized picture we saw in Chapter 2. At several points in the confessions, as will be seen, many of the ideals of the client–practitioner relationship, such as the practitioner being a mere mirror for the client, are not strictly followed. Also, we see additional themes and techniques being used alongside Naikan's main three themes of what one received, what one gave and what trouble one caused. One main additional theme is that of 'lying and stealing', whereby clients reflect on lies they have told and things they have stolen, again going year by year and giving reports to the practitioner. Another theme is that in which clients try to calculate how much money their parents have spent on them. A further technique, perhaps used only by Yanagita and shown below, involves the client making a list of complaints about a person's negative traits, inverting the list into positive traits, and then seeing how impossible it would be for a person to live up to those high expectations. Thereby the client realizes that the person being complained about cannot be perfect and should be accepted. We will see these turn up in the confessions below and at the end of the chapter I will provide an analysis of emergent trends.

I have had to be selective in my choice of confessions, and also, due to limitations of length, in what parts of each confession to present here. I have chosen to show some variety: confessions from three women and two men of various ages and backgrounds, taken between the 1970s and 1990s at two Naikan centres and under three practitioners.[2] I selected confessions to illustrate changes in the client's perception of self, others, experience, illness and imagery; the practitioner–client dynamic and the practitioner's role in shaping the Naikan process for the client; and the influence of external factors, such as the playing of confession tapes, on the client's Naikan experience.

Except in the case of Yanagita, who appears here both as client and practitioner, the names of the clients have been changed to protect their identities. The ellipsis [...] within a paragraph indicates that some material has been omitted within a single *mensetsu* session (each is usually five minutes long), while between paragraphs it indicates that the following material comes from a later *mensetsu* session. Editorial comments are given within brackets in italics.

Noriko

Noriko visited the *Meisō no Mori* Naikan centre in Tochigi, where Yanagita and Shimizu conduct Naikan, in January 1998, two years before the death of Yanagita. Noriko had been suffering from collagen disease for four years. Even though she had been on medication throughout, she was not getting better and her doctor told her that she had only two years left to live. She hoped to find some alternative methods of healing without relying on 'Western medicine' and visited the Naikan centre after trying *kikō* (or *Qigong*) and others. She tried analysing the cause of her disease and came to the conclusion that it was linked to the death of her parents. The following transcript begins from day two and continues through her seventh and final day of Naikan.

YANAGITA: How old are you?

NORIKO: Thirty-seven years old.

YANAGITA: I would like to ask the purpose of your visit and how you came to hear about Naikan.[3]

NORIKO: All right. I lost my parents nine years ago. My father killed my mother, then he tried to kill himself. Well, I consciously altered my memory on this issue so that I remembered instead that I lost my parents due to their illness. [*long pause*] So, I can't remember that time and [*long pause*] I sank deeply into my sorrow and I've been suffering from collagen disease for four years. When I started searching for the cause of my illness, I though that it must be that incident nine years ago. But I couldn't advance further than that. My pain has gone, but I suffocate and can't breathe if I walk three steps. I cough and my nose runs if I talk to other people, because I become so nervous and tense. So I thought I needed to change myself, and that's why I came here, to do so intensively.

YANAGITA: Was it a forced double-suicide?

NORIKO: No. My father was mentally disturbed at the time, though we weren't aware of it. He had been suffering from severe rheumatism for over ten years and was physically handicapped. He was so bossy that people didn't find him easy to be around. He refused to dine at home and always ate out. He only went home to sleep, so he was a lonely, sad person [*cynical laughter*]. He never told anyone about his pain, and he used to go to the hospital by himself and only asked my mother to accompany him for operations. My father blamed my mother for his suffering. He said he suffered from rheumatism all because of her [...] and he stabbed my mother. He went mad and killed her. My mother used to say that she wanted to separate from my father, even when my brother, sister and I were small. But she said that she stayed home because we were so important to her. She loved to drink. [...] She had been ill since her liver got bad and developed cirrhosis, and it was then complicated by diabetes. I wanted my parents to be on good terms, but they were always bitter towards each other. [When my father stabbed her] my mother died without knowing what was going on, but [right after that], my father said to me, 'Look good and hard at me. I have nothing to lose anymore', and he cut his throat right in front of me. His attempt to kill himself failed and he was sent to the hospital and recovered there. Then he was sent to prison where he became ill. He was hospitalized at the psychiatric hospital since no other hospitals would accept him. Later he died at the psychiatric hospital due to phlegm getting stuck in his throat while his hands were bound to prevent him from being violent, since even then he didn't keep still. After that I erased all my memories from around that time. Now I can talk about it like this, as I just tried to do, but I couldn't even dare to do so until now. I was filled with secrets and lies [*sobbing*].

YANAGITA: What is collagen disease like? Could you explain what it's like?

NORIKO: I suffered from a high fever and couldn't walk at the beginning. I was repeatedly hospitalized for three years. Medication was free, since it's recognized as a malignant disease. [...] Mine is a relatively mild collagen disease, and medicine was used to suppress the symptoms, but I still find it difficult to stand up, wash dishes or do laundry, since my hands and feet are numb and feel cold due to a lack of oxygen and blood. [...] I've been on medication for four years, but even the medicine has started becoming less effective. My doctor suggested that I get an oxygen machine and live everyday attached to it. He told me I have only two more years to live, since no medicine would be effective anymore. The amount of medicine has been increasing since I started taking it. I didn't want to live anymore. I am alone, I feel lonely, and I don't have anyone to rely on. So, I thought of dying and I stopped taking my medicine, since I didn't know how to die. My doctor told me that not taking my medicine would endanger my life. But nothing happened. I woke up in the morning as usual. The pain I felt and the degree of suffering was exactly the same, regardless of whether I took the medicine or not. So I stopped taking medicine and thought about the possibility of living without relying on a doctor. [...] I also had pulmonary tuberculosis due to overwork. I was working at the company and looking after my parents who were both ill. I can't remember things well from around that time and I felt that my illness couldn't be healed unless I could gain some awareness of what happened. I think that I would like to heal my heart [*kokoro*] and it doesn't matter whether I recover from my disease.

YANAGITA: [*silence*] Well, let's do Naikan by following its form [*kata dōri*]. [...]

[*During Noriko's first attempt to examine herself in relation to her father, she is able to remember what she received from him and what she returned to him, but not the trouble she caused him.*]

NORIKO: This time, I examined myself in relation to my father when I was twenty-five to twenty-seven years old. What I received from my father was that he built a new garage and bought a new laundry machine when the old one broke. What I returned to him was that I took him to the hospital by car. I prepared rice porridge for him in the morning. I cleaned his room. What trouble I caused him was he was staying home almost all the time because of his rheumatism and he often had a nap. He found our dog's barking very disturbing for his nap and told me to bring the dog to a public health centre. But I ignored his request, because I preferred our dog to my father. Now that I think about it, I remember that I felt so sad as a child when my father used to tell me to go away and when he didn't talk to me and what I did at the time was exactly the reverse situation. I ignored him, I didn't talk to him and I avoided him.

[…]

NORIKO: I examined myself in relation to my father when I was twenty-eight years old. I tried so hard to examine myself by following the three themes, but my memories from that time of sharing time with my father hardly pop up, since I forced myself to forget about what happened then and buried my memories as deeply as possible. […] I've tried in vain to get my memory into shape. Scattered memories pop up randomly and I don't know how to give my report. I'll report on the theme of what trouble I caused my father. My father's fingers, toes and waist were all bent due to his rheumatism. When he stabbed my mother with the knife, he held it by wrapping it onto his hand with layers and layers of dressing. At that moment his face looked like that of a demon, and he was blurting out some nonsense, something like he had to kill my mother since otherwise he would be killed. […] He said to me, 'Look at me. There's nothing I have to lose anymore' and slit his throat. The trouble I caused him was that I hadn't understood his feelings until that instant. He didn't die after slitting his throat. He was sent to the hospital, and I looked after him until he recovered, but I wasn't able to say anything gentle or warm to him. He asked me how my mother was doing one day, and I told him that she had actually died. He didn't cry or show any tears. He just said he was hungry and asked me to buy him some food. I couldn't believe such an utter lack of any sense of guilt in him, but I didn't think that his mental condition was disturbed. I only saw him with anger, hatred and remorse. He was sent to a psychiatric hospital in the end and died alone. He looked happy when I visited him but my feelings were cold. I regret that I couldn't understand his loneliness and pain.

[*Toward the end of the week, Noriko does Naikan in relation to her father a second time*:]

NORIKO: I examined myself in relation to my father when I was zero to three years old. This is a story of before I was born. I had one brother who was eight years older than I, and one sister who was two years older. Right after my sister was born, my mother returned to her parents' home and got divorced. After two years, she put my sister out to nurse, and she thought about putting my brother out to nurse as well to somebody who wanted to have him as a foster child. My father reconsidered their relationship and asked my mother to return to him. My mother, feeling sorry for my brother, decided to return to him. If my father hadn't asked my mother to return to him, my life would not have been given. Therefore, I thought that this could be the first thing I was given by my father. [...] There was nothing I did in return. I troubled my father, since as a child I cried so hard or went rigid when he held me, things I later heard from my mother. I apparently troubled him each time he held me.

[...]

NORIKO: I examined myself in relation to my father when I was ten to twelve years old. What I received from my father was that he let me start taking piano lessons when I was ten years old. He also bought me a piano at the same time, and he took my family on a trip. [...] It was our first family trip. He taught us fishing, swimming and he really entertained us. [...] I was so excited and happy. At night, we spread the futons in such a way that my father's was on the right and my mother's was on the left, so that my two brothers and I were comfortably sandwiched between our parents. My father kept eating ice cubes and I asked him to give me one. Then my father said 'No, children can't eat ice cubes, because they'll just wet their bed. Well, do you think you can go to pee without waking me up to accompany you?' Since I wasn't sure I could, I just said 'Hmm...' Then he said 'See, that's why it's no ice cubes for children!' I recalled this happy conversation with my father for the first time in my life. I realized that I was loved by my father so much. [...] What trouble I caused my father was that when I was twelve years old, I accidentally broke a glass window at school with my knees, and my knees got cut and I was taken to the hospital. My father drove to the hospital to pick me up, but he scolded me, which made me feel miserable at the time. On the way home, he suddenly told me that he forgot to bring his driving licence, and he became silent and slowed the car down. Now I realize that he must have been upset enough to forget bringing his driver's licence, because he was so worried about me. Now I am so grateful to him. But I think I troubled him at that time, since I was just being angry with him.

[...]

NORIKO: I examined myself in relation to my father when I was thirteen to fifteen years old. My father used to run three pachinko shops, but he closed one shop and turned it into a tea house, and he also opened a bakery in the front part of the tea house. [...] He bought me a dog. When I asked him to buy me a dog, he agreed with me happily, and told me that a dog makes a good guard, so it's good to have one. There was nothing that I returned to him. What trouble I caused him was that when I was fourteen years old, he developed rheumatism and I often heard him groaning in pain from his bedroom. [...] I was forbidden to play in the house or invite my friends over. So I used to complain that I couldn't watch TV with the sound up loud or have friends over. I didn't worry about his illness at all. At that time, I didn't know anything about rheumatism, and I thought that anything called a disease would be soon cured by taking medicine. Now I understand chronic pain, but I am so ashamed of myself for not being able to be kind to him and not taking care of him. I am regretful. I troubled him. I now remember that it was around the time he developed rheumatism that I started disliking him. I regret my lack of sympathy for him.

[…]

NORIKO: I examined myself in relation to my father when I was sixteen to eighteen years old. What he gave me was that he let me go to a private high school and paid the tuition. I used to believe that my parents were wealthy and it was only natural for them to allow me to go to a private school. I really was not grateful to my father. Father, thank you for letting me go to that high school. What I returned to my father was that when he had an operation when I was seventeen years old, I visited his hospital and collected his clothing and did laundry and brought the cleaned clothing to his hospital again. I was shocked to see my father in his hospital bed. He was lean and tall and always had a neat hair style. People called him 'president' [*shachō*] and I thought he was a very cool guy. However, lying in the hospital bed was this hunch-backed man with untidy and tattered hair. I thought he looked so bad, and I couldn't look in his eyes, because I was so embarrassed by him. He was suffering from his illness and here I was feeling embarrassed by him. […] I am ashamed of myself.

[…]

NORIKO: I examined myself in relation to my father when I was nineteen to twenty-two years old. What I received from my father was that he paid the tuition for the hairdressing school I enrolled in after graduating from high school. […] I was able to attend this school thanks to him. I am grateful for his support. I was such a fortunate person. Thank you very much. There was nothing I did in return.

[*Noriko explains that she refused to go to a college suggested by her father and left for Tokyo without discussing it with him first.*]

NORIKO: After I started living in Tokyo and started my course at the hair-dressing school, I wrote him an apology letter in which I wrote about my life in Tokyo, my course at school and dormitory life. I heard from my mother that he read my letter and was happy about it. For that reason I assumed that he had forgiven me. So when I returned home during the summer vacation, I went to his room and told my father I was back. Instead of greeting me, he just told me to go away. I thought my father was such a cold person after all, who couldn't even say a warm word to his own child. I decided that I should stop having any expectations of him and stopped even thinking about him, or even thinking about the fact that I had a father. […] I really disliked my father when I was twenty-two years old. Now I can understand the pain of rheumatism. My father must have been in pain, putting up with terrible pain all the time. He must have been so absorbed in coping with his illness that he couldn't be kind to other people. I feel so sorry for him since he must have had such a lonely life fighting with his rheumatism alone without relying on the family. [*sobbing*] If I were more mature, I could have listened to him complain. [...] I am led to the realization that he was being patient all by himself without being able to rely on his family.

[...]

NORIKO: I examined myself in relation to my father when I was twenty-six to twenty-seven years old. What he gave me was that when I was twenty-six years old, [*after having returned home from Tokyo*] I handled all the domestic matters. One day, our laundry machine broke and I asked him what to do about it. Then he immediately bought a new machine, he even went to the shop to look at various laundry machines. I remember feeling so happy. At the time, I used a car to take my mother to the hospital and my brother used another car to take my father to the hospital. Then my father built an additional garage. Since I had previously had to walk to the nearest parking space to fetch my car, I was so grateful for his support. I am truly grateful. What I returned to him was that he started taking meals at home frequently and I prepared rice porridge for him. He didn't like rice porridge made out of the cooked rice, he preferred it made from uncooked rice. He was very grateful when I prepared the rice porridge the way he liked. [...] When I was twenty-six years old, my older brother also returned home and he and I started to run a cake shop. Then we had my father, mother, younger brother, older brother and myself in our house and that made him so happy. When I was sweeping and cleaning, he used to follow me and smile and thank me and apologize to me. [...] What trouble I caused him was that when my father asked me to take our dog to the public health centre, since its barking was disturbing his sleep, I ignored his request and told him that it was the dog's job to bark, so he should be more patient. Then my father became furious and started insisting that he would take the dog to the public health centre by himself. I laughed at him and asked how he could do this, with his bent hands holding his robe and unable to drag the dog, which was stronger than he. Then he looked very sad and turned his back and returned to his room in silence. Now I regret so much that I said such harsh things to him.

[...]

NORIKO: I examined myself in relation to my father. He died right before I turned twenty-eight years old. I feel so grateful that I can see myself from the perspective of my father. It was not my father's problem that I hated him, but mine. My father was I, and I was he, we had the same heart. I do accept the fact that I have been loved by my father and I am grateful for his existence, that he was there, and I am grateful to him for raising me. Since my father was not peaceful in my mind or in my image of him, I helped him to achieve peace in my image of him. I dug up the anger toward him that was buried deep down in myself. For the first couple days of Naikan, I just couldn't find my father. When I finally found him, my father with a knife and bloodied hands, I was so scared and I felt nauseated. He was holding the knife and standing with blood all over him, that was my father when I was twenty-eight years old when he killed my mother and attempted to kill himself. All my bitterness, anger, tears and mortification were attached to him. I bathed him and washed him clean. Then I laid him on the bed that he liked, and I dissolved the bitterness, anger, tears and mortification, which were my own creation, in a bag made of light. I wrapped him with a quilt made of light and he became a ball of light, and I sent it flying into the universe. He was smiling, he looked comfortable being a ball of light, and he is still floating in the cosmos. I accept the fact that my father killed my mother. But as long as I have this memory of being loved by him, I will not hate him anymore. It was not his problem, it was my problem to hate him. It took me nine years, but I am all right. Thank you very much.

That concludes the transcript of Noriko's one-week session of Naikan. After concluding a session, clients are often asked to reflect on their experiences in an exit-interview or at a group *zadankai* meeting. Some of Noriko's most interesting statements come from this post-Naikan reflection time:

Hatred caused more hatred, distorting my mind. It created an imbalance in my mind and, as a result, it caused the distortion in my body that was this incurable collagen disease. This is the result of me being self-centred all through my life and leading a life only according to my convenience. I was utterly shocked when I realized that. I recognized it, accepted it and repented toward my body and mind. [...] I realized [*kizukaseteitadaku*] the difference between 'curing' and 'healing'. 'Healing' involves love and it heals both body and mind; even somebody like myself can heal other people. I think that 'curing' involves a strong feeling or desire of being cured; it also causes anxiety that some medicines work for certain parts, but not for other parts. It also causes greed in that you start hoping for so many things. [...] I explored my body by entering into my mouth: my throat was rough and the colour was stagnant. Then I visited my lungs, tracheas and small veins, which were all blocked as if by a spider cobweb being woven all over them. That must be why it was hard to breathe. My stomach was hanging down; what was shocking was that I could not enter the adrenal gland, it was like a hard concrete wall. I cried after coming out of my body, I was so sorry for my body. I will clean my body with the ball of light, a ball of love being given by my father. Coughing comes from problems in human relationships. I worry and become nervous when I talk to people, and that makes me cough.

Phlegm comes from a dissatisfaction with personal relations. I started enjoying talking to my body. I am going to be the person that I am. I love myself the way I am now. I am gracious that I am lived and full of happiness. I am you and you are I. It is the same thing. I want to return love, I will keep opening my hands. I have received such a bright light. I am feeling nature. I started seeing my true self. Thank you very much.

Noriko's case is an extraordinary one, raising several interesting questions. Her language towards the end, when she speaks of the unity of things ('My father was I, and I was he, we had the same heart' and 'I am you and you are I') and the 'light-ball', is remarkably mystical, resembling statements made by mystics across religious traditions, which we will explore later. At the same time, her metaphorical language and the symbols she employs connect with Littlewood and Lipsedge's (1997) discussion of 'private symbolism', as we shall see in Chapter 4. Noriko approaches her illness holistically, drawing a clear connection between body and mind, and placing holistic healing above the idea of a specific 'cure' for the disease. Although even at the time of starting Naikan Noriko felt there must be a connection between her illness and the incident of her father killing her mother, her image of her father changed considerably throughout the week. At the end of the week, the image of her father as a murderer is replaced by a beatific vision of him as a ball of light, and his restoration in her mind is connected with a healing of herself. As we observe with Noriko's narration, many Naikan clients claim that they found their 'true self', a topic which we will explore in greater detail later on.

Akina

Akina visited *Meisō no Mori* in the early autumn of 1995. At the time, she was a 25-year-old university student majoring in psychology, and had heard about Naikan from one of her professors. As she wanted to write about herself, Naikan sounded like an ideal way to explore herself. Unlike Noriko, she came with no illness or major problem that she wanted solved.

Akina's memories are vivid and detailed from the beginning. As the transcript of the first day shows, the practitioners Yanagita and Shimizu alternate in listening to her confessions. Also interesting is that at the end of her official 'reports' on what memories she recalled according to the Naikan themes, Akina appends more general comments about her current experiences and perception. Thus she begins to appreciate the scenery more, and notes that water starts to taste different to her, somehow better.

[DAY ONE]

YANAGITA: How old are you now?
AKINA: Twenty-five years old.

YANAGITA: I'd like to ask you the purpose and motive of your visit here.

AKINA: I came here to write my undergraduate thesis, and I wanted to write about myself. Then I heard about Naikan from Professor Nagayama,[4] and I came here hoping to learn something about myself.

[…]

SHIMIZU: It's 5.45 p.m. on 24 September 1995. What have you been examining at this time, at what age and in relation to whom?

AKINA: I examined myself in relation to my mother when I was zero to six years old. What I received from her was that I was given such a lovely name. […] There was nothing I returned to her. What trouble I caused her was that I crossed a street carelessly. My mother said 'Watch out!' with a shocked expression.

[DAY TWO]

AKINA: Although it's only the second day since I started Naikan, I have gradually started to deeply realize [*jikkan to shite kanjiru*] that my mother has been always at my side in all the memories I have recalled, including some unpleasant ones. I am filled with a warm feeling.

[DAY FOUR]

[Akina focuses on the theme of 'lies and secrets']

AKINA: Despite the fact that I did many bad things in the past, I can hear myself making excuses: that I was a small girl, or that these things happened a long time ago.

[…]

AKINA: [*After finishing her report:*] As I closed my eyes when it started getting dark, I heard the sound of insects, of club activities at the neighbourhood school and of everyday life like people's footsteps. When I closed my eyes in the evening, I felt how stable the world is.

[DAY FIVE]

AKINA: [*After finishing her report in relation to her grandmother*] Just now I went to the bathroom and the sun was bright and I saw laundry hanging, which made me feel calm and made me think how gentle the scenery was […] The water had a taste, it tasted good and cold.

[…]

AKINA: [*After giving a report in relation to her boyfriend*] The picture of Buddha that Mr Yanagita drew started looking like myself after two days. This picture has appeared to have various expressions at different times.

[DAY SIX]

AKINA: [*During her report in relation to her mother for the second time*] I was listening to a broadcast [of a confession] in the bathroom during the meal time, and when the person said 'I am so terrible, can I continue Naikan this way?' the wind blew, and I felt that I heard 'It's all right' coming from a plastic bag being blown by the wind. I was so surprised, wondering how a plastic bag could think such a sweet thing, and I looked around. Then I felt that the cups standing there, the hair spray and the other things that were there looked as if they were listening to the broadcast [of the taped confession] seriously, and I was the only one who wasn't listening to it seriously.

[...]

AKINA: I was able to sense that I have hands, shoulders and legs – that I am existing here. I felt that I am here now thanks to my father and mother who created me. I realized that I didn't grow up by myself just by eating food. [...] However, I still have such a shallow recognition of my guilt. [...] As for what trouble I caused my mother, I started living by myself when I was in my first year at university. [...] My mother gradually got used to not having me at home and she always welcomed me so warmly whenever I visited home. [...] Now I feel that I am very dirty. I never want to make her sad anymore. Now I think I can't separate from my mother until she dies. I might leave my house eventually, but I will return to her, and I don't want to make her feel sad again. Doing Naikan like this makes me feel like I'm dusting, and the more I dust, the more additional dust rises up. I'm concentrating on dusting. [...] Thinking about my mother's face now, her face looks like it's brightly shining. I don't know the meaning of the word 'divine' very well, but if I try to describe my mother's face in words, 'divine' seems to me to be the exact word.

[DAY SEVEN]

AKINA: [*Akina does the theme 'lying and stealing' and recalls that once while working in a department store, she stole an expensive package of green tea and made it for her parents*] While examining myself in relation to stealing, I've become so scared of myself. Doing Naikan doesn't erase all my guilt. Apologizing cannot undo the tea my parents drank. Now I see all the greed I have. I can see myself deeply submerged in a swamp and grinning. My parents come all the way to the swamp and even wash their face and brush their teeth in the dirty pond water. This is my last day of Naikan, but how can it be the end of my Naikan, since I'm in such a mess? Maybe it was good to realize [my sin] but I am so scared of myself before I was brought to this realization.

This concludes the transcript of Akina's Naikan confessions. Like many other clients, Akina felt that she was making real progress only at the end of her week-long session. Some of her comments resemble the mystical experience spoken of by Noriko. However, her descriptions are the most animistic. She comments on a drawing made by Yanagita of the Buddha that hangs in the bathroom of *Meisō no Mori*, and also says that objects in the bathroom appear to be speaking and listening to the broadcast confession. Also interesting is that she felt that becoming emotional and crying during Naikan was normal, a point we will return to later, and even worried about not being able to do this. This is revealed in her comments after the Naikan session:

> At the beginning, I was wondering whether I could ever become like other Naikan people, since I never had any dramatic experiences nor any serious troubles. I doubted I could ever say thank you from the bottom of my heart without pretending. However, once I started examining myself, I was in tears with the realization of being loved at the early stage of Naikan. Gradually, I started realizing how dirty I am, and how sinful I am. I did so many bad things knowing they were bad. I did not know the meaning of being bad. After I finished doing Naikan in relation to my mother for the first time, I felt the calmness of my mind and the taste of the rice. Meals really tasted delicious and I noticed the taste of the rice. I felt the feeling of a plastic bag and tap water, which must be the ultimate state of animism. I felt: Now I am feeling happiness.

Keiko

Keiko visited *Meisō no Mori* in the autumn of 1995. At the time she was 28 years old and an airline stewardess. Married for four years, she had been suffering from anxiety neurosis (*fuan shinkeishō*) for three years and had come to the Naikan centre on the advice of Dr Nagayama, the same doctor who recommended Akina. Keiko confessed that she thought she became ill because of her mother, whom she viewed as a crazy, mah-jong obsessed woman.

Interesting in Keiko's case is the change in her voice and language. As an airline stewardess, her voice during the first few days of Naikan is official-sounding and her language is formal. Yet after her rest on day five, her voice becomes much warmer and relaxed and her language more casual. This phenomenon, most pronounced in her case, is actually very common in Naikan and most confession tapes reflect this. Use of formal terms for mother and father such as *ha ha* and *chi chi* gives way to informal vocabulary such as *okāsan* and *otōsan*.

This recorded confession also reveals that occasionally practitioners insert their own commentary into the tapes. In the commentary, the practitioner may explain to those listening what difficulties the client was having with his or her progress, and what was done to remedy that. In this instance, for example, Yanagita's commentary appears half-way through and explains

an exercise he had Keiko do in order to help her make progress in her
Naikan.

[DAY ONE]

SHIMIZU: How old are you now?
KEIKO: Twenty-eight years old.
SHIMIZU: I would like to ask the purpose of your visit here, and how you
    came to hear about Naikan.
KEIKO: I developed anxiety neurosis (*fuan shinkeishō*) three years ago and
    have been treated by Dr Nagayama at Jikei University Hospital. I came
    here this time on the advice of my doctor.

[DAY TWO]

YANAGITA: How is your anxiety this morning?
KEIKO: I took my medicine this morning, so my symptoms are under control.
YANAGITA: Thank you very much.
[...]
KEIKO: I examined myself in relation to my mother [...] What trouble I
    caused her was that when I was a third year student at university, I was
    hospitalized for a month because of my pancreas. My mother had to
    come and visit me at the hospital and look after me. I assume that it must
    have been tough for her. Even after I left the hospital, I had to continue
    the diet-control therapy and she had to cook meals considering the
    number of calories in them. It must have been hard and I think I caused
    some trouble.

[DAY THREE]

KEIKO: What trouble I caused my mother was that I left home and started
    living on my own when I was twenty-one years old. Well, I didn't want to
    be with my mother and that was a part of the reason. [...] Even though it
    was only a year, it was fun being on my own and I had some good
    experiences. But, placing myself in my mother's position, she must have
    worried so much, letting me live on my own, and I think I troubled her a
    lot since she supported me financially, too.
[...]
KEIKO: What trouble I caused my mother was that I fainted during a flight,
    since I was suddenly struck by anaemia. I was prescribed a stabilizer and
    it was diagnosed as a mild autonomic imbalance at a hospital. I visited Dr
    Nagayama at Jikei Hospital and he diagnosed it as an anxiety neurosis.
    Since then, I tried counselling, took some Chinese medicine and tried
    kikō (Qigong). As a result, I realized that my environment growing up
    since when I was small has been a partial cause of my illness. I disliked

my mother even when I was small and I felt strongly that I didn't want to be like her. My parents were shocked to hear about my illness. Though I was already married by then, I found it painful to listen to my mother who kept calling me up and asking me insistently why I developed such an illness, so I hung up the phone when she rang me. I wrote her a ten page letter in which I expressed my feelings toward her and mailed it to her. I cried while writing it. It was the first time I ever expressed my feelings toward her and I felt better after that. It must have been quite a shock for her. She left me alone for a year or two. [...] A year, then two years passed that I didn't have to talk to her anymore, and it was a help that she didn't mention anything except business over the phone.

[...]

YANAGITA'S COMMENTARY: Up to this stage, Keiko reported what she received from others, what she returned and the trouble she caused in a very business-like tone. She tended to say things like 'Maybe I might have caused some trouble' or 'I think perhaps I caused some trouble'. Up to that point, her Naikan had not yet started. Finally, she told a story about her struggle with her mother, but she still had a deeply rooted grudge against her mother. Therefore, I asked her to make a list of her struggles with her mother and her portrait of her mother. [...] Well, this is outside of Naikan, but I sometimes ask clients [who are having difficulties] to itemize their problems with the particular person before going back to Naikan. Now I am going to read out this itemized list, which was her image of her mother:

1. She's a lazy person [...] 2. She plays mah-jong and sometimes stays over at somebody's place playing and doesn't come home [...] Sometimes I woke up and saw strangers sleeping in the living room, and there were tons of dirty dishes in the kitchen. I had to prepare breakfast by myself and brought it to my room and ate with my brother. 3. She doesn't wake up in the morning. 4. She doesn't cook breakfast [...] since she stays up until late playing mah-jong. 5. She really sleeps until late in the day during the weekend and holidays. 6. The house in untidy. 7. She went out even when I had fever and had to stay at home. [...] 9. We frequently had to eat delivered food at night. [...] 11. She is negligent in preparing meals. [...] 23. She never listens to me or lets me finish what I want to say. 24. When I was in my first year at junior high school, I felt my throat was clogged and I was taken to a hospital. There a doctor told my mother that this symptom was related to something psychological and she should take me to an amusement park or something like that, but she never did. [...] 26. When I was a university student, I got a pancreas inflammation and was hospitalised. My doctor scolded my mother, saying this was from malnutrition and she should cook meals properly. Then she replied that she always cooked, which was such a big lie. After I left the

hospital, I had to be on a special diet. But my mother was so rough about cooking and she rarely cared about it and only calculated the total number of calories. When I complained, she told me that I was too precise. I felt sad [...] 30. When my symptoms started [her anxiety neurosis], she said to me 'Cut it out'. 31. She told me it was so embarrassing to talk about my illness to other people [...] 33. She thinks she's always right. 34. She's selfish [...] 35. The way she thinks is so childish [...] 36. She is harsh and easily becomes very emotional [...] 42. I think that even when I was small there were some alarming signs regarding the state of my mental health, but she didn't notice or pay attention to my signals. I think I wouldn't have developed anxiety neurosis if she had taken good care of me. I really hate her when I think of that. [*The list continues to number 48.*]

[DAY FOUR]

[*On Yanagita's advice, Keiko does Naikan in relation to her father. She has no emotional problems accepting that he gave a lot to her. She feels great gratitude towards him and that he loved her very much.*]

[DAY FIVE]

[*On Yanagita's advice, Keiko stops Naikan and rests for the whole day.*]

[DAY SIX]

KEIKO: [*Keiko's tone of voice changes to a more relaxed, warm tone and she speaks more slowly*] I examined myself in relation to my mother when I was zero to three years old. I remembered many things I received from my mother. My mother held me in her stomach and gave me her nutrition for nine months and gave birth to me without any physical impediments. She breast-fed me and named me and taught me how to talk and walk. It is endless to count what she did for me. There was nothing I returned to her.

[...]

KEIKO: I examined myself in relation to my mother when I was four to six years old. [...] Since this morning I've felt that I've understood something. I've started being able to remember all the basic things my mother has done for me. I really didn't notice that I've always received infinite love from my mother. When I noticed this fact, I realized that I've been supported by other people like my parents. I'm here thanks to these people, and even though I understood this before in my head, I never felt the reality of it. When I realized that I've received so much affection from my parents, I could really feel – not only in my head, but as reality – that I am here now thanks to other people, I am lived thanks to other people. I wasn't aware until now that I never had a fundamental self-reflection, even though I did say 'sorry' verbally in the past.

[DAY SEVEN]

KEIKO: What trouble I caused my mother was that I always complained to her that she hardly cooked meals and she was always out. However, while doing Naikan, I started remembering many, many meals that my mother used to cook. I remembered meals like rolled cabbage, deep fried tofu and pumpkin dishes, and they were all so tasty. My mother always cooked me meals. I picked out some occasions when she didn't prepare a meal and blamed her for that. But it wasn't true. The meals I cook for my husband are extremely similar to the dishes my mother used to cook. My mother hardly taught me how to cook before I married, but all the meals she cooked for me from the time I was born until the time I married have permeated into me. I realized that I was brought up by eating meals cooked by her.

[...]

KEIKO: I examined myself in relation to my mother when I was a university student. [...] What trouble I caused her was that I thought that I got this stewardess job by my own ability. [...] I realized that my mother supported me so much and created the whole supportive environment for my preparation for the examination. Until now, I believed *I* took the exams, and *I* passed both the physical and written exams. After Naikan, I realized that it was my parents who prepared a supportive environment in which I could concentrate on preparing for the exams and financial support as well.

[...]

KEIKO: What trouble I caused my mother was that I always blamed my mother for being the source of my anxiety neurosis. I did believe that it was my mother's fault that I developed anxiety neurosis. After my Naikan, I realized that I always received an infinite amount of love from her. It wasn't because of her, but rather because I only paid attention to the things she did not do and grew in anger and dissatisfaction, that as a result I built up stress by myself and became sick. [...] I really feel sorry for my mother, thinking about how much worry I must have caused her these last three years. I'm filled with the emotion, wanting to apologize to her. [...] I would like to remind myself of this and be a dutiful daughter to my parents. [...] Thanks to Naikan, I can now firmly believe the twenty-eight years of affection I received from my mother. This realization came not through my head, but through my heart, which fell into my feelings. I gained security, and since I am certain of the affection I've received now, I think I can finally live in the present.

Keiko is an interesting case of someone whose perception of a significant other, in this case her mother, changed completely during Naikan. Her strong negative feelings towards her mother prevented her, in Yanagita's estimation, from making progress, hence he suggested she make the list and take a day off. In the end, however, she absolves her mother of guilt for her illness, and even identifies with her. An interesting parallel between Keiko and Akina is that they both considered leaving home and living alone to be something that troubled their parents, hinting at a strong negative notion about being separated from parents and being independent that might be less prominent in other cultures.

Yanagita

We have just seen three examples of Naikan being conducted by women under Yanagita at his *Meisō no Mori* Naikan centre in the 1990s. Now we will go back to August 1977, when Yanagita himself came for the second time to do Naikan at Yoshimoto's Naikan centre in Nara. He was a 47-year-old businessman at the time, and head of his company. His first visit had been a two-week long session in August 1976, twice as long as a normal Naikan session. His second visit, though only the normal one week, would also be an intense one, for it was 'deprivation Naikan', meaning that Yanagita would go without food, drink or sleep, having *mensetsu* conducted throughout the night as well as the day. Later, Yanagita would go on to found *Meisō no Mori*, which soon became the most popular centre besides Yoshimoto's.

The transcript below reveals a Yoshimoto who is a far cry from the idealized picture of a practitioner given in most explanations of Naikan by practitioners themselves. He frequently asks additional questions (i.e. beyond the set questions), even interrupting Yanagita at times. Yoshimoto's occasional farting has also been noted to affect a client's experience of Naikan, some of whom interpreted it as revealing his humanity, whereas others have wondered whether it represented his disapproval of the shallowness of their Naikan.[5] It should be further noted that at the time of this Naikan session he was suffering from the effects of his stroke in the summer of 1976. We now turn to the last two days of Yanagita's session.

[19 August 1977, evening]

YOSHIMOTO: What was the purpose of your first visit?

YANAGITA: My first visit was to conduct educational training for my employees.

YOSHIMOTO: How many employees does your company have?

YANAGITA: About 150. This time, however, I thought it was important to polish myself up before dealing with company matters. I think everything else will work out better indirectly if I work on myself first. My back pain, which troubled me for over thirty years, vanished at the end of my first Naikan session. I was diagnosed as having a stomach ulcer, duodenal ulcer, enlargement of the liver, and nephritis. I was told that I might have some kind of autonomic imbalance. My stomach hurt, and I had diarrhoea and constipation in turns. I also used to suffer from a sharp pain in the right shoulder when I got tired.

YOSHIMOTO: When did you notice that your health condition was getting better?

YANAGITA: In the early morning of Friday the thirteenth, bright morning light fell on me while I was doing Naikan. My body felt so light and I was struck for a while by the sensation of sitting in the middle of a religious painting by Rembrandt. At that moment, I sensed then that my back pain was gone.

YOSHIMOTO: How has the pain been since then?

YANAGITA: I have had hardly any pain since doing Naikan last year. [...]

YOSHIMOTO: What is the purpose of your visit this time?

YANAGITA: For a hundred days after returning from my first Naikan session, I did Naikan by myself two hours a day. It was not a painful thing. It was completely natural for me to go and do Naikan. But something started to prevent me from doing Naikan. I was in a state where I couldn't do it, even though I wanted to. In this state I gradually started drinking sake and alcohol again, something I had stopped doing after my first Naikan experience. I also felt that the feeling I received last year was fading away. So I came here again to review my last Naikan session.

YOSHIMOTO: When did you start drinking, and how long have you been doing it?

YANAGITA: I started when I was fifteen or sixteen years old and I've been drinking for thirty years. [...]

YOSHIMOTO: Looking back over the past year, in what other ways were you affected by having done Naikan?

YANAGITA: People whom I hadn't met for a long time told me that I looked lighter and more friendly. My company has been doing well, and I've had more accomplishments in business. There hasn't been much trouble in my family. What I am most grateful for, though, is that I could reconcile with my retarded child. I had always said that my stupid child was most adorable, but in reality I hadn't found him adorable – I had disliked him intensely among the other children in my family. My previous Naikan session allowed me to realize why I had come to dislike him, so that later my retarded child came to like me as best as he could, and we achieved reconciliation.

YOSHIMOTO: Why did he become retarded? What was the cause?

YANAGITA: I don't know why he became retarded, but I realized why I had started to dislike him. When I was a child, there was a retarded child in my neighbourhood whom I used to bully. I was shocked and stunned when I realized my child had been born retarded. I couldn't help having a negative reaction to my child, since I just could not accept that I could have a retarded child of my own. Until I did Naikan, I never remembered the fact that I used to look down on the retarded child in my neighbourhood, bully him and completely reject him. When I remembered that, I really felt so sorry for that person.

[…]

YOSHIMOTO: What did you examine about yourself this time, at what age and in relation to whom?

YANAGITA: I examined myself when I was forty to forty-one years old in relation to my child. What I received from my child was that I took my child to a special school for retarded children since the time he was old enough to start schooling. Thanks to that experience, I learned a lot about retarded children, despite the fact that I hadn't known anything about them until I took my child to that school. […]

YOSHIMOTO: Were you a good father or a bad father up to the period you have examined?

YANAGITA: I really feel sorry for my child. I made a lot of effort to take him to hospitals for the first three years after he was born, since he was physically very frail. However, after I learned that he was retarded, I stopped taking care of him. […] I should have looked after him much more than one would other children, since he needed a lot of care. […]

YOSHIMOTO: You can receive this as a gift from your son. Your son brought you to Naikan due to his retardation. If you see things this way, you can be grateful that your son was born retarded. Why don't you bring your child to Naikan, as a gift from you to him?

YANAGITA: Well, it would be so wonderful if that were possible, but my child can hardly speak, nor can he produce any sounds, and he can't understand what other people say. He cannot even go to the bathroom by himself. So I doubt it would be possible for him to do Naikan.

YOSHIMOTO: Don't give up so easily. You should at least try.

[19 AUGUST 1977, 11.00 P.M.]

YANAGITA: I've realized the kindness of other people through my experience with my son. When I get in the train with my son, he starts behaving very bizarrely. Then people often offer us their seats or help by carrying my bag. I never knew people were so warm and kind. I did not believe in the kindness of others, because I was never kind to other people. […] I used to think it would be better for such a retarded child to die while his parents were still healthy. Since I used to think this, I was afraid of seeing my child. I killed my son in my heart. My heart was like a demon wishing that something bad would happen to him. That must be why I couldn't even manage to keep my weekly visit to my son's boarding school, even though it was only once a week.

[19 AUGUST 1977, MIDNIGHT]

YANAGITA: Just before he turned three, after many visits to various hospitals, my son was diagnosed as brain damaged. This brain damage is what is commonly called retardation. Up to that point, I had visited every possible hospital, but after that day I completely abandoned my efforts. My wife and I cried all night that day. But the tears of the father and those of the mother were quite different. My tears were not due to worries about the future of my child, but rather tears of self-pity. I was scared for myself: What a terrible thing has happened to me! How could I have such a child? It can't be possible! I wondered what would happen to me. My feelings toward my son changed that day, and I started disliking him. It was the same as if I had abandoned him. I left all the responsibility for our son to my wife. [*sobbing*]

[20 AUGUST 1977, MORNING]

YANAGITA: I used to think that a child that stupid would have to do something like farming, and I tried to make things easier by thinking in that way. But when he turned five, it turned out that he was suffering from being severely mentally handicapped. He started smashing and destroying everything in the room. He also had a habit of climbing higher and higher whenever he found a high place. He would climb up to the roof top. My house became a complete mess. [...] Through Naikan, I've come to realize that I formulated this attitude of looking down on mentally weak people when I was a small child.

Yanagita, too, had mystical experiences, such as seeing himself in the middle of a Rembrandt painting. As in the case of the women, his perception of his son changes over the course of Naikan and is accompanied by feelings of guilt. Yoshimoto's role as practitioner is especially interesting in that he makes frequent and lengthy comments during the *mensetsu*. He almost seems impatient, probing Yanagita further and seeking to influence the way Yanagita evaluates his memories and experiences. Thus he asks leading questions such as 'Were you a good father or a bad father?' and even tells Yanagita to view Naikan as a gift from his son which he ought to return. The following and final case also illustrates this aspect of Yoshimoto.

Hiroshi

Hiroshi came to Yoshimoto's Naikan centre to begin a Naikan session on 3 February 1971. A psychiatrist, he had worked briefly in a hospital and then later at a temple. On the third day of his Naikan session, he decided to do 'deprivation Naikan' and go without food, drink or sleep. On the following day, where we begin our transcript, he has been examining himself on the theme of 'lying and stealing' during his second year of university. Following this Naikan session, Hiroshi, who was a Christian, went on to become a pastor.

[DAY FOUR, 8.00 P.M.]

YOSHIMOTO: Why did you start doing Naikan without food, water and sleep?

HIROSHI: Because I thought that someone like me, who is so sinful and far from sensing the impermanence of all things [*mujōkan*], would not be able to do Naikan without being ready to face death by not eating, drinking or sleeping.

YOSHIMOTO: You sat [*i.e. did Naikan*] here last October for seventeen days and then you became an assistant at a temple. How was that? Did you sense the impermanence of all things?

HIROSHI: It was my first experience working at a temple and every day was a succession of surprises.

YOSHIMOTO: How was it? Could you get closer to the sense of impermanence?

HIROSHI: Yes. Even now, I can't help crying when I think about the sight of my parents gathering my ashes if I die, after writing a will to my father.

YOSHIMOTO: For what purpose do you think you were born into this world?

HIROSHI: I believe in Christianity. Therefore, I believe the purpose of this life is to know God.

YOSHIMOTO: Do you know God now? Or not yet?

HIROSHI: I used to think I knew Him. However, doing Naikan last time, I realized I did not know anything about Him.

YOSHIMOTO: Do you think you are doing Naikan seriously, with all your heart, by valuing highly each minute, each second?

HIROSHI: Not at all, not yet.

YOSHIMOTO: Are you determined not to get up and leave this place, no matter what happens to you?

HIROSHI: I am.

YOSHIMOTO: Your next subject is when you were in your third year at university, isn't it? Please examine yourself firmly.

[DAY FOUR, 9.30 P.M.][6]

YOSHIMOTO: What did you examine this time?

HIROSHI: When I was shopping at a store, I was given more change than was correct. Although I knew I had been given extra change, I just kept it to myself. Sorry, but I was letting my mind wander.

[DAY FOUR, 11.00 P.M.]

HIROSHI: I'm so sorry for my previous report. I fell asleep, since I couldn't conquer the cold and heavy feeling of my head. When you visited me, I just woke up and reported whatever popped in my head. It was not the only time. I fell asleep a couple of times before as well.

YOSHIMOTO: Mrs —— did Naikan for fifteen days, but I never sensed even once that she lost her intensity in doing Naikan. Well, what did you examine at this time?

HIROSHI: [*sobbing*] I think I am lacking in seriousness.

YOSHIMOTO: What did you reflect on this time?

HIROSHI: I was examining myself with regard to the issues of lying and stealing during my fourth year of university. My bus pass only allowed me to take one route, but I used to ride other routes as well with it. I also stole a ride on the bus without paying the whole fare. I didn't feel guilty about it at all. Rather, I thought that if I couldn't even do that kind of thing, I wasn't a man, so I repeatedly did so.

YOSHIMOTO: [*silence*] Is the next theme about when you were in your fifth year at university?

HIROSHI: Yes.

[DAY FIVE, 4.40 A.M.]

YOSHIMOTO: It is now 4.40 a.m. on the morning of 7 February. What did you examine this time?

HIROSHI: I was examining myself with regard to the issues of lying and stealing when I was a fifth-year university student. I sat in on a class in another department without first asking for permission. I borrowed notes from a friend for a class I didn't attend, but I pretended as if I was attending it when I submitted a paper. [...] I used to use up wastefully a lot of materials and utensils for experiments, since I figured they were provided by the state. I was also seeing a woman whom I didn't like by pretending to like her. I have no idea how much I hurt her feelings. One can replace a broken item with a new one, but there's no way to mend a broken heart.

YOSHIMOTO: Your next Naikan is about the time when you were in your sixth year at university. This time of day is the most quiet. I've found that it's easiest to concentrate on Naikan at this time of the twenty-four hours in the day. So please do Naikan seriously by fighting back drowsiness. [...] Stay alert.

[DAY FIVE, 5.30 A.M.]

YOSHIMOTO: It is now 5.30 a.m. on 7 February. What did you examine this time?

HIROSHI: I was examining myself with regard to the issues of lying and stealing when I was in my sixth year of university. I studied with two friends at the flat of one of them. We became hungry at night and I went out to get a snack. They both gave me some money and I bought some snacks. I received change from the shop, but I kept it for myself instead of returning it to my friends, thinking that such an insignificant amount would be useless to anyone. During my graduate examination, I showed my paper to others and saw others' papers as well. I didn't take the examination seriously and assumed it was just a formality for allowing students to graduate. When a friend of mine was hospitalized, I didn't pray for him, I didn't even care about him. But when I visited him at the hospital, I pretended in front of him as if I was so concerned about him. I always kept up appearances in front of other people then and there [*sobbing*]. I was full of sin.

YOSHIMOTO: Your next Naikan is about the time one year after your graduation. Please examine yourself with regard to the issues of lying and stealing and seriously ask whether you were a good psychiatrist or not.

[…]

YOSHIMOTO: It is just the end of the fourth full day since you started Naikan and the end of second day since you stopped eating, drinking and sleeping. I assume that it will be very hard and tough for you from now on. If you feel the urge to sleep, eat or drink, please freely do so, since these things are not the main line of Naikan. Please do Naikan seriously.

HIROSHI: I was examining myself a year after my graduation with regard to the issues of lying and stealing. I was so exhausted by working at the psychiatric hospital. For someone like me, who only had a basic knowledge of psychiatry without much experience, it had been a succession of tense and nervous moments. I didn't even talk to anyone until 3.00 p.m. every day, and I used to go back to my office and smoke, or visit my senior doctor's office to chat. I was stealing my monthly salary [by slacking off at work]. There were always some sweets for people to eat at the hospital, which I never ate when I was around other people. When I was on night duty and alone at the hospital, however, I ate a lot of sweets. I always considered that kind of nature[7] to be the most dirty. But I was the one with such a dirty nature. I was also such a failure as a doctor, because I only took the time to examine patients thoroughly if I liked them, but other patients, whom I didn't like, I didn't treat seriously. It scares me so much to think that I will keep spreading such seeds.

YOSHIMOTO: Are you going to examine yourself with regard to your latest year, which is two years after your graduation? Please do Naikan seriously and stay alert.

[…]

YOSHIMOTO: What kind of things did you remember?

HIROSHI: I was examining myself with regard to the issues of lying and stealing up to the present. While working as an assistant at the temple,[8] when I got hungry in the morning while sweeping the living room I used to steal and eat sweets that were on the table there. I told the other trainees at the temple that I always ate food like *udon* or *soba* for lunch, but actually I sometimes went out to a restaurant and ate whatever I felt like eating. I had to wake up at 4.00 a.m., but I sometimes didn't wake up until 4.30 or even until 5.00. But I always lied to people who visited the temple, saying that I woke up at 4.00 a.m. Yesterday, I was dozing when you visited me for the *mensetsu*, but I promptly lied by saying I was thinking about other things. I can't detach myself from lying even while doing Naikan like this.

YOSHIMOTO: Please examine yourself in the first two months after you started working at the hospital with regard to whether you were a good psychiatrist to your patients.

[...]

HIROSHI: I was examining myself with regard to whether I was a good doctor in relation to my patients in May and June after I started working at the hospital. [...] I treated my patients with a cold attitude, without making any effort to understand what their problems were. To the best of my ability, I was busy diagnosing my patients' symptoms and conditions. After I diagnosed a patient, I sometimes wrote out a prescription by selecting one of the patient's previous prescriptions, even if I didn't know the effects of that medicine. I also didn't pay enough respect to some nurses who had much more experience than I, ignoring their advice and causing trouble for my patients in the end.

YOSHIMOTO: Then is your next Naikan during the periods of July and August? Please do Naikan seriously.

[...]

HIROSHI: I examined myself in July and August in relation to my patients. What I received from them was that I learned various conditions, symptoms and examination methods, thanks to my patients coming before me and allowing me to have these experiences. Reading text books isn't enough to understand these things. I never realized this or thought this way until doing Naikan.

YOSHIMOTO: You were having some delusion whereby you considered yourself to be of a higher class than your patients.

HIROSHI: You are absolutely right.

YOSHIMOTO: Even though there were many things that you were taught by them.

HIROSHI: What I returned to them was that I arranged for patients to be able to return to their homes during the summer *obon* week,[9] since there were many patients who had not been back home for many years. However, it was just my natural obligation as a doctor to do this, now that I look back on it. What trouble I caused was that I hospitalized a patient who was living with his old father who was eighty years old and his mother who was seventy-five years old. They were living in the middle of nowhere in a mountain. When I received a phone call from the parents of the patient that his condition had deteriorated, I went to visit their house and judged that he needed to be hospitalized. Looking back upon it now, I feel so sorry for the old parents who were left alone after I hospitalized their child. Later I heard that the father of the patient died while he was at the hospital. Thinking about the elderly mother living alone in the middle of a mountain, I am troubled. Another thing is that there is an examination method which extracts water from a patient's back. Since my skill wasn't good, I could never insert the needle into my patients' backs smoothly the first time, and I had to try repeatedly, causing them incredible pain. I didn't think anything of it.

[…]

HIROSHI: I examined myself in relation to my patients in the period of September and October. […] There was a retarded child who couldn't understand what I said and it was impossible to train him. I wasn't patient enough. Instead I used to scold him and shout at him.

YOSHIMOTO: I wonder how his parents would have felt if they had seen such a sight.

HIROSHI: [*sobbing*] I am so sorry.

YOSHIMOTO: Your next Naikan is during the periods of December and January. Please do Naikan as seriously as you can.

[…]

HIROSHI: I was examining myself in relation to my patients during the periods of December and January. What I received from my patients was that they gave me a farewell when I left the hospital. I was to quit by the end of December. […] What trouble I caused them was that when one patient died of tuberculosis, I wasn't at his deathbed. I could have stayed with him after my duty was finished. Instead, I went home and left the patient to another doctor who was on night duty, since I thought I had to start my duties early on the following day. However, looking back upon that time now, I should have stayed with the patient until the last moment of his life.

[…]

YOSHIMOTO: What was the reason you asked to take a bath today?

HIROSHI: I smelled something, perhaps because I haven't been drinking anything. When I go and urinate, the smell of my urine is so strong that I thought I should at least wipe my body.

YOSHIMOTO: That's only natural after doing Naikan without food and water for two or three days. I had this experience four times when I was young. I thought: 'My urine has started to smell nice, so perhaps my Naikan is getting on the right track'. The smell of the urine and of my breath were like some sign to me, as an amateur, of judging how deeply I was doing Naikan. Of course, in reality these things don't indicate anything. Anyway, the smell won't go away by taking a bath. Is your next Naikan about the periods of July and August? Please examine yourself in relation to your superior, not your patients.

HIROSHI: Yes, I understand.

The practitioner

In the analysis that follows, I will examine the experiences of altered perception by Naikan clients and the mystical and somatic elements of this experience. First, however, I would like to address the involvement of the practitioner and his or her influence in the process of the formulation of Naikan confessions. The emphasis in Naikan is on the autonomous self-realization of the Naikan client and, as we noted in Chapter 2, the idealized image of the practitioner is that of a mirror that merely reflects the client and does not directly interfere in the process. Practitioners say that their job is not to 'help' or 'guide' the Naikan client, but merely to be *mensetsu-sha*, i.e. those who do *mensetsu*. Yoshimoto, for example, has said that Naikan can be done without having a practitioner, *mensetsu* or a Naikan centre, once one has learned the Naikan method. We see from Yanagita's case above that Yanagita did conduct Naikan on his own for over three months after his first Naikan session with Yoshimoto.

Still, there are some obvious contradictions revealed in the confessions above to this 'official' Naikan model of the practitioner, highlighting some tension between the representational model and the actual practice, which is much more complicated and difficult to fit into an explanatory model. Indeed, we see that the representational model is violated most clearly by Yoshimoto himself. His questions are probing and loaded, often pushing clients towards evaluating their experiences in a certain way, usually in the direction of acknowledging their own guilt and sinfulness. Furthermore, at several points the interaction stops being a one-way channel from the client to the practitioner (as it is supposed to be in the idealized model), and becomes dialogical.

The confession tapes also prove the operative aspect of the Naikan settings and environment and show the active way in which practitioners take part in shaping the Naikan experience for clients. Although Naikan clients are supposed to gain insight about themselves autonomously, confession tapes have a strong influence on the way clients recall memories. Naikan practitioners carefully select and edit tapes for the purpose of broadcasting, occasionally including their own commentary.

The broadcasting of recorded confessions, which takes place only at meal times, starts from the first day and the choice of confessions to broadcast is carefully thought out.[10] At *Meisō no Mori*, for example, Shimizu told me that he will arrange the order of tapes so that clients can start listening to something which is not too emotionally intense. He said clients can react very strongly and even negatively to confession tapes which contain a lot of crying, so he tends to choose tapes like Akina's (above) which are easy to listen to without having a negative reaction. On the third day, Shimizu broadcasts a recorded lecture by Yanagita on how clients have commonly misunderstood Naikan, which is very humorous, but also contains guidance about 'non-Naikan modes of thinking' as opposed to 'Naikan modes of thinking'. Shimizu and Yanagita told me that while selecting tapes they also take into account the clients doing Naikan at that time and try to find tapes that bear some resemblance to the problems, backgrounds or ages of the clients. At Nagashima's Naikan centre in Toyama, this is taken further to the point where each client listens on headphones to tapes that are individually selected by Nagashima for that specific client.

The interaction with the practitioner during *mensetsu*, the playing of recorded confession tapes during meal times and recorded lectures on how to do Naikan correctly, and the hearing of other clients' confessions as they are making them nearby in the same room all take part in shaping the way the client experiences Naikan. It may help to explain, for example, why crying is not an uncommon phenomenon in Naikan. If clients frequently hear other clients cry, either in the same room or in recorded confessions, they may receive this as an acceptable or even 'correct' way of doing Naikan.

Altered perception

Throughout the course of the Naikan week, it is common for numerous changes to occur with regard to one's perception. A client such as Keiko begins with a wholly negative image of her mother, yet ends her week of Naikan with a much more positive image. Later, she comes to a different awareness of her illness and its causes. Thus, it seems that these changes occur on various levels and perhaps even in stages.

Such changes in perception have been illustrated in the five cases given above, in my own Naikan experience described in Chapter 1, and are present in all the other confessional tapes that were given to me. I have showed up to this point what I consider to be the most important factors that lead to this process of altered perception: the Naikan setting with its sensory deprivation and 'tomb and womb' environment; the three themes of Naikan which focus on what trouble one has caused others but not the trouble others have caused; the practitioner, who carefully selects tapes, subtly conditions how the client is to understand 'correct' Naikan, and whose role during *mensetsu* is more complicated than generally acknowledged; and other factors, such as the physiological state of sitting for fifteen hours a day for a week, the embodied process of memory recall and the reconstruction of autobiography, which I will discuss in the following chapter.

The causes for this altered perception are therefore numerous and difficult to evaluate precisely. However, one can identify the kinds of altered perception that are common to Naikan and the order in which they usually occur in clients. I suggest that there are four such stages.

The first is an altered perception of the Other. Usually this follows the form of the client doing Naikan with relation to a certain significant other, such as the client's father, mother, husband, wife or child. When the client begins Naikan in relation to that person, the client brings to mind his or her pre-existing image of that person, which is really a static idea. By recalling memories year by year from that person's perspective and by being forced to concentrate on the trouble the client caused that person and not on the trouble caused by that person, this pre-existing image is problematized and called into question. Concomitantly a new image of that person is constructed, usually emphasizing the good qualities of that person (patient, giving, kind, etc.).

In the case of very important persons in the client's life, such as Noriko's father or Keiko's mother, the practitioner may suggest that the client do Naikan on that person twice. Exercises such as that provided by Yanagita for Keiko (listing negative traits and then reversing them) further encourage the client in this process. By the end of the process, the client has constructed a new image that often bears little resemblance to the initial image, accompanied by a feeling that the client now understands the significant other much better. Thus, Keiko begins with an image of her mother being a lazy woman who never cooked properly (in fact, she lists 48 grievances against her), yet concludes with an image of her mother who always cooked tasty meals. Noriko begins by describing her father as 'a lonely, sad person', who looked like 'a demon' when he killed Noriko's mother, but she ends her week of Naikan by describing him as a 'ball of light' and completely identifies with him.

The second stage is a corresponding change in the client's view of the self. Again, the client begins with a pre-existing image, a static idea, of him- or herself. Once the client recognizes the immeasurability of what he or she has received from others, any sense of being a self-made person collapses, and the client feels profound regret for things that cannot be undone and a sense of indebtedness to others that cannot be repaid. However, not only does the client's view of self change, but the view of the 'old self' changes dramatically. Clients may come to feel that in the past they were callous, self-centred, cruel and lacking in understanding. Thus when Yoshimoto suggests to Hiroshi that he was proud and saw himself as better than his patients, Hiroshi agrees. Yanagita sees his old self as self-centred, selfish and insincere regarding the condition of his retarded child, saying 'I killed my son in my heart. My heart was like a demon'. Just as in the case of reconstructing an image of the significant other, in this stage the client creates a strongly negative image of the previous self, against which a new self can be constructed, one that is better than the old self.

This new self, however, is not necessarily seen as 'good' or 'sinless', but rather one that is aware of interconnectedness with others, a topic we will explore in much greater detail in the next two chapters. Since this takes place concomitantly with the first stage of alteration of the images of significant others, clients frequently conclude that they do not live by themselves, but are 'lived' by others. Noriko concludes: 'as long as I have this memory of being loved by him, I will not hate him anymore'. Keiko says: 'I am here now thanks to other people, I am lived thanks to other people'. Another client reports: 'I was not aware that I talked very harshly to other people until I did Naikan. [...] I was convinced that I had been living, but I realized that I am lived. A sinful person like me is also being lived'. Yet another says: 'When I woke up this morning, I did not feel that *I* woke up, but rather that I was given life today as well'.

The third alteration is in the perception of the client's illness or problem. As seen in the case of Noriko, in some cases clients come with an idea that their illness may have a psychosomatic element. It is common for clients in the course of Naikan to give meaning to their illness, often concluding that the cause of their illness was a denial of the interdependence of their self with others. If the illness was previously seen as caused by another person, the illness is reinterpreted as having been caused by the client him- or herself. Thus, Noriko says 'Hatred caused more hatred, distorting my mind. It created an imbalance in my mind and, as a result, it caused the distortion in my body that was this incurable collagen disease. This is the result of me being self-centred all through my life and leading a life only according to my convenience.' Similarly, Keiko reports: 'I always blamed my mother for being the source of my anxiety neurosis. [...] It wasn't because of her, but rather because I only paid attention to the things she did not do and grew in anger and dissatisfaction that as a result I built up stress by myself and became sick'.

The fourth stage is an altered perception of the client's surroundings and a change in the way the client reports his or her sensory experience. There are some commonalities in the images clients use to describe this, such as a bright light of some kind; one's body feeling weightless; people and nature suddenly appearing beautiful; food and water tasting better; a feeling that some deep and ineffable truth has been discovered, even if it cannot be fully articulated in words; a sense of great happiness; a feeling that one has suddenly become meek or obedient (*sunao*); a willingness to serve and a great desire to share the joy and the feeling of gratitude; the feeling that one has been reborn; increased self-worth and the accompanying desire to take better care of oneself; fulfilment and peace of mind without any sense of anxiety.[11]

This fourfold perception alteration experienced by clients undergoing Naikan is clearly connected with the therapeutic efficacy of Naikan, or what we might call the process of healing. Yet we have still not answered how this process of healing takes place. In this chapter and the last I have provided some of the relevant background information for answering this question in our examinations of the Naikan setting, its themes, individual confessions and the client–practitioner relationship. In the next chapter I will turn to a theoretical explanation by investigating the interrelated issues of memory, illness narrative, autobiography and the self in Japanese and Western perspective, and we will explore how a relatively simple method such as Naikan can have such a transformative effect upon those who practice it.

Plate 3.1 The ritualistic motions of the *mensetsu*. The practitioner presses his hands together.

Plate 3.2 The ritualistic motions of the *mensetsu*. The practitioner bows. He will repeat these motions four times each *mensetsu*: before and after opening the screen, and then before and after closing it.

4   Embodied memory and the reconstruction of autobiography in Naikan

Naikan brings our attention to the interrelationships between autobiographical memory, life narrative and the sense of self. In analysing the therapeutic structure and mechanisms of Naikan, it is clear that recalling memory is a crucial component of Naikan. All other components such as the physical environment of the Naikan centre, the rigid time-framework, and the restrictions of no talking, reading or television, seem to be provided to create the most conducive environment for clients to recall their past in order to reconstruct their autobiography. However, what is of central importance in Naikan is not necessarily the recalled memories themselves, but the interpretations given to them within the framework of the client's narrative and the light such interpretations cast on the client's self-image and view of others. In my observation, Naikan's aim is actually to adjust the interpretive lens of the client from one that is distortedly self-justifying and impossibly self-sufficient to one that acknowledges past misdeeds honestly and recognizes the valuable role other people have played in ensuring one's well-being.

As Lowenthal rightly points out, 'we place unjustified confidence in our own memories, seldom questioning their reliability' (1997: 200). This enables us to maintain confidence in our life history and our identity. In Naikan, however, this confidence is called into question when clients are forced to view their life history from the perspectives of others. In this chapter, we will explore how the recollection of memory along Naikan's three themes reveals the subjectivity of the client's life story by revising it from a static, literally 'self-centred' (in privileging one's own perspective over that of others), seemingly fixed-in-the-past and 'objective' story into a negotiated, relative and vividly present re-experiencing. In other words, the recollection of memory along the prescribed lines of Naikan is primarily a means to help clients gain insight into the way they construct a life-narrative and self-image, and to recognize a self that exists not autonomously, as previously thought, but interdependently. It is known that memory can cause pain as well as heal. Ironically, although Naikan often gives the impression that focusing on one's misdeeds rather than one's positive traits would cause more pain, the movement from an apparently fixed-in-the-past and therefore unchangeable past to a present re-experiencing seems to have the potential to bring significant healing.

I begin with a discussion of how memory is central to one's concept of oneself as well as the relationship between self and other. In Naikan, this is particularly evident in the sense that a client's narration of an autobiographical life history reveals, and is deeply connected with, that client's self-image and view of significant others. Therefore, any marked alteration in the client's narrative often reveals a change in the client's view of him- or herself. In fact, it is through changes in their clients' narrative styles that practitioners often evaluate whether the clients are succeeding in doing proper Naikan and making progress.

Next I point out how memory recollection is often negotiated interactively – between practitioners and clients in Naikan's case. Client–practitioner interaction, the playing of confession tapes, the characteristics of the Naikan setting and the overhearing of other clients' confessions in the same room all predispose clients to recall autobiographical memory along certain patterns. All this points to the negotiated, improvised and constructed nature of autobiographical memory. This in turn reveals a third point, which is that memory should be considered as social – not merely individual – and this holds true for autobiographical memory as well, as Naikan illustrates. Indeed, the social vs individual dichotomy often does not seem appropriate in dealing with memory.

Fourth, in considering the social aspects of memory, it is only natural that cultural and social values will enter into the process of memory recall and reconstruction. Illness metaphors are one way this happens. Since major illness is a solid framework through which a life story may be narrated, a revision in the way that illness is viewed can result in a marked transformation in that person's whole self-understanding, often leading to experiences of great healing. Furthermore, exploring the constructed nature of illness narratives indicates that speaking of narratives as 'true' or 'false' may be inappropriate.

Fifth, if memory is constructed, then inner and outer conditions will naturally affect memory recall, and here the Naikan environment again becomes very important. The Naikan environment and the recollection of memories about the past trigger vivid sensory experiences in the present. These vivid *experiences* in the present interact with the static *ideas* that were used to narrate the past. This differentiation between vivid experience and static ideas comes out of Buddhist models of mental states (Berzin 1997): by 'memory-idea' I mean a constructed, static image or thought (one that has usually evolved or been developed over time) about something that happened in the past that is not experienced anew. So, for example, Noriko's static memory-idea of her father killing her mother, which caused her so much pain, comes to be liberated through a vivid experiencing *in the present* of seeing her father, washing him with light and sending him off as a ball of light. Keiko's static idea of her mother as a mah-jong obsessed woman comes to be replaced by a vivid experience of seeing her mother in the present with a brilliant, shining face that she describes as 'divine'. What is remarkable in these accounts is that the client is not remembering something new, nor is she replacing one memory-idea with a new one, as one might expect. Rather, she is having a completely new, present-tense experience involving the other person (father, mother) in the very Naikan environment, and it is this new experiencing that effects healing and dislodges the old memory-idea.

Naikan is of course not alone in employing memory as a means for therapy, and it is therefore unsurprising that many scholars find Naikan the most 'psychoanalytic' of Japanese therapies. However, Naikan's use of memory in therapy is quite different from Freud's. Freud seemed to believe that uncovering the past would lead to liberation from it and the treatment of neurosis, and although he may have later become rather pessimistic about the therapeutic effects of psychoanalysis, nevertheless, he still held it as a scientific study of the mind. In his framework, there is a strong assumption that memory is like a 'static object' that people can access and literally dig out. The notion that there are true and false memories (i.e. bad psycho-analysis can lead to the client constructing false memories) itself indicates a deeply embedded belief that memory is either correct or not. The focus in Naikan seems different. Although Naikan practitioners usually ask their clients to recall merely 'the facts' regarding their past, the entire Naikan practice seems to be questioning the 'mere factuality' of memories by draw-ing attention to the interpretive lenses that are used in the present-tense process of memory creation and recall. Through this process, therefore, Naikan clients begin to see a certain relativity in what they once considered to be objective facts about their past.

Thus, much of Naikan's engagement with memory has more to do with the present than the past, and Naikan's so-called 'reliving the past' is very much an engagement with the present. This leads to vivid experiences that cannot really be considered 'memories', as seen in the case of the confession transcripts in Chapter 3. The great importance of these vivid experiences, some of which appear to be quite remarkable and bear resemblance to religious and mystical experience, leads us to the final section of the chapter, which takes up that comparison.

Memory, life story and self

Although anthropologists have studied the constructive and continually reconstructing nature of the self (Kondo 1989; Roland 1991; Rosenberger 1992a; Cohen 1994; Morris 1994), too often they have neglected the import-ance of memory in this process. Naikan invites us to confront this issue and theoretically develop the vital role of memory in the reconstruction of the self. First, Naikan suggests the crucial tie between memory and selfhood. Second, the rearrangement of autobiographical memory, which is also the simultaneous process of reassessment of the sense of self, is effected by the client providing one week of consecutive life-story narrations. Although we may think of memory as ever-changing, there is in fact a static element to memory once a person has establish one version about their life-history, and such static memory-ideas can become crucial constituents of the self, such that their revision could effect rather fundamental changes in the client.

When clients are approached for the confessional interview, their report inevitably reveals their current self-image, due to the structure of Naikan's three themes. However, being forced to view the past from the perspectives of other persons is a way to shake up the existing static picture of the past that clients may have. One of the first things I observed about the way memory is used in Naikan is that it questions the reliability and objectivity of the client's life story, that is, his or her confidence in that story. The positive side of such confidence is that it provides the client with a sense of who he or she is as a continuity. At the same time, the static feature of such stories is such that when there is a negative or traumatic element, it can be experienced as unbearably painful, and the client feels unable to free him- or herself from that pain, as the event is fixed and stuck in the past.

I was intrigued when I heard practitioners say that nobody can do Naikan for the first couple of days – that it took a few days, if not longer, for a client to start doing real Naikan. This is similar to Yanagita's statement, quoted in Chapter 3, that Keiko's Naikan 'had not yet begun'. After going through Naikan as a client myself and listening to other clients' Naikan confessional narrations, I began to understand what they meant by such statements. At the beginning, clients are not actually engaged in actively recalling past memories afresh. Instead, they tend to just replay their existing static memory-ideas and report them to the practitioner. This is only natural as clients believe their story is a true history that happened in the past, therefore, it is a given (as opposed to a fabricated, i.e. constructed, story being continually re-created in the present). Especially traumatic events such as abuse are quickly reified as objective, immutable facts independent of any interpretation and impossible to view from any alternative angle. Only through re-remembering the past within a relational context are clients able to begin to shake up their static image of the past.

The differentiation between static memory 'ideas' and vivid 'experiences' I am drawing here comes from the Buddhist study of mental states and the way conceptual thought is differentiated from non-conceptual thought and experience, and I think it is particularly helpful in investigating what is happening in the Naikan process. To further explain the background of this distinction, here is an explanation by the Buddhist scholar Alexander Berzin:

> Ideas are static phenomena – usually translated as 'permanent pheno-mena.' This means they remain fixed so long as we think in terms of them, and do not undergo organic change from moment to moment. While we are thinking of our mother, for example, our idea of her does

not become tired or hungry. We can imagine her walking, in which case our idea of her walking is a semblance of movement. The sequence of images entailed, however, taken as a whole, constitutes a single idea. The mental pictures that compose this idea, like frames in a movie, are not actually walking.

Our idea of something, of course, may change, but this occurs in a special way. One idea is replaced by another. The latter version does not arise from the former through an organic process of depending on causes and circumstances ...

We can now begin to understand why conceptual thoughts are not vivid. When we think of something that changes from moment to moment, such as our mother, through the medium of an idea of her, we are mixing our mother with an idea of her. Our mother changes from moment to moment, while our idea of her does not. The appearing object of our thought – the idea of our mother – and its object of engagement – our actual mother – are not in the same category of phenomena. Because the focal object of our thought – our mother through the filter of our idea of her – is a hybrid object, the conceptual mind with which we think of our mother cannot give rise to a vivid experience.

(Berzin 1997: 87)

We will pick up again on the importance of vivid experience later in this chapter.

Although no one has yet theorized it in this way, Naikan, to my mind, ultimately points to the relational or intersubjective aspects of our experience and memory. For example, the more self-centred one is, the more one tends to see other people as objects, like machines, and one sees the world from an overly self-oriented way. Such a person hardly recognizes the simple fact that other people are also experiencing the world simultaneously. Yanagita used to say that people who suffer from severe illness often have a harder time following Naikan's three themes, as they are so trapped by their illness that they find it difficult to see things from other people's perspectives. As in the example of Noriko in Chapter 3, the transformation such people go through is often more dramatic than that of clients who were not suffering from a major illness.

The interactive negotiation of memory

Not only are memory and the sense of self deeply interconnected and mutually influential, but memory is also a continuous process of interactive negotiation. Recalling the confessions transcribed in Chapter 3, we have seen that, in contrast to the idealized portrait of client–practitioner relations often given by practitioners, the mirror is not as transparent as it is described to be. Naikan is often described as a sensory deprivation therapy due to its distinctive environment and setting of having no television, talking, reading, and so on. Yet even in such an environment, the interaction between the Naikan practitioner and the client cannot be neglected, and might even take on a more heightened significance.

Practitioners do not merely reflect back clients' narratives. Instead, they operate within a carefully structured environment, keep clients focused on Naikan's themes, and occasionally go further by asking probing questions or making suggestions that influence the client's narrative or affect the way clients engage with their memory. Even when the practitioner is silent, the client feels the presence of the practitioner. The client will still view the practitioner in a certain light – for example, as a teacher or parental figure, as we discussed in Chapter 2 – and this will affect the client's experience accordingly. Even if a client then goes on to do Naikan individually without a practitioner, the client will still be influenced by his or her earlier experience.

The fact that a client must make his or her narrative intelligible and acceptable to the practitioner underscores the interactive nature of Naikan confession. In fact, not only the client's verbalization, but also his or her recall of autobiographical memory itself may be affected by interaction with the practitioner. Such a point has been illustrated by Fivush *et al.* (1996) in their study on how children's memories are affected by their mothers' guidance. They point out that a mother asks questions about what the child remembers about a certain occasion, and if the child does not remember well, she repeats the question with additional details within the question, thereby elaborating on the event under discussion and directing the child's response (1996: 350–51). Reconstructed memories, they claim, are not complete fictions but rather 'negotiated' memories: changed, but not reinvented (1996: 344). They write:

> By telling a past event in a story form, the event is ordered in a way that maps onto experience and is coherent to listeners. Thus, an important part of the development of autobiographical memory is learning the culturally appropriate narrative forms for recounting the past.
>
> (Fivush *et al.* 1996: 344)

This is paralleled in Naikan when practitioners encourage clients to be more specific about their memories. Such specificity is viewed by practitioners as crucial for proper Naikan, while a free-association style of recalling the past is seen as least appropriate, and they direct clients accordingly. The increased vividness in memory caused by being forced to be specific may affect the client in particular ways, as we will explore below, but by intervening in such a way the practitioner is participating in the negotiation of memory in a similar way as the mother is with her child.

Autobiographical memory, therefore, is a part of social interaction and consequently must follow culturally appropriate narrative forms in order to make sense to a listener. Linde makes this point when she writes:

Life stories express our sense of self: who we are and how we got that way. They are also one very important means by which we communicate this sense of self and negotiate it with others. Further, we use these stories to claim or negotiate group membership and to demonstrate that we are in fact worthy members of those groups, understanding and properly following their moral standards. Finally, life stories touch on the widest of social constructions, since they make presuppositions about what can be taken as expected, what the norms are, and what common or special belief systems can be used to establish coherence.

(Linde 1993: 3)

Social memory and metaphor

If Naikan practice is inherently interactive, through the narrative structure of confessions during *mensetsu*, then it cannot be free of social and cultural norms that will affect the recall and construction of autobiographical memory. There is a strong notion that there is *individual* memory and *social* memory, with individual memory being private, self-possessed and not shared, whereas social memory is collective, shared and public; however, this dichotomy is challenged by Naikan. Naikan clients often come to realize that their life story was highly coloured by their subjective perspectives and that their current life story is constructed by their own *interpretation* through their Naikan. For example, Keiko's judgement that her mother was a bad mother because she hardly cooked for her while she was at college reveals Keiko's own expectation that a mother should take care of her children by not failing to provide cooked food three times a day, even after they are grown up. This clearly comes from a Japanese cultural norm; if an American or European heard such a narrative, they might think that Keiko was rather demanding and not very independent for her age. Not only do cultural norms, values, symbols and images inevitably enter into how people construct their life story, they also enter in naturally as the client attempts to communicate his or her autobiographical memory in a way intelligible to the practitioner.

Rubin discusses how the narrative structure of autobiographical memory resembles those of other social communication and claims that the act of recalling autobiographical memory is nothing but a 'social act' (1996b: 2–3). Tonkin also develops the idea that narratives of the past are socially constructed in her book *Narrating Our Pasts: The Social Construction of Oral History* (1992). This develops from her view of individuals as being fundamentally social, 'formed in interaction, reproducing and also altering the societies of which they are members' (1992: 1). She insists on the inseparable relationship of teller and audience in our oral representation of the past, rejecting a Cartesian dichotomy that also dichotomizes individual and society. Memory is for her the locus of social practices 'that makes us, together with the cognitive practices through which we understand society'

(1992: 12). This leads to her discussion of understanding memory as a key mediation between individual and society: Memory makes us, we make memory (1992: 97–8).

In her discussion of memory, Tonkin looks to Halbwachs, who saw memory as external. When I remember something, what I recall is my past responses to the outside world; thus it is the outside world that gives me understanding of what I am (Tonkin 1992: 104). Regardless of my wish to see my memories as unique to myself, memory is a 'social fact', coded in language and not the choice of any individual. For Halbwachs, therefore, there is only society, and 'memory ... mediates between the social world and the mind, but only so as to reproduce society' (Tonkin 1992: 105). Yet Tonkin goes further than Halbwachs by including the importance of socialization, which she defines as the ways and means by which we internalize the external world (1992: 105). In a sense, then, Tonkin is employing Halbwachs' views on memory to develop a line set out already in *The Sacred Canopy* (1967), where Berger writes of internalization:

> the socialization of the individual also occurs in a dialectic manner. The individual is not molded as a passive, inert thing. Rather, he is formed in the course of a protracted conversation (a dialectic, in the literal sense of the word) in which he is a *participant* ... he must continue to participate in the conversation that sustains him as a person in his ongoing biography.
>
> (Berger 1967: 18)

Clearly this ongoing conversation, in which autobiographical memory plays a crucial role, is shaped by the values, beliefs and norms of each particular culture. Bruner and Feldman, in their analysis of autobiographical memory in three groups, make this point (1996: 291–317) and go on to claim that 'Autobiographical memory, to be communicable, must be constructed of cultural materials' (1996: 293). Fitzgerald also attempts to broaden the framework of personal identity in his discussion of self-narratives by considering the effect of social environment: even simple questions such as 'What is your name?' can be taken as referring to personal or social identity. He therefore emphasizes the need for qualitative methodologies (1996: 379–80).

Barclay, too, suggests that autobiographical remembering is lodged in 'affective, interpersonal, sociocultural, and historical contexts' (1996: 94). His notion of 'improvisation' connects with the interactive negotiation of autobiographical memory discussed above:

> Improvised selves are created in present contexts to serve psychosocial, cultural, and historical purposes ... The root metaphor underlying my thinking about the nature, functions, and dysfunctions of autobiographical remembering and self-composition is "a moment of being ('selfless')

and is a product of improvisational reconstructive remembering activities" … Understanding the nature and functions of improvisation in
the reconstruction of autobiographical remembering clearly involves
specifying the referents from which memories are reconstructed and
extrapolated.

(Barclay 1996: 94–5)

Echoing in a sense the conclusions of Halbwachs, Schudson goes so far as
to say that there are no purely individual memories at all:

Even when memories are located idiosyncratically in individual minds,
they remain social and cultural in that (a) they operate through the supra-
individual cultural construction of language; (b) they generally come
into play in response to social stimulation, rehearsal, or social cues – the
act of remembering is itself interactive, prompted by cultural artifacts and
social cues, employed for social purposes, and even enacted by cooperative
activity; and (c) there are socially structured patterns of recall.

(Schudson 1997: 347)

Here Schudson is referring primarily to what he calls 'cultural memory',
which, while 'available for the use of individuals, is distributed across social
institutions and cultural artifacts' (1997: 347). He continues:

In broad terms, collective memory is characterized by four general
principles. First, memory is in fact social. People remember collectively,
publicly, interactively. This is true even of individual memory that is
sustained only by social interaction, by rehearsal, review, and the
language people have by virtue of being social beings. Second, memory
is selective. Remembering one thing requires forgetting another. Third,
selection is driven by various processes, both willful and unconscious …
Fourth, collective memory, at least in liberal pluralistic societies, is
provisional, always open to contestation and often actually contested.

(Schudson 1997: 360–1)

Here, the most compelling point they make is to demonstrate how even
what people consider individual memory (autobiographical memory, for
example) is social in nature. In my opinion, however, it might be clearer to
say that the 'individual vs social' dichotomy itself has certain limitations that
become exposed when considering memory. This point will become clearer
when we connect it with examinations of selfhood in the next chapter.
Anthropologists have thoroughly examined how selfhood is constantly in
flux, revision and reconstruction through work, gender roles, interaction and
so on. Once we recognize the interconnected relationship between selfhood
and memory, how memory is affected by these factors becomes obvious, as
does the sometimes arbitrary split between social and individual.

Thus Naikan is an example of how personal life story, which seemed at first objective (not relative or subjective), not dependent on other people, not biased by perspective, and so on, is actually a product of *selection* as Schudson (1997: 247) states. In the Naikan context, this selection includes one's perception and interpretation. Recognizing that one's memory is not free from interpretation, tragic memories move from the realm of what *cannot be changed* to the realm of what *can be changed*, because while it is clear that an 'objective' past event cannot be changed, a present-tense subjective interpretation of that event can be. As long as memory (and therefore one's life history) is seen as residing in the former, transformation is not possible, but when the focus is shifted to subjectivity, as happens in Naikan, this becomes a critical aspect of the therapeutic process.

Conversion and transformation in illness narratives

We might wonder, then, in what specific ways cultural norms and values might enter in. Here it may be useful to look to Sontag and her discussion of the illness metaphors. Sontag (1977, 1989) warns of the danger of attaching metaphors to diseases such as cancer, tuberculosis and AIDS, which can create negative associations (such as leprosy being seen as God's punishment). She argues that giving meanings to the disease causes the sense of pollution and danger; then the disease becomes a metaphor, it appears as fearful, making it harder for us to evaluate and treat the disease as it is. The medical anthropologist Namihira, however, rightly suggests that if we replace the term 'metaphor' with 'symbol', we see that 'illness as symbol' has been well-known in the field of cultural anthropology for a long time (1993: 13–22). As I will discuss in further detail below, it is too narrow to see 'illness as metaphor' in a purely negative light, since symbols can never be independently analysed, but rather exist within a complex and shifting symbol system. The signifier–signified relation is never a simple one-to-one correlation; rather one symbol can refer to a number of things.

Sontag's emphasis on the scientific, objective approach to illness also leaves out the cultural belief in causation and cognition of illness (Crapanzano 1973; Kapferer 1983). She ends up neglecting the importance and positive aspects of our activity of 'giving meanings to' and 'symbolizing' illness. Good criticizes Sontag's assertion that the metaphors of AIDS need 'to be exposed, criticized, belabored, used up' (1989: 94), suggesting instead:

> Ironically, Sontag's desire to do away with metaphors, to 'use them up,' reproduces the Enlightenment ideal of a culture-free representation of disease, of disease as objective reality, the biosciences as providing neutral and realistic representations, and folk culture as rife with dangerous and ultimately mistaken metaphors. Surely it is important to 'expose' the stigmatizing aspects of both scientific and popular accounts of disease and participate in the work of refiguring disease, gender, and

the human body. But for the anthropologist, replacing mistaken folk culture with the 'value-free information of science' seems a deeply inadequate goal for either cultural analysis or common action.

(Good 1995: 45)

Accepting this criticism, we may retain Sontag's insight into illness metaphors as a way in which cultural values enter in, if we expand it with the above points on the importance of cultural beliefs and the social character of memory. In the following sections we will see how, in contrast to Sontag's primarily negative view, giving meaning to illness may be an important part of how healing takes place in Naikan.

'Memory not only causes pain, it heals' (Butler 1989: 26), but it does do so along culturally specific lines. The appearance of Buddhist imagery in Naikan clients' accounts of their experience is a clear example. Also of crucial importance is the idiom in which healing prescriptions and subsequent healing narratives are presented. Not only is the discontinuous life story subject to constant revision and reconfiguring as one ages, meets different people or goes through fresh experiences, but it is imbued with moral meaning: 'The narratability of a given sequence of events is not fixed, rather, it is crucially related to the potential speaker's ability to perceive that a reportable event has happened and that it can be seen as having a particular moral relevance' (Linde 1993: 23).

As the process of the recovery of memory progresses, the clients' perception of their past changes and they 'reshape the past to accord with present self-images' (Lowenthal 1997: 201). The connection between a shift in the client's narrative tone and that client's sense of self is exactly what the Naikan practitioner seems to pay attention to. It seems that, as much as the life story is reshaped according to the present self-image of clients, self-image is reshaped according to the revised understanding about their life story. In other words, these processes occur simultaneously, so once clients start describing themselves in a different way, that indicates that their life-story has changed. Also, it is to be noted that reshaping the past is not a simple act of replacing an old story for a new story. Oftentimes, it is not the actual story or event that changes, but how it is understood. Once Noriko realizes that, although her father killing her mother is a fact, her father was also kind to her countless times, her story becomes differentiated such that her father is a figure who both helped and harmed her. As a result, Noriko's life story changed without changing the event itself. The past is revealed to be not a static object that can be approached in a non-contextualized manner, but rather made up of many different components such as how one connects and makes sense of events.

Listening to confession tapes, what is remarkable is the very short time in which such significant revision and change takes place. There is often a marked contrast in perception from the first day to the last, as we saw in the cases presented in Chapter 3. The success of Naikan in this regard may be compared to that of other transformative experiences such as near-death experiences and perhaps even religious conversion. Although one might remain sceptical of the ability of Naikan to cure clients of their illnesses and solve their problems, once clients achieve this transformative experience, a completely different light is shed on the same old past. One thinks of St Augustine's *Confessions* and the transformative power of conversion experiences to reshape one's entire picture of oneself and one's remembered and hence reconstructed autobiographical past.

Although Naikan confession is officially a report of the client's recollection of the past in relation to a significant other by following the three themes, and therefore not autobiographical narratives of the client's life or illness, many clients still start by providing a life story and explaining at length their suffering and what they believe caused it. We saw this in the cases of Noriko and Keiko in Chapter 3. Yanagita, understanding the human need to get such a thing out of one's system, tended to listen to clients' illness narratives for the first two days or so, and occasionally even specifically asked about a client's illness at the beginning of a Naikan session.

A severe illness can dominate a client's life so that the illness becomes the solid framework for their life story, making it hard or unthinkable for them to reflect on their life from outside of this framework. Therefore, once this framework is removed, the transformation they experience can be earth-shattering and liberating. Noriko's case, for example, is an example of a client spending a great deal of time explaining in detail her disease and what she believed caused it (the traumatic death of her parents). Such cases point to the meaning illnesses can provide in clients' lives, and how clients can be trapped in their illness and in their past, but the positive side is the significant transformation that is possible when such frameworks are revised.

If illness narratives can be transformed so comprehensively and in such a short time, what does this say about their veracity? Could it be that one fictional account is merely being replaced by another? We have already noted how this is not the most adequate way of viewing this process. Good, who has long studied illness narratives, writes that 'although illness experiences are far from "fictional," there are reasons to reduce the gap between fiction and reality in the context of cultural studies of illness' (1995: 163–4). His reasons for this are:

1   An illness has a narrative structure such as stories told by the sick about their experiences, by family members, doctors, healers, etc.
2   Stories are not only the means by which illness experience is objectified, communicated, and reported to others, but they are also a primary means for 'giving shape to experience'.
3   There is an element of fiction in illness stories, since narratives are organized as an unfolding of human desire.
4   The sufferer is not only a narrator of stories but is, similar to a 'reader', helpless to affect its outcomes.

I would agree with Good that the gap between 'fiction' and 'reality' is problematic, but I would push this claim further to argue that the very conception of 'fiction' vs 'reality' is not entirely appropriate in dealing with illness narratives, because of the particular picture of autobiographical memory it connotes. First of all, illness narratives are considered 'narratives' for those who are not suffering from the illness, but for a person who is experiencing suffering, it is not considered a 'narrative' but the mere facts of the illness. Therefore, the model of illness narratives provides a good example of how one's life story functions as seemingly objective fact until one recognizes its constructed nature. Second, although a narrative is usually understood as a verbally expressed statement to others, I would argue that there is an *inner narrative* which is one's own recollection and the story one tells to oneself. This would then serve as the basis for the *outer narrative* told to others. Furthermore, due to the interactive and constructed nature of memory, as we have explored, there is every reason to believe that these two narratives would be mutually influencing.

Another point I would like to push further regarding Good's argument is that the sufferer may not be completely helpless to affect the outcome, as Good claims. I would say the extent of 'helplessness' depends a great deal on the kind of narrative shape the client chooses to give his or her experience; it, too, is an interpretation, not a given. Noriko's case is perhaps most compelling here, as the facts about her father killing her mother and her incurable disease do not change, but her sense of helplessness transforms once her pre-established framework breaks down. Indeed, a feeling of helplessness seems not to be beneficial for recovery; at least in Naikan, a common observation by clients at the end of their sessions is the realization of the role they themselves played in holding on to negativity and trauma, which actually empowers them away from feelings of helplessness towards acting differently and in a way that will facilitate recovery.

Imagination, imagery and healing: the effects of internal and external conditions on memory

Internal and external conditions also affect how Naikan clients recall memories. For most Japanese, the external conditions of staying at a house of practitioners where someone cooks three meals a day and prepares a bath for clients creates a nostalgic sensation of going back home and experiencing life as a child again, being looked after by one's parents. The internal conditions are the changing perspectives clients experience through following Naikan's three themes to reflect on their past within a relational context. Imagination, emotion and perspective are therefore essential internal conditions that affect the construction of memory. Imagination often stirs vivid sensory experiences, triggering memories and playing a role in healing the body and mind during the Naikan practice. Akina and Noriko provide reports that reveal the important role of imagination in their memories.

Although imagination is often associated with being non-factual or false, 'true vs false' is not the most appropriate framework to understand a life story or illness narrative. Once we recognize that memory is inescapably bound to a process of fabrication, the role of imagination fits naturally into this process.

Since Rubin's collection of essays (Rubin 1986), the subject of 'auto-biographical memory' has become a rapidly expanding field in cognitive psychology. Freeman (1993), Ross (1991), Rubin (1996a), Schacter (1997a), and Schacter and Scarry (2000) have all attempted to supplement laboratory methods-based psychology with anthropological and sociological approaches.[2] They all emphasize the nature of autobiographical memory as constructed by imagination, narratives, social condition, cultural environment, and emotion, and search for alternative methodologies and paradigms. Thus, several psychologists and anthropologists agree that autobiographical memory is constructed[3] and, as Rubin argues, 'If memory is constructive, conditions at the time of construction will affect recall' (1996b: 9).[4]

Already in 1932, according to Schacter, 'Bartlett concluded that memories are imaginative reconstructions of past events that are heavily influenced by the rememberer's preexisting knowledge structures or *schemas* ... remembering is a fundamentally social activity that is inevitably distorted by the attitudes and needs of the rememberer' (Schacter 1997b: 9). In 1967 Neisser expanded this view, as Schacter summarizes:

> remembering the past is not a simple matter of reawakening a dormant engram or memory trace; past events are constructed using preexisting knowledge and schemas to piece together whatever fragmentary remains of the initial episode are available in memory ... all memories are constructions because they include general knowledge that was not part of a specific event, but is necessary to reconstruct it. The fundamentally constructive nature of memory in turn makes it susceptible to various kinds of distortions and inaccuracies.
>
> (Schacter 1997b: 10)

Connerton claims that in social memory, 'images of the past commonly legitimate a present social order' (1995: 3). Rubin writes, 'This does not mean that they are either accurate or inaccurate, but that they are not encoded, stored, and retrieved as wholes but rather are created at retrieval using components like the narrative, imagery, emotion division' (1996b: 4). Thus, it is not an issue of fiction or reality, for autobiographical memory is always partial and never fully accurate. Rather, the point is that we perceive our autobiographical memories as being true.[5] Imagery itself may be the major cause of this paradox (Rubin 1996b: 5), since images provide specific details of the past events which convince us the memory is true and accurate.

These images can connect with one's illness problems, along the lines we examined in looking at Sontag. In other words, they are an avenue for cultural norms to enter in to the healing process. The medical anthropologist Ueda has sought a more holistic approach to the topic of healing by combining brain physiology and image psychology (1994: 178). He takes the well-known image treatment founded by the American cancer specialist Dr Simonton as an example. Simonton discovered that people with strong will and positive attitudes tend to recover from cancer much better than people who are negative and pessimistic. From this fact, he discovered a correlation between the patient's psychological state and the advance of cancer, which led him to invent the Simonton method, which consists of relaxation and guided image treatment. Relaxation is done in a dim, quiet room and patients are told to sit in a comfortable chair and pay attention to their breathing. Patients are directed to imagine the cancer as tiny, frail lumps and the radiation treatment as energy penetrating the cancer like bullets. Patients imagine that energy starts to fill their bodies, that they are loved by their beloved and that their human relations are becoming more positive.

Ueda compares Simonton treatment to a Sri Lankan demon ritual, in which the healer calls for the demon that is possessing the patient (1994: 195). The patient imagines the demon vividly as a weak figure in front of Buddha, and then imagines the demon leaving each part of his body. The next morning, the patient is surrounded by his family and neighbours and shares their laughter, which emphasizes and actualizes warm human relations. Ueda proposes that the main difference between Simonton treatment and the demon ritual is that in the former treatment, the image is created only individually, while in the latter the image is produced and shared cooperatively. Since the image of the demon and Buddha are shared and maintained as a mythic cosmology, it is easy for the patient to imagine them, while it could be very hard for some patients who have cancer to imagine the cancer as frail since society believes cancer to be a fatal illness. These examples demonstrate how imagination not only activates and stirs vivid sensory experiences and triggers memories, but it can participate in effecting healing of the body and mind, a fact not yet fully understood by Western biomedicine. The use of imagining coloured lights entering one's body to cleanse diseases and impurities is a common practice in several different spiritual traditions including Buddhism (Zopa Rinpoche 2001).

Ueda's discussion raises some interesting points. First, the close link he makes between the body and imagination suggests that in Naikan the bodily engagement of sitting for fifteen hours a day for an entire week is central to the heightened imagination and intensity of the images produced by clients. Second, his discussion also suggests the function that a shared cosmology in a social community might have with regard to 'imagination healings'. This would suggest a connection between the role imagination plays in healing and the symbols employed in Naikan taken from the broader Japanese cultural background (for example, the role of the mother), a topic we will further address in the following chapter. Third, Ueda's emphasis on the importance of the imagination in sickness stands in contrast to Sontag's hostile attitude to the idea of the 'metaphor' of the illness. Simonton treatment, for example, is only possible by making patients create certain images and symbols about the cancer in their body. In other words, illness metaphors serve positive as well as negative ends.

Although image and metaphor are not the same, both engage and require the imagination for the construction of meaning. In religious language, metaphors exist within a rich symbol system; similarly, symbol systems affect illness metaphors. For a long time, philosophers of language such as John Searle (1969, 1979) have treated metaphor as parasitic on real language and translatable in a rather straightforward manner. However, such views are highly questionable. As Donald Davidson (1979) points out, the interpretation of even the simplest of metaphors seems limitless; metaphors draw us into a participation in the creation of meaning that can lead us infinitely on. Richard Moran writes:

> To make progress from here, it may be useful to re-orient our approach to the whole phenomenon, to consider cognition and communication outside the context of strictly linguistic activity, and to begin investigating them from this broader perspective prior to explicit theorizing about the case of metaphor. That is, instead of taking the determinate proposition expressible in a simple sentence as our paradigm, and then asking how closely metaphor may or may not approach this model, we might begin with communicative situations that are non-verbal, indefinite, and unstructured, and ask where we might locate metaphorical speech on a continuum of cases from there to explicit, literal speech.
>
> (Moran 1997: 265)

Others such as Lakoff and Johnson (1980, 1999) have argued the centrality and inevitability of metaphor in all complex forms of human thought, based on the fact that a vast number of basic metaphors are grounded in sensory-motor experience.

Imagination plays an important role in healing as well. Csordas sees 'imagination as an important self process in Charismatic healing, focusing on the revelatory imagery of healers and the relation between imagination and perception in the intersubjective milieu of ritual performance' (1994: 109). This notion is shared by Tonkin, who writes, 'Any representation of pastness is identity-constitutive and can be elaborated into an identity-support as well' (1992: 135). Csordas notes a 'characteristic Charismatic notion that healing of memories can divinely achieve in one session what would take months in psychotherapy' (1994: 123).

This healing is inextricably linked to the creation of a new self along the lines outlined at the end of Chapter 3. As Csordas writes, 'The negative goal of removing suffering is strictly complementary to the positive one of creating the sacred self' (1994: 109).[6] Once one is released from the negative self-image of the past, one can feel that one is in the present, and this occurs by using one's imagination to connect with reality (1994: 123–4). Such ideas parallel Naikan, as does the idea that a static reality cannot be changed, but perception can. Csordas writes:

> First of all, memory is a powerful symbol of the self, such that access to memory is access to a privileged zone of communication with that 'other who becomes myself.' In that invocation of others any psychotherapeutic or religious technique that offers such access to memory can have overtones of the sacred ... Because of the symbolic value of memory, in a sense it does not matter whether it is literally accurate. Secondly, if memory is a symbol of the self, the array of specific memories invoked and re-invoked by techniques such as healing of memories constitutes a *pastiche* of the self.
>
> (Csordas 1994: 110)

In Chapter 2 we explored the issue of Naikan and death, and how the setting of Naikan might be called a 'tomb and womb' environment. This is a clear example of how the imagination of clients is engaged in Naikan and even directed towards specific concepts such as birth, death and rebirth. The Naikan practitioner Ishii often conducts five-minute long mini-Naikan sessions at Naikan meetings and conferences. He asks the audience, most if not all of whom have already done Naikan, to close their eyes. Then he instructs them in an imagination exercise, saying 'Now you are on the way home from your elementary school. You are wearing school uniform and carrying a leather school backpack. Here is the street to your home, your home when you lived when you were that age. Now you are opening the door. Is your mother there waiting for you at home? What is she doing? Is she preparing some tea and sweets for you? Now it's dinner time. What kind of meals are on the table prepared by your mother or your grandmother? What was your favourite food?' and so on. Audiences therefore recall their past in a heavily guided manner, one that is rich with Japanese cultural norms and one that assumes a host of common experiences among the audience members.

Another favourite technique of Ishii, again showing guidance, is 'Death Naikan'. This exercise is also carried out at Naikan meetings and conferences. Ishii asks the audience to close their eyes and tells them that they have only ten minutes left before they die. They are on their deathbed and can barely move. As Ishii continues, he counts down the minutes they have left to live. 'It's time', he says, 'to speak with your friends and close relatives, and thank them and say the things you never had the chance to say before.' With only five minutes left, he says, 'It's time to call your mother, father, wife, or husband. Apologize to them and thank them.' Finally, Ishii says, 'It's time now. You cannot hear any more, your sight is getting blurred. Everything starts looking dark. It's time.' After a moment of silence, he asks the audience to open their eyes. When I experienced this, I saw many people crying.

Embodied memory

Unless we are to posit a disembodied mind, our examination of how imagination and memory affect healing cannot ignore the fundamental importance of the body. To achieve a full picture, we must take into account factors as varied as embodiment and body practice, the mind–body problem, neurology and physiology, mental states and physical states, and parallels to Naikan experiences in mysticism, and altered consciousness. We should also consider how repetitive body acts recall culturally specific connotations and images, revealing the embodied nature of social memory. This will not only help us in our understanding of Naikan, but also, I hope, provide insights into memory, healing and the body that will carry over into a number of other areas as well.

We have seen that clients normally begin Naikan with only vague memories and have difficulty remembering past events. By the fourth or fifth day of constant sitting, however, memories come flooding out almost spontaneously and without effort, and are surprisingly vivid. An important aspect of these memories are images, and we have explored that avenue and what it can tell us about the process of healing. Yet these memories are not just images; they are also accompanied by somatic experience. One client confessed that she could feel her grandmother was rubbing her stomach to help her digestion when she was three. Others speak of 'ice cubes suddenly melting in my body', 'a solid lump under my right shoulder suddenly falling off with a sound', and so on. Quite commonly, clients feel their palms getting warm. Many, in fact – and this was also my experience – feel their entire body becoming so warm that they no longer need a blanket at night.

It seems clear that some physiological changes are happening here, and one can only regret that studies of such phenomena from this perspective are scant, although recent studies on the physiological changes brought about by meditation are promising (Goleman 2003). Yet, as one would conclude from our earlier examination of imagination, a physiological investigation would not be likely to explain enough. The experiences of clients even go beyond the physical sensations described above. As noted earlier, the language clients use reverts back to childhood terms and levels of politeness. Some confess that they see an image of Buddha on the paper screen before them, or even feel an actual living presence within their meditation space. Others even recall events such as being born.

It seems, then, that in deep Naikan clients lose their sense of distance to the past, and are actually in some cases re-experiencing and reliving their past (yet this time in a radically different way, according to the guidelines and themes of Naikan) or in other cases having new experiences that did not happen in the past, but that are connected with past events or persons. To see how this might be happening, we will have to bring together a variety of elements. In Chapter 2 I discussed the discomfort and disharmony between mind and body caused by the Naikan practice of sitting for such long periods of time, and brought in the philosophers Ichikawa and Yuasa to suggest that breakthroughs might occur when this disharmony was overcome. I also explained the Naikan setting and the ritualistic elements of Naikan. Already, this material presents part of the explanation, but it remains necessary to bring in our discussion of memory, and especially memory as social and embodied.

We have seen that cultural influences enter into Naikan through the interactional nature of the confessional *mensetsu* session, but this also takes place in the repetitive, ritualistic acts of the practitioner. When the practitioner comes to the client for *mensetsu*, moves aside the paper screen, kneels, presses his palms together and bows, these are far from innocent acts. Rather, they bring with them a great deal of cultural weight. In Japan, pressing one's hands together is reserved typically for the sacred; it may be done in a Buddhist temple before an image of Buddha, in a Shinto shrine before the altar or by a Christian praying. It has strong religious connotations, therefore, and it is not often done before other people. Bowing, on the other hand, is done before other people, but carries with it meanings of greeting, gratefulness, apologizing or shame (as in kowtowing).

For these reasons, when a practitioner does these ritualistic acts before clients, it is not just normal practice in Japanese culture. On the contrary, clients are often puzzled by this and may feel strongly resistent to reciprocating by pressing their palms together and bowing back. Some Naikan centres have even removed this element for the very reason that it is too religious. Yet the resistance of clients usually disappears after the first few days, and clients engage in the same ritualistic acts as the practitioner.

These repetitive body acts recall culturally specific prior connotations and images. To use Connerton's phrase, they recall a past that is 'sedimented in the body' (1995: 72). This is again an instance of social memory. Although the client may not go regularly to a Buddhist temple or Shinto shrine, it is unlikely that he or she would never have encountered such practices in any way. Many Japanese make an annual visit to a Shinto shrine on the New Year's Day, pressing their hands together and then throwing some change into the *osaisen bako*, or offertory chest. When the client participates in the ritualistic body acts of Naikan, memories of experiences that were registered in earlier life are engaged anew.

By bringing in broader cultural activities that will resonate with the client, the particular body acts in Naikan create a solemn, even reverent atmosphere. It is easier to feel grateful, apologetic and ashamed while bowing and pressing one's hands together than it is to feel angry, bitter or proud. Physical states, then, are being used to conjure up or influence particular mental states. This recalls Jackson's (1983) findings on patterns of body use resulting in mental images and establishing moral qualities, when he studied the importance of the imitation of practical skills such as hoeing, dancing and lighting lanterns in Kuranko village. He writes:

> We are all familiar with the way deconstruction of muscular 'sets' and the freeing of energies bound up in habitual deformations of posture or movement produce an altered sense of self, in particular a dissolution of those conceptual 'sets' such as role, gender and status which customarily define our social identity. My argument is that the distinctive modes of body use during initiation tend to throw up images in the mind whose form is most immediately determined by the pattern of body use. This is not to say that all mental forms should be reduced to bodily practices; rather, that within the unitary field of mind-body-habitus it is possible to intervene and effect changes from any one of these points.
>
> (Jackson 1983: 336)

A similar point might be made about the importance of sitting posture in many forms of meditation.[7] Would it even be possible, one wonders, for the same experiences to be had if the ritual postures were ignored?[8] Similar to Jackson's work is Ikuta's study of the continuous imitation and repetition of students training under their master typical in Japanese traditional art forms. Ikuta sees habitus as a useful concept in understanding this process (1992: 36). Together, the creation of mental images, morality, 'altered sense of self' and our 'social identity' through certain body postures, as discussed by Jackson and Ikuta, help to explain the emphasis on body practice in Naikan.

Experiencing the past in the present

Looking at the body acts in Naikan as an example of embodied social memory is helpful, but it is still insufficient in explaining how Naikan clients seem to be vividly re-living their past, even to the point of having somatic experiences, and how this can have such a transformative effect on their sense of self. I would suggest that part of the problem has to do with the way in which memory has often been dealt with. There are different kinds of memory, tied together, as Wittgenstein would say, more by a family resemblance rather than by a strict definition of what 'memory' is. If we fail to recognize this, we fall prey to the essentialist fallacy that because we use one word to describe different activities, there must be one distinct thing to which this word refers. Remembering what the capital of France is, remembering how to ride a bicycle and remembering one's past are not the same thing. On the one hand, it is easy to recognize this, and several scholars have. Yet at the same time, I would argue, the difficulty in differentiating between different kinds of memory has resulted in the weakening of many of the theories we have looked at in this chapter.

Part of the problem stems from the idea that memory must deal primarily with the past. Tulving and Lepage, based on their PET studies of the brain, counter this notion, writing that 'most forms of memory and learning studies in many areas of the life sciences have to do with the present and the future, not with the past' (2000: 209) and the only exception is episodic memory. While other forms of memory are proscopic, i.e. forward-looking, episodic memory alone deals with a person's experienced past and makes possible what Tulving and Lepage call 'mental time travel', namely going back and re-living past experiences.

> All of the many different forms of memory, with a single exception, serve the same purpose as do the 'instincts': they provide organisms with the means of behaving more effectively than would have been possible in the absence of the relevant knowledge or skill ... The singular exception to the ubiquity and evolutionary significance of proscopic memory that serves the future without bothering about the past is episodic memory. It does exactly what the other forms of memory do not and cannot do; it enables the individual to mentally travel back into the personal past.
>
> (Tulving and Lepage 2000: 211)

Unlike other forms of memory such as semantic memory, episodic memory involves 'autonoetic' awareness, a special form of conscious awareness that is missing in habitual acts. To prove their point, Tulving and Lepage give the example of a brain-damaged patient who lacks autonoetic awareness.[9] Although his other cognitive functions remain intact and he can acquire new semantic information at a slow rate, they write, 'he cannot consciously recollect any single or even repeated event from his entire life, regardless of how memorable the event by ordinary standards and regardless of how heavily he is cued or prompted' (2000: 217).

Recognizing this distinction clears up a lot of the conceptual confusion caused by assuming that all memory must be about the past. When Connerton presents the act of swimming as an example of the past 'sedimented in the body' (1995: 72), he seems to be making this error. Swimming is a forward-looking skill; it does not evoke images or engage the imagination, nor is it prone to distortion. Though we may use the word 'memory' to refer to our ability to swim as well as our ability to reflect upon our past and create a narrative out of our recollections, we should not confuse the two and think that because both are 'memory', both have to do with the past.

As mentioned earlier, Naikan seems to illustrate how, when asked to narrate something about our past, we typically narrate a 'static idea'-story, and do not engage in an actual act of critical remembering. This would seem especially true if it is a story we have recounted numerous times either to ourselves or others. Usually the more we recount the story, the more static it becomes and the further removed it is from experience. Moreover, the story is inherently subjective because it is created out of selection criteria of what is deemed important, and it is given a narrative structure in order to render it intelligible to ourselves and others (rather than being a mere collection of meaningless, uninterpreted sensory data). In one sense, memories as static ideas do not have to do with the past – just as when we use words we have learned in the past, we are not actively remembering when we learned them – and they are not vivid in terms of sensory experience. A reliving of past events as present experience, however, can be accompanied by a vivid sensory dimension since it is a present experience. So in this important sense, Naikan's so-called 're-living the past' is actually experienced in the present.

Shinagawa suggests that our brain has difficulty distinguishing between a real event and a vivid image; therefore, if vivid images are created successfully, the brain can react to this as reality and affect the entire body correspondingly (Ueda 1994: 197–8). Combined with Tulving and Lepage's findings on episodic memory, and our earlier discussions above, we can now paint a reasonably complete picture of what is happening in Naikan. We are able to say that autobiographical memory, as distinct from other kinds of memory, is particularly social in nature, affected by the environment and conditions of recall, and influenced by narrative structure. In the 'tomb and womb' environment of Naikan, guided by practitioners, and influenced by their very body posture and body acts, which are culturally distinctive, clients recall and narrate their past. This past by necessity engages their imagination and brings images to mind, images that are made vivid by the specificity required by practitioners and the environmental factors we have described, and images that are grasped as 'true'. In an altered physiological state, and altered state of consciousness, and in 'autonoetic' awareness, clients re-live their past. They re-experience past events as if they were happening again, complete with somatic experiences that are far from imaginary, except this time from the perspective of others and with a different moral valence. And since they are re-living their past, they are constructing a new past, and hence a new self.

Mystical experience in Naikan

The well-known non-fiction writer Yanagita Kunio wrote that while experiencing Naikan he often fell asleep during the first five days. Suddenly, on the sixth day, he felt he was in the middle of a mandala. He saw the Buddha in the middle of a cosmic whirlpool with innumerable small Buddhas revolving around him. Then he realized that he was the central Buddha, and the smaller Buddhas were his relatives, friends and others who were supporting him as they revolved around his shining being. It was a trance-like, rapturous experience (Yanagita and Kawai 1998: 276).

The parallels between Naikan experience and religious experience, especially that of mysticism, invite explication, yet at the same time, perhaps unsurprisingly, they defy it. I would like to conclude this highly analytical chapter, therefore, with a postscript on mysticism that will be primarily descriptive. Still, I hope that in view of the above discussion it will prove enlightening.

William James, in his classic *The Varieties of Religious Experience*, suggested 'four marks which, when an experience has them, may justify us in calling it mystical' (1999: 414). These are:

1   Ineffability ... The subject of it immediately says that it defies expression, that no adequate report of its contents can be given in words ...

2   Noetic quality ... They are states of insight into depths of truth unplumbed by the discursive intellect. They are illuminations revelations, full of significance and importance, all inarticulate though they remain; and as a rule they carry with them a curious sense of authority for after-time.

3   Transiency ... Often, when faded, their quality can but imperfectly be reproduced in memory; but when they recur it is recognized; and from one recurrence to another it is susceptible of continuous development in what is felt as inner richness and importance.

4   Passivity. Although the oncoming of mystical states may be facilitated by preliminary voluntary operations, as by fixing the attention, or going through certain bodily performances ... yet when the characteristic sort of consciousness once has set in, the mystic feels as if his own will were in abeyance, and indeed sometimes as if he were grasped and held by a superior power.

(James 1999: 414–15)

James goes on to give a broad survey of mystical experiences as reported over centuries and across religious traditions. As space does not permit such a selection here, I will instead present a few experiences reported by Naikan clients that resemble other accounts of mystical experience and that also fit James' four marks. We have, in fact, already seen some examples in the confessions transcribed in Chapter 3.

A PhD student at Tokyo university wrote of his experience:

While continuing the work of recalling the past, with the sensation that all segments of my past memories merged and harmonized, 'realizations' came to me ... I realized my true self by seeing all the deeds I had done as they were, especially deeds that I had been unconsciously avoiding because I did not want to be forced to see them ... These realizations sometimes visited me suddenly, at other times they were more gradual like feelings that seemed to carry some meaning. These feelings were vague sensations within my stomach and around my chest ... While trying to see and feel these vague feelings as they were, without framing them by logical or conceptual thought, and focusing on past facts, the feelings gradually grew stronger and developed into realizations that 'This is true'. The moment these feelings became realizations, a word that perfectly fit the first sensation of the feeling appeared. By repeating this word over and over, and ringing the sound in my mind (*kokoro*), I came to understand that it really was the truth. Whenever I went through this process, something was pushing up from the bottom of my stomach and my breathing became deep and I could not help crying. My body was shaken, sobbing and crying. After some time, something which was hanging in my body dropped with a sound – something like a sea cucumber dislodged from my left rib-bone, blockages disappeared and my body became very meek (*sunao*).

(Yanagita 1997: 122–4)

Yanagita Kakusei, the practitioner, describes the following experience of his journey home after his week of Naikan at Nagashima's Naikan centre in 1985:

I suddenly found myself in the middle of a strange imaginary world. I saw a mountain of guilt, which just exploded in front of me. It was a mountain of my guilt, the mountain that had always existed in the depths of my heart. The mountain had been nourished and cultivated over the last fifty-five years ... The mountain of guilt was rushing toward me. I felt the sensation of losing my strength of both body and mind. Yet it was not with fear, but rather more like a sense of relief, that I saw my true colours. Then, at that moment, a strange, gigantic impact struck inside my body. My intestines were all twisted, all my muscles danced, my blood was boiling, my heart was filled with emotion, endless energy was pushing both upwards and downwards, my body was about to be hurled to the edge of the cosmos, and I felt a powerful excitement that nearly made me scream ... The next second, infinite logic about the philosophy of life started formulating with accuracy and precision in my brain. This epiphany of one second would be five hundred pages' worth on paper ... I accepted all my guilt and all my experiences – in other words, my whole life ... The moment I accepted both my guilt and experiences, I understood my real self and I understood the unity of myself and the cosmos. This truth has infinite logic and spreads like the cosmos. The moment I understood the truth, I laughed so uncontrollably that my whole body shook endlessly.

(Yanagita 1997: 114–17)

This whole experience, he reports, lasted for thirty minutes while he was on the way home. The following week he slept for only one or two hours a day, yet he claims that afterwards he did not feel tired and was full of energy in a state of excitement that lasted for half a month (1997: 118).[10]

As James noted in his criterion of ineffability, when it comes to mystical experience, language fails. I conclude this chapter with one client, a businessman, who attempted to better capture his Naikan experience in the form of a poem.[11]

The World of the Unity of the Self and Others

I am a lighthouse, an island, a wave, and a grain of sand.
I am a fishing line, a needle, and the fish being caught.
I am a mountain, a cloud, rain and a breeze.
I am a tree, the grass, and a pretty flower.
I am an ant, a butterfly, and an insect.
I am a wall, a sliding door, and a paper screen.
I am you and you are I.
I am a father, a mother, a wife and a child.
I am music, painting and art.
I am courage, beauty and love.
I am the moon, the earth, and the sun. I am the cosmos.
I am myself, and all in all.

Conclusion

In the Naikan process the client re-lives the past through the perspective of others; through this process his or her previous story comes under critique and eventually collapses. The key here is seeing that collapse, seeing one's own bias, and having one's fixed ideas and story be replaced by vivid experience, which, unlike the fixed ideas and story, cannot be easily expressed in language. However, the client must then express his or her experiences to the practitioner. At this point, the client may construct another story, a new revised story, and this may replace the previous story. Although this is what we occasionally see in the confession transcripts, the point is not that the new story replaces the old story. If that is all that happens, the new story – which has also become an idea and not an experience – can merely become another fixed, set story, so that one story gets replaced by another. But this is not the main point – the main point is the insight the client gains while undergoing the process of seeing his or her previous story collapse in the face of new vivid experiences: this is what is therapeutically effective, in my opinion. And if the client can gain a deeper insight into the process of biased, self-centred story-creation, then this insight can be applied in future, and this is much better than just having a new, revised story.

This is an implicit aspect of Naikan's therapeutic mechanism. Naikan practitioners occasionally speak about 'replacing an old negative past life-story with a new positive life story', to use a statement of Yanagita. Other practitioners are even more hesitant to state something like this and say that clients are merely asked to recall the facts about their past deeds. I am not sure what Naikan practitioners themselves believe about the factuality of the memories or not, but my impression is that many practitioners seem to see that our past memory is always biased due to the self-centred nature of human beings which tend to view things and events from an 'I-centred' perspective, yet see that perspective as being 'objective' at the same time.

The newly revised self-story, on the contrary, appears less subjective, less narrow and therefore closer to the objective facts as the new version includes and acknowledges the subjectivity, existence and perspectives of others.

Although the Naikan method is centred around memory recall, ironically – as evident from Yoshimoto's comments especially in the transcripts in Chapter 3 – the Naikan practitioner is not actually concerned about the actual past events of the client's life, but rather how the client views those events. Although Yoshimoto frequently asked whether the client was good or not, he was not asking to find out objectively whether the client was good or not, which was irrelevant. Rather, what was of ultimate importance was the client's self-image, their understanding of themselves. Asking clients to narrate the past is primarily a *means* through which this self-image comes out, becoming evident to practitioner and client alike, and is also the very means to critique it. This is why Yanagita says – in his commentary on Keiko's case presented in the last chapter – that what is important is not what Keiko is narrating, but the fact that she is doing it in a business-like tone, without any sense of remorse. That is a sign to him that her Naikan has not yet begun. If Naikan were just the process of recalling autobiographical memory or reconstructing one's life story, or even re-writing it, there would be no grounds for Yanagita to claim that her Naikan had not yet begun. But the principal aspect of Naikan is not memory recall in itself, but the re-evaluation of oneself and one's relationships to others that occurs in the present through the critique of the self-image that is triggered by recollecting one's past from the perspective of Naikan's three themes.

If Naikan were merely about re-writing the facts of one's life, it would not make sense why serious *Naikan-sha* would engage in it again and again. Rather, it is not the facts of the past that change or are rewritten, but the interpretive lens that the client uses to narrate them and indicate their significance. This interpretive lens can be polished again and again, as clients delve deeper into the Naikan experience and gain deeper insight into their dependent co-existence with others. Similarly, it is not the facts of the client's past that the practitioner is interested in, but the interpretive lens that they are bringing to those facts. This is why the practitioner might be more interested in the client's tone of voice or interpretive comments in narrating an event than in what he or she actually did. A smooth narration of a story at the beginning of Naikan may indicate that the client is just using a pre-existing interpretive lens, and has not yet begun the actual process of reflection and introspection.

This distinction between the facts of the past and the attitude, perspective or interpretive lens of the client towards them is extremely important in terms of Naikan's therapeutic efficacy, because while the actual events of the past cannot be changed, and the past cannot be rewritten, one's attitude towards those events can always undergo change, and this change happens in the present. When the client comes to actually realize this for him- or herself, it is certainly empowering, since the scenario changes from something that cannot be changed to something that can be changed, and indeed, can even be changed by oneself alone. And this is likely what Yanagita meant in speaking of a 'rearrangement of self-history' (1979: 30).

Plate 4.1 Yanagita at *Meisō no Mori* Naikan Centre in Tochigi during an interview with myself. He holds up a picture of the 'relational self' drawn by one of his clients, showing a person surrounded by others.

Plate 4.2 A mandala made by another of Yanagita's clients. The central Buddha-like figure represents the client. The inner circle represents family; further circles represent friends and others.

5 Interdependent selfhood, Buddhism, and the role of mother

Due to its emphasis on mother and its effect of restoring relationships, Naikan is often regarded as a culturally conservative, conformist practice aimed at conditioning clients and re-socializing them. In Chapter 2 we saw Reynolds' list of characteristics of Japanese forms of psychotherapy, which includes 're-socialization', and Reynolds has also mentioned that he feels that any psychotherapy which criticizes the mother would not succeed in Japan. There are reasons why some might have this view. In principle Naikan requires clients to start with recalling memory with regard to their mother on the first and last day of the week-long session. 'Start with mother and conclude with mother' is the theme. Yoshimoto explained that we are all protected and fed by our mother when we are small. 'Mother is the starting point and origin', he said, and 'Everything is symbolized through how you are to your mother'. Moreover, Japan is well known as a culture that places great significance on the role of mothers.

Nevertheless, I believe classifying Naikan as an essentially conservative practice oriented towards the re-socialization of its clients may be a bit of a simplification. Furthermore, Naikan's emphasis on mother may not merely be a reflection of conservative Japanese cultural norms, but may play a deeper role in the process of transformation that can occur in Naikan. These questions and the debates surrounding them revolve around how scholars have approached the study of self and society in Japan, and whether there is a distinctively Japanese sense of self, which may account for the effectiveness of Naikan, or whether the Naikan method is actually dealing with psychological and cognitive structures that would make it of more general, and less culturally specific, relevance. In exploring these questions, this chapter will focus on three interrelated topics: first, the way selfhood is reconfigured in Naikan and how this relates to various existing theories on the Japanese sense of self; second, the Buddhist heritage of Naikan, which is the source of this method of insight and transformation; and third, the focus on the role of 'mother' as a principal means in Naikan to effect such insight.

Regarding the first of these points, it seems to me that successful Naikan is the development of insight within the client from a construal of an impossibly self-sufficient and independent self, and completely distinct and separate 'others', to a recognition of the interdependent nature of self and others. The first is a dualistic view of self and others; the second is a view of interconnection and inter-penetration of self and others. If this is not properly understood, one might conclude, as many observers of Naikan have, that Naikan is a process of downplaying independence in favour of re-socialization and reintegration. Yet to see things in this way is to remain within the first dichotomy, where the only alternative to independence is an integration into social norms and structures within which individuality disappears. This is quite different from the view that such a dichotomy is misleading to begin with, and that the reality of our existence is quite otherwise: namely that the individual exists and remains as an individual, but is only made that very individual in reliance or dependence upon others. In other words, it is not a rejection of the individual, but a different view of what it means to be an individual, of how individuals exist. The Naikan method itself can therefore be seen as a process of systematically bringing the first dualistic view under critique, whereby the client's self-conception changes from viewing him- or herself as a person who came into existence and continues to exist self-sufficiently and autonomously, to a person whose existence has always depended upon, and continues to depend entirely upon, others.

This view of how persons exist comes to Naikan from the Buddhist tradition. According to Buddhist philosophy, it is impossible for anything to exist in a completely self-sufficient, independent manner – that is to say, not dependent on anything or anyone else for its existence. On its most basic level, this means that human beings require, for their existence, such things as air, food, companionship and, of course, parents, without whom they could not even be born. Nevertheless, human beings have a strong tendency to disregard this and instead act and think as if they did exist self-sufficiently and independently of anything else. Since this is in total opposition to reality, living one's life out of such an impossible stance inevitably causes mental suffering.

Thus, according to Buddhism, while the individual person does exist conventionally, introspective analysis (*vipassana*) reveals that nothing has an essential self that exists in an autonomous or independent way, but rather only in dependence on other factors. Unawareness of this results in an overly dualistic view of 'self and other' that in turn naturally gives rise to the afflictive mental states of attachment, aversion, confusion, jealousy, pride, and so on. From these states of mind, one projects a world and constructs a life story that leads to, and is full of, suffering. Moreover, although this is one's own projection and construction, it is experienced as completely real and objective. Therefore, the solution Buddha proposed was to eliminate the mistaken view of an independent self, since by removing that, the subsequent processes of self-grasping, views of self and other, afflictions and the suffering they cause will all cease. Hence, according to Buddhist psychology, there is every reason to believe that the Naikan process of moving individuals from a mistaken construal of independent selfhood to one of interdependent selfhood would lead to the alleviation of much suffering and the revision of one's life narrative.

What, then, would be the best way to effect this change? The centrality of the role of 'mother' in Naikan has been alluded to, and much can be made of the place of mother in Japanese culture. Reynolds has drawn attention to this, and has proposed that for American clients or even Japanese of younger generations, the focus on mother may be less appropriate, and one may attain similar results by focusing instead on a 'wife or girlfriend'. It may be, however, that the chief significance of focusing on mother here is not really a reflection of Japanese cultural norms, but pragmatic in nature. I would contend that the principal reason the figure of the mother is stressed so heavily in Naikan is because of the unique relationship we all – regardless of our culture – have with our mothers. Unlike other relationships in life, our relationship with our mother is one of total and incontrovertible dependence.

This point should not be mistaken to mean psychological dependence, or that everything that happens in our life is directly dependent on our mother at that moment. Rather, it is merely to point out that our very coming into existence and survival early in life depended entirely on the support of our mother, and since everything else in our life in turn depends on that coming into existence (e.g. being cared for in the womb, at birth and during infancy), everything in our life indirectly depends upon our mother, in the way that in a chain of events, every subsequent event is dependent upon the very first link in the chain, because if that had not happened, nothing subsequent would have happened.

Thus, it is a certain perspective on our life that Naikan is proposing, an angle on things that one would not normally take in ordinary life. This perspective can be most clearly seen when we consider the time we spent in the womb and shortly after birth, and this is precisely where Naikan starts: with the client recalling his or her past in relation to his or her mother in the first few years of life, or even including the time in the womb, along Naikan's three themes of 'What did you receive?', 'What did you return?' and 'What trouble did you cause that person?' Unlike other situations, other times in one's life, and other relationships, here virtually everyone is compelled to answer in the same way: As a foetus, infant and very young child, I received almost constant love, care and food from my mother in a large variety of ways, without which I could not possibly have survived; I caused significant trouble or inconvenience for her; and I gave nothing back in return.

Taking this perspective can be quite a shift for many clients, especially those who have developed strongly negative views of their mothers, and this may be the reason it generally takes clients a few days, or even most of the week, to open up to the Naikan process. From the framework of Naikan, however, it is held that restoring positive relationships to the people in one's life, and in particular to one's mother, can result in healthier physical and mental well-being. Recent medical studies show that for both human beings and many animal species a good early relationship with one's mother is a primary indicator for physical well-being throughout one's life. It may be that such studies will find increasing scientific support for the efficacy of Naikan's therapeutic structure.

Searching for self

Naikan is a secular therapeutic method that does not require any religious beliefs or commitment, yet it is based upon a Buddhist view of the nature of suffering, the nature of mind and self, and the goal of therapy. Thus, it serves as a good model for comparison with Western psychotherapies. Whether they are regarded as religious or secular, it seems that all therapeutic methods, including many traditional religious practices that are not necessarily associated with therapy, share one thing in common: they are different means for working on one's sense of self, thereby helping one to deal with the inner suffering caused by trauma, anger, hatred, suppressed feelings, and so on. As both Naikan and Western psychotherapies, such as psychoanalysis, present systems of healing that evolved over time within their respective cultures, they are permeated by different conceptions of what the self is, how it exists, its relation to its environment and to others, and so on, reflecting the conceptual framework of the founder, his or her clients, and their cultural milieu.

The existing scholarship on Japan tends to view selfhood in Japan as relational, harmonious, and so on, as opposed to the individualistic notion of selfhood found in the West. However, if this view leads to a dualistic framework within which being an individual (with connotations of having free will, choice, independence, etc.) is contrasted with being merely a faceless member of a group (without free will, etc.), and therefore not an individual, then it is certainly misleading. Indeed, in certain extreme cases, one could almost get the impression from some accounts that the Japanese have no sense of individual selfhood at all, that is to say, that a Japanese person would not relate to himself or herself as an individual person, but merely as part of some larger organism. This kind of orientalism can lead to absurdity and make the Japanese appear as if they were some other type of creature altogether, rather than human beings like anyone else. Rather than accept such a dualism of self and society, it is perhaps more helpful to think of interdependence as that which transcends or moves beyond this dichotomy.

As Naikan is a practice that encourages gaining insight of oneself, clients often spontaneously report how their sense of who they are changes over the week. Therefore, the ethnography of Naikan provides rich source material for analysing how selfhood is understood in Japan. The Japanese self has been a popular subject to be studied since Ruth Benedict (1989 [1946]), and overall, scholars agree that the sense of self in Japan is more communal, harmonious and group-oriented than the individualistic and independent model of selfhood valued in the West. Although recent scholarship has criticized the implicit hierarchy of this comparison, whereby the Western sense of self is valorized as independent, creative, dynamic, etc., and some have argued that the Japanese have a much less harmonious sense of self than is portrayed in Western scholarship, I nevertheless still find the entire predominant framework to be unsatisfactory. As we shall see, some of the current scholarship on Japanese selfhood refutes the notion that there is a single, solid Japanese self; rather, they present the self as something that is always being cultivated, which is in accord with Naikan's view. At the same time, these models still operate within a framework that holds being socialized as something that overpowers being an individual.

The reason I find this framework to be unsatisfactory is because it is too simplistic to place individualism and independence on one side, and interdependence, communalism, society, etc., on the other. A better approach, in my opinion, would be the view presented in Buddhist thought, whereby interdependence should not be understood as the binary opposite of independence, nor as negating individual existence; rather it transcends the very dichotomy of individual vs society by deconstructing both terms to reveal that the individual exists *as* individual because of society, and society exists *as* society because of individuals. It is therefore a different way of understanding and employing the same terms of individual and social, seeing how each term depends on the other. Thus, neither 'individual' nor 'society' need to be hypostasized as if they could exist independently of the other. This helps to explain why, although Naikan is often viewed as a culturally conservative practice that reinforces interdependence and re-socialization to clients, many Naikan clients feel liberated after their week of practice, and in many cases gain the confidence to say 'No' to the people they interact with when they re-enter everyday life, while at the same time feeling more intimately connected to others.

Studies of Japanese selfhood

Despite the innate sense of self we all have and our corresponding tendency to consider the self as something very concrete, there is actually little consensus regarding what the nature of the self really is. Is 'self' something independent of society and culture; is it a part of culture, and therefore there is no self apart from culture; or is there really no such thing as a self at all?

'Self-discovery' (*jiko hakken*) or 'Discovering your true self' is a favourite way Naikan practitioners describe the goal of their practice. Such expressions are quite different from the contemporary psychoanalytic sensibility of 'developing a healthy sense of self', 'constructing authentic sense of self' or 'strengthening one's self-esteem'. There is no connotation of building up one's self in Naikan.

In Naikan, the self is something to be 'discovered' and what is most important is to find one's 'true self'. That being the case, there must be a 'false self' and a 'true self' which are not equal. Furthermore, as a method to approach 'one's true self', Naikan practitioners speak of 'diminishing one's ego', which literally means to diminish the sense of '*I am* (so and so, like this)', or the sense of needing to assert our self with thoughts or feelings of 'me, me!'

Naturally, one might wonder whether Naikan and Western psychodynamic therapies are even talking about the same kind of self or not. The thorny issue is to enquire whether the notion of self in Naikan is different from the notion of self in the Western psychodynamic (or psychoanalytic) discourse, or more generally, whether Japanese notions of self are different to Western notions of self, and whether Buddhist notions of the self are different from Western psychological notions of the self.

A common notion about the self in the West is that it is bounded, individual, unique, independent and autonomous, with some inner core that is stable and unchanging, despite having certain aspects that undergo constant change and development.[1] Such a notion of the self is prevalent in literature, some schools of philosophy, Christianity and in popular culture. It is almost like the notion of an 'inner-sanctuary' we all possess as human beings: some aspects of our personality surely do change over time, but there remains a sense of a concrete self, which constitutes who we are, and nothing external can invade this sanctuary. This sense of 'autonomous and independent self' is not quite the same as the character description we might give to other people when someone asks what kind of person we are; we probably have a couple of distinctive characteristic features about our personality (e.g. stubborn, proud, honest, short-tempered, etc.), yet we are fine about some aspects of our personality changing, developing or even being eliminated altogether. This sense of a concrete self seems in many ways linked to the notion of a soul, although the latter can be understood quite differently.

Of the many scholars who have come up with theories regarding the Japanese sense of self, let us start with Ruth Benedict (1989 [1946]), one of the first cultural anthropologists to write on this subject. Although her theories have been hotly contested since her writing, especially her idea of Japan as a culture of shame (Doi 1981; Murase 1981b; Okonogi 1982, 1991, 2001) and are problematic in certain ways, her basic points are as follows. Benedict characterizes the Japanese as highly bound to obligations (*giri*), very conscious about fitting in to the correct social or hierarchical 'place', and always trying to behave according to their appropriate social role. This affects their sense of self in various ways; for example, husband and wife call each other 'mother' and 'father' once they have a child, and husbands may seek outside lovers, as their wives are 'mothers' and therefore not sexual objects anymore.

Benedict also distinguishes between the 'shame culture' of Japan, as opposed to the 'guilt culture' of the US. For Benedict, shame is based on an external force, such as being laughed at or humiliated in front of others, whereas guilt stems from an inner feeling of the individual. Thus, individuals in a 'guilt culture' are controlled by internal sanctions against breaking moral standards. Such a sense of guilt can be eased by the practice of confession, whereas a culture of shame would not practice confession. By contrast, the Japanese are controlled by social force, rather than an individual, inner sense of morality. Furthermore, as shame is a reaction to other people's reactions, the Japanese are highly sensitive to their personal honour and reputation and behave according to the expected judgements of other people. This stands in contrast with the notion of individualism, where people are encouraged to behave according to their own beliefs and decisions, not external factors such as other people's opinions.

Benedict's portrayal of Japanese culture and Japanese behaviour has been highly influential in contemporary study of Japan, even among Japanese scholars. It contributes to the idea that the Japanese are 'group-oriented' and clearly places this in opposition to notions of individualism. Several Japanese scholars have supported Benedict's analysis, and have turned her insights into criticisms of Japan's supposedly group-oriented mentality. The Japanese Freudian psychologist, Doi Takeo, for example, seems torn between praising individualism and criticizing it in his classic discussion of *amae* (Doi 1981). According to Doi, the Japanese are driven by *amae*, or 'dependency', a desire to be 'united' with the other person, 'an attempt to draw close to the other person', 'the craving of a newborn child for close contact with its mother ... the desire to deny the fact of separation' (Doi 1981: 167). According to Doi, there is no equivalent of the Japanese word *amae* in other languages such as English. Nevertheless, although *amae* is not 'socially recognized' in the West, according to Doi, it is practised and the 'psychology of *amae*' exists in the West, such that Freud should have included it in his theories.

Several provoking attempts to uncover the subject of Japanese selfhood appeared in the early 1990s. Rosenberger's edited book *Japanese Sense of Self* (1992a) is in a way a response to the Benedictian/orientalist approach to the Japanese self, whereby an underlying assumption exists that the Western individualistic self is ideal, and the Japanese sense of self is inferior. Rosenberger states that Benedict portrayed the Japanese as 'foreign others' with a dangerous self, and further correctly points out some of the major limitations and problems with existing anthropological approaches to studying selfhood in non-Western cultures. She writes:

A dichotomy of Western ('us') versus non-Western ('them') became embedded in the dichotomy of individual versus society, with the first term superior in each case. Westerners living in industrial, economically 'modern' societies idealize themselves as individuals, in control of emotions and social relations, able to think abstractly by cause-and-effect logic. Westerners often affirm this ideal by viewing non-Westerners as swayed by emotion, relation, and context – only able to think in the specific case and then only by metaphor. It follows that Western societies can take the 'higher' form of democracy because decision making can be entrusted to the hands of rational individuals, whereas non-Western societies require a strong collectivity for cohesion and control of people enmeshed in the immediacy of relationship and superstition. This point of view remains with anthropologists, even those studying complex, industrialized non-Western societies. Whether anthropologists characterize Japanese as disciplined and submissive (overcontrolled from within), we still tend to locate them on the negative side of the individual/society dichotomy. We often portray Japanese as the opposite of our ideal selves: as concrete thinkers, particularistic moralists, situational conformists, unintegrated selves; as intuitive rather than rational, animistic (undivided from their environment), and unable to separate body and mind. The temptation of such general conclusions continually bedevils Western-trained scholars of Japan.

(Rosenberger 1992b: 2)

Dualistic thinking is innate for human beings, and not just a characteristic of Western thinking, and it rarely exists without an implicit or explicit value judgement. However, it is interesting to wonder why certain of the above characteristics would be seen as better or worse than their opposites. Why, for example, should intuition be seen as inferior to rationality? Why is a more interconnected understanding of body and mind labelled an inability or failure to recognize the difference between the two? Why would a sense of being integrated with nature be seen as bad? All of these value judgements reveal an underlying world view and bias, such that studies of the Japanese operating out of such a perspective may reveal more about the observant's own cultural assumptions than his or her object of study.

It is usual for people, when facing something new and unfamiliar, for which they have not been prepared, to compare it with their own pre-existing assumptions and judge the unfamiliar as lesser. The same has been done by numerous anthropologists even after the colonialist history of the discipline was brought under critique. It was a contribution of anthropology to bring attention to the existence of other kinds of selfhood in the world and reveal, whether consciously or unconsciously, that the Western individualistic notion of self is not simply the 'truth' about the self, not necessarily the innate nature of the self as various disciplines such as psychology had tended to assume. Then, other anthropologists started bringing their search for the self to the next level by questioning the validity of the Western notion of selfhood itself.

The fact that there is no single, essentialist, image of the Japanese self is a point captured in Dorinne Kondo's *Crafting Selves* (1989). Kondo, a third-generation Japanese American, shows how in Japan the self is known through its presentation. First, identity as self is gendered and gender is not just an accidental attribute of selfhood, but is essential and central. Second, there is no 'self', but rather 'selves' in the plural – shifting, variable, contextual. Third, selves and power are inextricably mixed: Kondo writes of the 'intertwining of power and identity in the disciplinary production of selves' (1989: 304). Apart from the influence of Foucault (a resource that pervades Kondo's work), Kondo's key notion is that Japanese adult identities are largely constituted through work, and work is a major arena for the exercise of everyday power in contemporary Japan. Selves in Kondo's view are not 'given', but rather constructed through narratives; they are made up in the telling, they are in a sense stories.[2]

Building off of Doi's and Kondo's work, Rosenberger suggests that the Japanese self can be conceptualized in a three-part model of intersecting levels:

1 *ki*, movements of psycho-social energy;
2 *amae*, the taking and giving of indulgence; and
3 movements in context between formality and informality (1992c: 67–91).

The third level refers to the *uchi/soto* relationship identified by Kondo, and to similar instances such as Doi's concepts of *omote/ura* (front/back) or *tatemae/honne* (on-stage meaning/off-stage meaning in a Goffmanesque sense), but the other two move the debate beyond Kondo into Japanese cosmology and psychology. The self in Rosenberger's view is presumably the mechanism through which reciprocal or relational selves are constituted on a day-to-day basis.

Takie Sugiyama Lebra (1992: 106) suggests another three-part model:

1 the 'interactional' or presentational self, which refers to the 'awareness of self as defined, sustained, enhanced, or blemished through social interaction';
2 the 'inner' self, seen as *kokoro* (heart or mind), true subjectivity, or the seat of the *kami* or god that each person is believed to be endowed with; and
3 the 'boundless' self, the source of which she sees in Buddhism in the idea of the self being merged with the rest of the world, beyond normal social constraints.

The inner self is considered by Lebra to be in a constant state of dialogue with the outer, but here she makes a point that distinguishes her concept of Japanese selfhood from that of others: 'It is the inner self that provides a fixed core for self-identity and subjectivity, and forms a potential basis of autonomy from the ever insatiable demands of the social world' (1992: 112). Lebra's typology is interesting in that it also contains one 'anthropological' version of selfhood and two that are closer to Rosenberger's schema in which certain essential features of the self are somehow outside of society – in nature rather than in culture. In her view the three are not mutually exclusive, but overlapping, and all three converge around 'the highest value in Japanese culture, namely purity' (1992: 117).

Several points can be made about these accounts of self identity. First, they are not entirely consistent with one another, although this could be interpreted as simply a difference in emphasis (Kondo focusing on work and power, Lebra and Rosenberger on transcendental aspects of identity). Second, none of these scholars see the self as being in a state of blissful rest. In all cases it is a project, something to be cultivated, formed in power, mutable and – in contrast to images of Japan as a group-oriented society of high conformity – in many ways opposed to the hegemony of society. However, we should also recall our earlier discussion of Yuasa in Chapter 2, and the idea of the achievement of mind–body unity through self-cultivation and body practice. The self is not just formed by society, it is also an area of freedom from that society. Third, the self is not purely sociological or cultural. Japanese conceptions of the self appear to resist the 'over-socialized conception' of humanity still prevalent in Western anthropology. In the Japanese view the self cannot be over-socialized because it is linked to the cosmic, to the 'Great Self' of which it is in a sense a manifestation or channel of energy (*ki*), and to its relationship with nature.

Self-esteem and self-derogation also form a point of contrast between Western and Japanese conceptions of self, and this can be seen in Naikan. Even though both Naikan and some Western psychotherapies emphasize the recovery of memory, in one sense their uses for it are completely different. Naikan encourages clients to focus on the negative aspects of their past, generating feelings of guilt and shame, whereby they come to seek forgiveness from others, rather than blaming others for their problems. In contrast, some Western psychotherapies focus on establishing self-esteem by enabling clients to focus on positive aspects of themselves, such that they come to love themselves and are thereby able to forgive and love others.

Derogation of one's past self can, of course, be a hidden means for establishing present-tense self-esteem, and while this is a common narrative strategy in cultures such as the US, this is clearly not what is supposed to be happening in Naikan. In their study of Americans, Ross and Wilson (2000) examine the role of derogation of past-selves in self-appraisal. The partici-pants in their research repeatedly appraised their current self as higher than past selves, indicating a perceived improvement over time.

> We propose, metaphorically, to consider past selves as other individuals who range in closeness to current self, and have achievements or failures on attributes that vary in importance to the present self. We suggest that people can maintain their favorable view of current self by shifting their evaluation of past selves, by modifying the significance they attach to the attributes in question, or by altering their judgments of the temporal distance between present and past selves.
>
> (Ross and Wilson 2000: 240).[3]

Ross and Wilson's study is limited by its cultural specificity to North America,[4] but their differentiation between the present self and past 'selves' in the plural applies also to Naikan. Past selves are constructed and mutable, and any change in one's image of past selves necessarily involves an evaluation of them and concomitantly a re-evaluation of one's present self. Moreover, the significance attached to attributes is also changed in Naikan; what was before a white lie is now a significant downfall. Yet regarding the temporal distance between past selves and the present self, the picture is more problematic; there is at once change and continuity. On the one hand, a client may have a 'born again' experience, in which the old self has died; at the same time, a client may feel that the insight provided by Naikan is that he was sinful, is sinful, and will for the rest of his life be sinful, yet this insight comes as a healing, transformative epiphany, because despite his infirmities, he is still cared for and supported by others.

It may appear counterintuitive, but it seems that the fact that Naikan compels clients to face the negative aspects of their past (and therefore themselves) is an essential part of the client's healing process. Facing the less savoury aspects of one's past is precisely what clients, and indeed most people, refrain from doing on an everyday basis. Rather, there is a tendency to gloss such past embarrassments with self-justification or denial. Yet Reynolds (1983: 86) argues that popular Western psychotherapeutic approaches of the 'I am okay, and so are you' variety have severe limitations, since we are self-critical in that we know that we are not really okay. This is the view taken by Ian Craib (1994), who has argued that the fallacy at the root of much contemporary psychotherapy is the belief that total happiness, integration and psychic harmony can indeed be achieved. In fact, Craib argues, disappointment is a basic and unavoidable ingredient in the human condition; frustrated desire, sickness, aging and the other less appealing qualities of the existential condition are intrinsic to therapeutic (and all other) contexts. Psychotherapies of the 'fashionable' kind that ignore this are doomed, according to Craib, not only to ineffectiveness, but to actually increasing the incidence of the very problems that they exist to solve, since patients' doubts and anxieties will be multiplied by the lack of results flowing from their participation in therapy.

Interestingly, Naikan follows Buddhism in believing, like Craib, that there is value in facing directly the unavoidable aspects of life, such as death, separation and so forth, and yet it proposes this as a very means towards the happiness, integration and harmony that Craib discounts as impossible. This is because, unlike Craib, but in line with Buddhist thought, it recognizes the difference between an object or event (sickness, ageing, death, a past trauma, another person) and the attitude one takes towards it. Happiness does not come from removing such events or persons from one's life, but through transforming one's attitude towards them.

Naikan and Buddhist thought

The reasons for Naikan's effectiveness in treating disorders, especially addictions, become clearer when one considers the strong focus in Buddhist teaching on how craving leads to suffering, and how the process can be reversed to bring about healing. There is also a strong emphasis in Buddhism on ignorance or misperception: namely, that we selectively interpret our situations and our past, take that selective interpretation to be the objective truth, and then suffer when this 'reality' we have constructed gets threatened or undermined by the actual course of events. To see the way these points interrelate, I believe it is very helpful to include here a section on the fundamental points of basic Buddhist philosophy and psychology. Thus, the next section is an edited transcript from an oral teaching on the central Buddhist teaching of the Four Noble Truths given by Geshe Lobsang Tenzin, a Tibetan Buddhist teacher educated at the doctoral level both in a traditional Buddhist monastic setting and a Western university setting.[5] As I believe it is important that these ideas be presented by someone who understands them deeply, rather than filtered and possibly distorted through my own interpretation, I think there is value in reproducing his own words.

The Four Noble Truths[6]

Of all the important deeds of Buddha's life, that of teaching, or 'turning the wheel of dharma', is the supreme one. Had he not taught, his attainment of enlightenment would have been good enough for him, but of not much benefit for others. That there have been many great masters since then, and that many people have attained enlightenment since Buddha's time, is possible because he taught and his teachings have been transmitted. This shows his great kindness in passing on the knowledge that he had.

It is said that Buddha himself wondered how to speak of his experience after he attained enlightenment, saying, 'This profound, peaceful, clear light, unborn awareness I have attained – who can I share it with? Nobody will relate to it. So let me just wander in the jungle for a while.'[7] So he wandered for forty-nine days after attaining full enlightenment, which happened on the full moon of the fourth month, called Saka Dawa, in Bodh Gaya.

Eventually he wound up in Sarnath on the outskirts of the ancient town of Varanasi and went to Deer Park there. There he met the five ascetics who had formerly been his companions in meditation, but who had left him after he had received some food to eat, rejecting their style of severe food depri-vation. In considering who might be able to understand him, he thought that these five ascetics who had meditated with him before would be the ones who could relate to his awakening.

In the traditional accounts, it was actually Brahma, king of gods, who in Sarnath had offered the golden wheel to Buddha, asking him to teach; so among his audience for this first teaching there were many beings – gods and other beings – but the humans in attendance were those five ascetics. He taught there a very precise and simple teaching, yet one that was profound and vast in scope, which became the foundation for all the Buddha's subsequent teachings. Whether one considers the Theravada, or basic approach to inner development, or the Mahayana with its very extensive and elaborate forms of meditation for cultivating bodhichitta and attaining full enlightenment, or the tantric practices, they are all founded on the first teaching of the Four Noble Truths. So the Buddha was very clear from the beginning, knowing what exactly he was teaching, as an enlightened being should, as that is what enlightenment is.

The Four Noble Truths is a deceptively simple teaching when one looks at it initially. It says that sufferings are true; they have sources; such sources of suffering can be ended; and there are methods to end the sources of suffering, and hence suffering itself. Especially in today's world, when we understand medicine, the medical model he used seems obvious and commonsensical: that, of course, if one wants to be healed from an illness, one needs to first acknowledge that the illness is there; one needs to know that such problems do not arise out of the blue, but from certain causes and conditions; if they arise from certain causes and conditions, then it is possible to end them; and lastly, there are means for ending them.

Maitreyanatha later said about the Four Noble Truths, using the medical model, 'Just as the disease needs to be diagnosed, its cause eliminated, a healthy state achieved, and the remedy implemented, so also should suffering, its causes, its cessation and the path be known, removed, attained, and undertaken.' Anyone who is suffering, who is not completely at peace, who is struggling, can relate to this message. The importance of this message can be understood by anyone who has problems, who is unable to experience true, genuine peace and joy – and that is impossible to experience in ordinary life, because ordinary life is full of suffering, just as Buddha says in the first noble truth, 'Sufferings are true.'

Buddha used a very graphic image to describe this, saying, 'The world is burning with suffering, and desires are its source; one who puts an end to desires will be free from such suffering.' Suffering is all around, because here suffering is not understood merely as what we understand as illness, such as headaches, cancer and so on, which are certainly intense sufferings, but ageing also is suffering, dissatisfaction is suffering (some people translate the Sanskrit word *dukkha*, or suffering, as dissatisfaction), our mind not being at true peace is suffering. From this perspective, we can see that there is some dissatisfaction that pervades our life. The problem is that we recognise some things as suffering, but not others, although they are really suffering in disguise, and so as a result we pursue things and engage in activities that do not yield true happiness.

For example, we are very susceptible to desires and cravings, be it alcoholism, drug addiction, food addiction, self-image, sex addiction, and so on. If we take the extreme example of alcohol or substance addiction, we see that a person in denial does not see the fact that craving the substance or the high it produces is itself the problem, and if they do not see that, they are likely to go on craving it and chasing after it. Of course, the reason they pursue the substance, be it drugs or alcohol, is because what they are really seeking is happiness. This is what drives us fundamentally: to have joy and happiness, and to avoid suffering and discomfort; this is what we all want. As the eighth-century Buddhist scholar and meditator, Shantideva, said so well: 'All living beings have the desire for happiness, yet they destroy the very source of their happiness. They want to avoid suffering, yet they are constantly chasing after it.' This shows that out of ignorance, a person who is not truly aware, who does not genuinely understand that the very craving of that high is the real problem, will keep going after such drugs and so forth, but will never be satisfied thereby. Rather, their situation will just get worse and worse and lead to all manner of problems.

Substance addiction is simply an extreme example of this, because such cravings take on many forms. If we consider how we spend our time and where our priorities lie, we see it is all governed by the 'eight worldly concerns': seeking pleasure, avoiding pain, seeking material or possessions, avoiding loss of possessions, seeking praise, avoiding criticism, seeking status or self-elevation, avoiding loss of status. Even a great deal of religious and social work is contaminated by the eight worldly concerns. If one is not careful, all such activities become means for the eight worldly concerns, and as long as we are driven by the eight worldly concerns, by such desires for fame, name, possessions, pleasure, and so on, it is no different from the craving of the alcoholic; it is a source of suffering, from the Buddhist perspective.

It is not hard to develop the wish to avoid manifest suffering, what Buddha called 'the suffering of suffering', and even animals desire to avoid this, but the wish to avoid what is known as 'the suffering of change' is difficult to develop. This is where Buddha's insight into suffering comes in. When he said, 'Sufferings are true' and that one must recognise suffering, he was not saying this to depress us, but rather to tell us to wake up and understand that pleasurable feelings themselves, if conjoined with desire, are really suffering and a source of suffering. So suffering is not just pain, but also the craving for fame and so on. Of course, having wealth and joy is no problem by itself, and one should of course have joy, but if one becomes so attached emotionally to them, then that is a problem.

Buddha did not just teach these two kinds of suffering, but also that our very body-mind, our psycho-physical aggregates, are so conditioned by attachment and aversion, that they are themselves a source of suffering, an all-pervasive suffering, like the body of an alcoholic who craves alcohol. Given this, awakening will not happen all at once. It will take time to decondition the body-mind.

It is therefore important to understand suffering as well as its sources, which Buddha said were the afflictive emotions (*klesha*) and the actions they lead to (*karma*), which in turn reinforce the afflictive emotions. Karma is thus not merely action, but the patterns and conditioning such actions leave behind in our body-mind. It is this conditioning that lasts a long time and stays with us, formed as it is in the mind and the mind's related energy. If these karmic conditionings are there, they will manifest and colour our experiences of things in the future. This is because how we are conditioned affects our experience; for example, someone who was abused as a child will react differently later in life to someone who was not. Thus, karma is like a kind of memory. Unhealthy emotions and ways of thinking lead to this conditioning, as does our unawareness of our interconnectedness: that you are the same as I am in wanting happiness and wanting to avoid suffering.

So the third noble truth is evident: that cessations are true. If our suffering comes from ignorance, then if we develop an understanding of our inter-connectedness, of our impermanence, namely that we will be gone one day, too, then this can be transformative. Ordinarily we suppress such thoughts, and think instead that others will die, but we will go on to live for a hundred years or even longer. If we are able to change that misperception and raise our awareness, by asking how long will we be on this earth, for example, then that can be effective, just as we know from people who come face to face with death that their perspective changes significantly. What we need is to develop right now the perspective that this day could be our last. As the Kadampa masters of Tibet used to say, 'If you don't recall the immediacy of death in the morning, your morning will be wasted. If you don't recall the immediacy of death in the afternoon, your afternoon will be wasted. If you don't recall the immediacy of death in the evening, your evening will be wasted.'

Our unhealthy attitudes and ways of thinking are due to ignorance, due to not tuning ourselves in to reality, the reality of impermanence, selflessness, and interconnectedness. If we tune into that reality, such ignorance will weaken. Gradually our understanding will become so powerful that our love, compassion, and so on, will become limitless, a limitless force. The *kleshas* and sources of suffering have no place in our true nature, our natural state of mind. They cease in the reality of our being; they do not exist there. They arise in ignorance, and we then mistakenly take that to be reality. This was the tremendous insight of the Buddha: that each being has Buddha nature. Each being in its true authentic state is pure, free from defilements, and perfect.

If so, then how does one actualize this? This is the fourth noble truth of the path: discipline, meditation, and the development of wisdom, which are called the three higher trainings. If suffering comes from ignorance, *karma* and the *kleshas*, then the path is the undoing of all that. How are we to do this: by going to the root first, or by choosing a place where we can make a dent in it? The deeply rooted ignorance of a permanent self is hard to undo right away, but we can look to our actions first. If we are someone who uses harsh words with our family or co-workers, or if we are someone who is violent with our body, we can look at that and try to curb our behaviour. We should see the disadvantages of doing harm and the advantages of refraining from it, because to stop it entirely through willpower alone is hard to do.

At the same time, we need a way to calm our mind, or to detect early on these afflictive emotions before they arise and hijack our consciousness. This is done through meditation, and this is especially necessary nowadays when people find it hard to find fifteen minutes a day to meditate. But if we cannot find the time to meditate, how are we to develop the mental strength to stop the afflictive emotions? Thus, we need to know our own inner demons, our jealousies, fears, and anxieties. We need to explore these in the safe, calm, secure place of meditation – not out in a conflict situation, where we could not handle it. Most of the time we are unaware of our inner emotions and we simply react to external stimuli; we simply let our inner forces, which are there from so much conditioning, build up.

Thus Buddha spoke simply of right speech, right action (meaning non-abusive action), right livelihood (not harming others), right mindfulness (being mindful of our thoughts), right concentration, and so on. Right concentration means developing the ability to keep the mind in a positive, balanced state, where you are the master and owner, where, if you choose to, you can just be with the breath, or whatever you want, instead of your emotions taking you wherever they want to. For this we need to be able to notice and just let go, to extend the moments where we are free from just reacting with thoughts like 'Yes! This is good!' or 'No! That is bad!'

Instead of such chain reactions, if we can prolong our concentration to a few minutes at a time, this will help a great deal, for example in our interaction with others in the world. If one can notice anger, for example, or the thought to take advantage of someone, when it arises, then one can hold off on an action that one would later regret. Later, when the anger has passed, one can communicate what it was that was bothering oneself. Because we do not communicate well when we are afflicted. The word for 'afflictive emotion' in Tibetan is *nyon-mong*. The meaning of *nyon* is something that makes you crazy or unclear. Afflictive emotions prevent clarity of mind, and wars arise because we do not control our emotions, but rather let them guide us.

We might think that if there is no desire, there will also be no joy, that life will become flat, or that we will not enjoy things as much. That is what we think, but experienced yogis do not experience it that way. Milarepa, for example, whose life would seem an extreme case for us, survived on nettles, yet his life was full of joy. He was not just some crazy person; rather, he mentions that the tremendous joy he experienced came from inner contentment. He said, 'Without inner contentment, pursuing joy from external things is just a source of more suffering.' Imagine a person who is an alcoholic; they might think, 'If I can't drink, I might as well die. There would be no point to life.' Maybe not consciously, but subconsciously they would think that. Yet it is just the opposite, in fact. The more you drink, the more you suffer. When the person sees that craving drink is itself the problem, and they stop, their happiness actually increases.

We are all afraid, thinking, 'Oh, if I don't have more wealth or a bigger name, then there will be no joy.' But actually, in that mentality there are a lot of fears, struggles, and disappointments. So to develop contentment, if you think, 'Oh, I must have a second home', then you are not going to enjoy your first home. Later, you might save up some money, and you might in fact buy a second home, but not out of attachment.

Detachment is not about not having motivation, being lazy, a couch potato. Rather, it is about being happy with what you have. What one does beyond that comes out of compassion. So you work, not to gain more for yourself, but out of concern for others, not to be a burden on others, on society, and so on. Great bodhisattvas sacrifice their own pleasures completely to work for others.

We do not experience joy in the mind when it is afflicted by fears, jealousy, attachment, and so on. What causes those? It is the eight worldly concerns. The natural state of mind is infinitely blissful. So when you see those who are really content, they radiate joy and happiness. In Maitreya's *Sublime Continuum*, he says joy, peace, and so on, are the true, natural qualities of the mind, whereas fears, afflictions, and so on, are not. So the more the mind comes into its natural state, the more these positive qualities will come out, and the more the negative ones will disappear. Therefore, in remembering this important day when Buddha first turned the wheel of dharma, the best way to honour the Buddha is to make a resolve to put into practice what he taught.

Shin Buddhism

The previous section on the Four Noble Truths will be helpful in our discussion for a number of reasons, as will become increasingly clear. First of all, it is a central teaching that is foundational for Buddhist thought in general, and not just one particular school or sect. Second, it shows the Buddhist perspective on suffering and the human mind. Suffering is not seen as something entirely separate from our own mind; indeed, suffering is seen as originating from the way our mind reacts to things and situations. Third, Geshe Lobsang's characterization of the mind as pure and luminous (which aligns with the way 'Buddha nature' is talked about in Naikan) appears to contrast with Shin Buddhism's emphasis on sinfulness and guilt, which we will be exploring in this chapter, but in my opinion they represent two approaches to the same situation. Many Western scholars, as we shall see, whose area of expertise is usually not Shin Buddhism, have misunderstood and misrepresented Shin Buddhism by depicting it as a degenerate form of Buddhism that parallels Protestant Christianity in its total reliance on an 'other power', describes the human condition as one of utter depravity (along the lines of Calvinism), and believes in something akin to original sin.

Although on a popular level it is quite possible that various devotees might hold such views, I believe, for reasons that will be discussed below, that Shin Buddhism can still be placed more squarely within the Buddhist tradition as a whole and need not be seen as a complete deviation.

Naikan's classification is ambiguous: some call it psychotherapy, others say it is a religious practice, and still others call it merely a method. Nevertheless, Yoshimoto Ishin was a Shin Buddhist priest and believed that the ultimate goal of Naikan was to achieve enlightenment, though he did not force this view upon his clients. It is therefore unsurprising that Naikan reflects a strong Buddhist influence. Having covered some of the basics of Buddhist thought in the preceding section regarding the fundamental teaching of the Four Noble Truths, we can now turn to the Shin Buddhist sect in particular to see how its influence lives on in Naikan.

Shin Buddhism, which is the English term for the sect of Buddhism called *Jōdo Shinshū*, or 'True Pure Land School', was founded by Shinran (1173–1262). After spending twenty years, from the age of nine, practising the Tendai School's Buddhist practices, Shinran left the mountain out of dissatisfaction and visited the hexagonal temple in Kyoto supposedly founded by Shōtoku Taishi. In his ninety-fifth day of prayer, Shinran received a message from Shōtoku Taishi in a dream. Dobbins cites the following from the 'Record of Shinran's Dreams':

> The Great World-Saving Bodhisattva [Kannon] of the Rokkakudō was revealed in the form of a monk of upright appearance. Dressed in simple white clerical robes and seated on a giant white lotus, he made this pronouncement to Shinran:
>
> If the believer, because of the fruition of karma, is driven by
>   sexual desire,
> Then I shall take on the body of a beautiful woman to be ravished
>   by him.
> Throughout his entire life I shall adorn him well,
> And at death I shall lead him to birth in Pure Land.
>
> The World-Saving Bodhisattva recited this message and then made the following pronouncement: 'This message is my vow. Expound it to all living beings.' Based on this pronouncement, I realized that I should tell this to millions of sentient beings, and I then awoke from my dream.
>
> (Dobbins 1989: 24)

Shinran is known to have taken his dreams and visions into account during his religious development. After this dream, he gave up the Tendai school's clerical practice based on *jiriki* (reliance on one's own effort to attain salvation) and became a disciple of Hōnen, the founder of *Jōdo Shū*, or the Pure Land School. Hōnen rejected the idea that one could attain salvation, that is, rebirth in the Pure Land of Amida (Amitabha) Buddha, through one's own efforts, which had been the mainstream practice in Japanese Buddhism. Instead, he claimed it was necessary to rely on *tariki* (other-power, namely the power of Buddha), by reciting the name of Amida Buddha (*nembutsu*).

According to Hōnen, 'Even the sinner can attain salvation' by reciting *nembutsu*. Shinran developed the concept of *tariki* further and claimed *akunin shōki setsu*, or 'Even the good man can attain salvation, let alone the sinner'. Not only was it impossible for human beings to attain enlightenment through their own efforts, but human beings were incapable of doing a completely selfless act due to self-consciousness. Some have interpreted this to mean that Shinran taught that human beings were 'sinners' by nature. Bloom, for example, writes:

> As to the essential depravity of finite natures, Shinran came to the conclusion that it was entirely impossible for a person to do a good act. Whatever good deed he appeared to do on the finite level was still evil, because it was done with a calculation in mind and was ultimately intended to redound to his benefit. Thus all good deeds performed by individuals were seen as essentially self-centered and involved in the entire web of passion.
>
> (Bloom 1965: 30)

Bloom's comment clearly allies Shinran's concept of 'sinfulness' and 'depravity' with Protestant Christian notions, such as Calvin's theology of 'utter depravity'. There has been a tendency in Western scholarship to describe Shin Buddhism in Protestant terms, but this parallel can be very misleading, as similar terms in Buddhism (sin, hell, evil) do not correspond to the usage of such terms in Christianity, but rather have their own specific meaning. For example, to speak of 'essential depravity' in the context of Mahayana Buddhism, of which Shin Buddhism is a sub-sect, might be misleading, first because nothing is regarded as having a true or fixed 'essence' according to Buddhism, and second because all beings are believed to have 'Buddha nature', an innate capacity for enlightenment.

It is better, in my opinion, to explain Shin Buddhism in strictly Buddhist terms, rather than Protestant Christian ones. Until enlightenment, Buddhism teaches, beings believe that they have an independent, truly existing self set apart from everything and everyone else. This ignorance causes them to perceive the world in a self-centred way, and to perform self-centred actions (*karma*). The law of karma, also called the law of cause and effect, states that good actions lead to good results, and negative actions lead to suffering. Yet a being who still believes in a separate, independent self, even if he or she does good actions, is still calculating that that self will be the recipient of the positive outcomes. Therefore, such action, even if conventionally 'good', can never break free from the cycle of unenlightened existence and suffering (*samsara*), and both seemingly 'good' and 'bad' actions (the concept of metaphysical 'evil', as understood in the West, is not accepted in Buddhism) stand in direct contrast to the selfless activity of enlightened beings (Buddhas), who fully understand the interdependency of all things, and therefore have transcended confined notions of selfhood. Therefore, in dealing with the same topic as Bloom, but using more appropriate and less loaded language, Unno Taitetsu writes:

> As long as our thoughts, feelings, and intuitions come from a limited, finite, and karma-bound being, they are all delusions. It is not a matter of right or wrong, good or bad; this is our naked reality. They are delusions because they make us see the world from a deeply self-centered perspective – a fact that eludes our normal conscious awareness. Our myopic vision distorts reality; hence, our thinking, doing and saying are invariably flawed and defective, even though we may not admit it. Religiously speaking, delusions arise from the darkness of ignorance (*avidya*), producing insatiable greed (*trishna*), and manifesting as blind passions (*klesha*). This is the cause of endless pain and suffering (*dukkha*).
>
> (Unno 1998: 11–12)

The reason Shin Buddhism is often compared with Protestantism seems to lie in the fact that Shin Buddhism teaches that faith in Amida Buddha is most important for uprooting delusions and attaining enlightenment.[8] In this reverence for Amida, some scholars claim that Shin Buddhism approaches monotheism, although such a comparison obscures more than it illuminates.[9] Shin Buddhism is also non-monastic, an entirely lay community. Such factors differentiate Shin Buddhism from most other sects of Buddhism.

Part of the complexity in understanding Shin Buddhism, and doubtless part of the reason why it is so often misrepresented, comes from the difficulty in understanding non-dualism, which is central to all Mahayana Buddhist schools. For example, *The Encyclopedia of Eastern Philosophy and Religion* (1989) has this to say in its entry on Shin Buddhism:

> In contrast to the Jōdo-shū, in which the recitation of Amida's name serves essentially for the strengthening of trust in Amida, the Shin school sees in it an act of gratitude on the part of the individual. This arises from the insight that the Buddha Amida exerts his entire force for the sake of saving this individual. In the Shin school only Amida is venerated; he may not, however, be called upon for the sake of purely private interests. The Jōdo-shin-shū represents the most extreme form of the 'easy path,' in which the practitioner relies on the 'power of the other,' (*tariki*), i.e., of Amida. Besides the absolute trust in Amida, no other effort on one's own is required to attain enlightenment. Trust and reliance toward Amida alone effect liberation. In this school, the old Buddhist idea of adapting oneself to the world to the greatest possible extent is logically extended: If members of the school live like all other men, i.e., as lay

people, they avoid building up barriers between themselves and the world around them. Thus the Shin school is inclined to do away with all religious rules. Thus, for example, marriage is a way to participate in the life of ordinary people as well as to serve the Buddha.

(*The Encyclopedia of Eastern Philosophy and Religion* 1989: 163)

Here again it will likely mislead readers to characterize Shin Buddhism as 'the most extreme form of the "easy path"' and to say that 'Besides the absolute trust in Amida, no other effort on one's own is required', gives the false impression that 'absolute trust' is easy or can be effortlessly achieved. All of this comes, however, from failing to see that the 'own-power' (*jiriki*) and 'other-power' (*tariki*) dichotomy is what is ultimately to be transcended in Mahayana Buddhism.

Thus, Suzuki writes that some people may wonder how Shin Buddhism, which seems to rely on other-power solely, could arise from the Mahayana which teaches self-reliance. To answer this, he points to the very meaning of the *nembutsu*:

When we say NAMU-AMIDA-BUTSU, *namu* is self-power, or *ki. Amida-butsu* is Other-power, or *ho.* Thus, NAMU-AMIDA-BUTSU is the unity of *ki* and *ho.* This unification is the oneness of Amida and ordinary beings, Other-power and self-power, this world and the Pure Land. So, when NAMU-AMIDA-BUTSU is pronounced, it represents or symbolizes the unification of the two.

(Suzuki 1998: 28)

He goes on to mention how 'unification' is not an adequate term. This, I assume, is because 'unification' or 'oneness' still remains within the realm of dualistic thought, whereas non-dualism transcends categories of singularity and multiplicity.

Similarly, Seki Hozen writes of 'other-power' in such a way that we can see how it directly relates to the central project of Naikan, explaining it by means of the Japanese word *Oya-sama*, one of the ways Amida is referred to, which has no exact equivalent in English, but which roughly means 'parent' or 'mother and father':

I came alone into this world and am departing alone to the next world. If there were no compassion toward me from the Other-power, my past, present and future would not exist. To protect and to guide me, there are countless powers. For example – my parents, my society, my nation, the air, earth, sun, etc. – all these powers of compassion are called *Oya-sama.* I cannot live in this world without Oya-sama. Oya-sama and I are in Oneness. Oya-sama is the infinite light and life that is called Amida Buddha.

(Seki 1998: 9)

Here Seki clearly equates Amida Buddha not with some external deity-figure, but with the countless powers of compassion. Since the individual is other-powered, in the sense that without such compassionate powers one would not be able to come into existence or remain existing, self-sufficiency is revealed to be an illusion, and self-power is seen as inextricable (non-dual) from other-power.

Shinran's influence on Yoshimoto

There are clear parallels between the lives of Shinran and Yoshimoto. Not only did Shinran drop the monastic ideals, he also married and had a family at a time when ordained priests were not allowed to marry. According to some records, Shinran signed his name with the word 'priest' or *sō* in 1204, but in 1207 after his marriage he described himself as 'neither priest nor layman' (*sō ni arazu zoku ni arazu*) and simply referred to himself as 'bald-head' (*toku*) (Dobbins 1989: 26).[10] Yoshimoto's Shin Buddhist faith permeated his Naikan practice. For example, he refused to be called the founder of Naikan, saying that the founder was Shinran or Amida Buddha (e.g. 1978b:1).[11] He himself was a mere 'comedian', who just 'talked about Naikan', a statement that parallels Shinran calling himself a 'foolish, bald-headed old man' (*gutoku*) (Bloom 1965: 29). Shinran was a defrocked priest, and rather than in temples, his followers met in private houses (Williams 1989: 269). Yoshimoto often mentioned Shinran in his autobiography, where he explains his decision to follow Shinran's way of life as 'neither monk nor layman' (*hisou hizoku*) in spreading the teaching of *michi*, the way of living as a lay person with both feet on the ground (Yoshimoto 1997: 106).

According to Yoshimoto, the moment he realized that even if everyone else in the world achieved salvation, he was a helpless sinner destined for rebirth in hell, he achieved enlightenment and attained faith in Buddha (Yoshimoto 1985: 25, 47). His understanding of sin was clearly inherited from Shinran. As Williams writes:

> Shinran abstracted from his own sense of sin and powerlessness to the general human condition itself. Not only is he riddled with sin, but we are all like this. We cannot perform a non-egoistic act, and for this reason we cannot perform a truly good act. We are self-centred, and therefore, compared with the Buddha, we as unenlightened beings are evil by our very nature.
>
> (Williams 1989: 271)

In taking this rather extreme view, Shin Buddhism seems to deviate from traditional Buddhist teachings, which would not claim that beings are evil by nature, but merely ignorant. Another deviation regards what happens upon death. In Shin Buddhism, it is believed that one's faith in Buddha is the only way to attain salvation at one's death. As Ueda Yoshifumi writes, 'The traditional view was that a long period of spiritual discipleship in the Pure Land was necessary before one could attain supreme enlightenment, but Shinran taught that the person of faith attains Buddhahood at the moment of death, having become free from karmic limitations' (1979: 13). The Shin Buddhist priest K. K. Tanaka explains of the experience of faith (*shinjin*) as follows:

> Once this is realized, there is a total sense of interconnectedness, a sense of being embraced by the other-power or the greater reality we call 'Amida Buddha'. How to describe that experience is a separate question. In a modern context I think you say it is finding a oneness with all beings and that is the soteriological solution. So it is no longer a question of what happens to my body or me. That is not a significant concern. Of course, doctrinally we say that upon death one attains full enlightenment, full Buddhahood. In this life one attains complete assurance of becoming a Buddha upon death.
>
> (Andreasen 1998: 175)

It seems, however, that this can be interpreted in various ways. Andreasen provides an interview of 15 December 1992 with Rev. Nakatsu Isao:

> Q: Do ordinary Shinshu followers believe in a cycle of birth-and-death before they end in the Pure Land – or is there only one life?
> A: For myself my life is only once but when my life ends, that is the Pure Land. And so we were taught by Shinran Shonin. The life of delusions finishes with this life. We have no belief in transmigration, in a substantial form of rebirth. But we are told in our sutras that we have been drifting in the ocean of birth-and-death since the beginning of our era (*kalpa*). This term expresses the working of the true dharma which reaches the bottom of delusion at the same time as it expresses the depth of human delusion.
>
> In household Shinshu (*ie no shukyo*) there is maybe a belief in transmigration or rebirth, but only few believe it. We regard it as superstition if we take it as substantial.[12]
>
> (Andreasen 1998: 135)

However, it is clear that Yoshimoto did believe in past and future lives, as it appears in his comments now and again. He had a great respect for his oldest son Kiyonobu, and it was related to me that in a conversation Yoshimoto said that Kiyonobu must have spread good seeds before he was born and must have had a past quite different to Yoshimoto. At another occasion, he said:

> [Kiyonobu] is an interesting child, it is really a case of a kite breeding a hawk, and I am often taught a lot by him. When he was in his first year at

elementary school, he insisted that he would not go with my wife unless she purchased an extra ticket for him [a child would not need one]. When he visits us, he takes the bullet train but he even purchases a ticket for his baby. He said the national railway company has been in the red. When I think about how I ended up having such a child, I cannot help but think that there are past lives.

(Soya 1989: 100–1)

In Yoshimoto's autobiography, *Naikan: Forty Years* (1997 [1965]),[13] a tension persists between a desire to present Naikan as non-religious, and portrayal of Naikan as informed by his strong beliefs. For example, he describes Kinuko, his future wife, as 'coming to believe in Naikan' (*nyūshin*), a phrase with religious connotations, after she attained the enlightenment through *mishirabe* (1997: 91). Yoshimoto's desire to spread Naikan and his decision to remove it from the framework of an established religion in order to do so were likely influenced by Shinran. One might say, then, that he extended Shinran's notion of an entirely lay community even further by removing the name of Buddha from the official philosophy of Naikan, while he himself sustained strong faith in Buddha and maintained this faith as a part of the Naikan method without overt expression.

At first, Naikan does not seem to fit the notion of *tariki* (other-power) at the core of Shin Buddhism. Naikan might appear closer to Zen meditation than Shin Buddhism's recitation of the name of Amida for salvation. My interpretation, however, is that Naikan requires one's autonomous power to bring out various insights toward the self, including remorse for past misdeeds. In short, Naikan is a method to enable one to realize the limitations of oneself (i.e. how one commits misdeeds, how helpless one is about this fact, the realization that one will continue to commit misdeeds again and again in this life), and to bring one to the point of admitting that one cannot exist without depending on others and seeing this as the truth. This moment of insight is the moment one realizes *tariki* and rejects the illusion of being a 'self-made' person.

The role of mother

This enables us to rethink the 'mother–child bond' in Japan, a well-known phenomenon discussed by numerous scholars (DeVos 1960; Doi 1981; Benedict 1989 [1946]; Buruma 1995; Murase 1996). Japan has often been described as a 'maternal society' (Kawai 1975), in which people are fixated on 'mother'. The dominant role of the mother permeates many husband–wife relationships as well. Some have noted that expectations toward wives in Japan often seem almost identical with those toward mothers. Traditionally, men can expect their wives to prepare meals for them, wait on them, prepare baths, do their laundry and iron their clothing, and men will even call their wives 'mother'.

Images of the mother in Japan, therefore, represent a rather conservative model containing elements such as self-sacrifice, caring, warmth and self-abandonment. Such images are favoured by certain kinds of Japanese cinema, soap operas and songs (*enka* music): the so-called *hahamono*, or 'mother things'. Male audiences watch or listen to these 'mother things' with feelings of nostalgic sweet guilt towards their mother. Yoshimoto loved such 'mother things', and used to play *enka* music and maudlin Japanese pop songs every morning at his Naikan centre (a practice which persists even after his death) to make clients think of their good old mothers. 'Mother-thing' *enka* songs usually have a common theme: mothers are described as suffering, sacrificing and warm loving maternal figures, whom grown-up children miss with nostalgic feelings.

Such representations of the mother may tie in closely with the concept of guilt, which is central to Naikan in its stress on how much one has received from others and how much trouble one has caused others. In Japan guilt is associated with 'indebtedness'. For Yoshimoto, awareness of one's guilt was a prerequisite for achieving enlightenment. Such awareness, he felt, could be best achieved by focusing on one's indebtedness to others, encapsulated in Naikan's three themes. The mother is therefore a central figure, since a strong emphasis on the affection and love one has received from one's mother, especially at an age when one was incapable of giving anything back in return, would create a powerful sense of indebtedness, and hence an awareness of one's guilt, thereby bringing one closer to enlightenment. Murase has pointed out that there is an aspect of the absolute dependency between the client and the practitioner which shares the nature of the infant–mother relationship (Murase 1996: 39). This recalls our earlier discussion in Chapter 2 on the 'womb' environment created by the Naikan setting, and what effect this has on clients in their recall of memory and reconstruction of autobiography.

Though there is no overt suggestion or advice from the practitioner to remember their mothers in a fixed form, previous clients' confession tapes that are broadcast during meal times as a guide or stimulation give new clients some idea of ideal Naikan confession. In addition, women in the kitchen (usually practitioners' wives) may remind clients of how their mother used to prepare meals when they were small. Many clients appreciate meals at Naikan centres and they comment that even when their Naikan was not smooth or deep, they appreciated the meals and were grateful to the practitioner's wife for preparing them. Many clients also say that they never appreciated food this much before, and that they have an increased gratitude towards their own mothers, who prepared such meals every day. Many Naikan centres are aware of the effect these 'home cooked meals' have on clients and avoid having food delivered from outside, which would otherwise be quite common in Japan. If a Naikan practitioner's wife has some occasion when she has to depend on delivered food, she will often either add one home-cooked dish or make sure to transfer the meals from their plastic containers to plates.

This psychological structure of a strong desire to be forgiven by and to achieve reunion with one's mother is often seen in Japanese films, soap dramas and novels.[14] Similarly, complaints of being an 'unwanted child' or undesired by one's mother are common in Japanese culture.[15] Not only do many Japanese men frequently refer to their wives as 'mother', but after work some may turn to bar hostesses, whose job is to listen to them complain about their jobs and wives, as if they were mothers listening to their children. The head lady at the bar is even called *mama-san* or 'mom'. However, I would not say that such phenomena are limited to Japan.

This brings us to theories about the tiny 'sacred space' (*hōza*) created by the screen. Two Naikan practitioners described it to me as a 'womb environment'.[16] One told me that the recovery of very early memories often deepens Naikan, and so he conducts 'womb Naikan' occasionally as a part of the standard Naikan practice. He has clients wrap themselves up in a blanket and lie on the floor until 'they are born', a process that takes about three hours.

The Naikan setting contributes to the recreation of an idealized mother, by using its enclosed, womb-like setting to create an absolute dependency of the client on the practitioner (Murase 1996: 39). The client is fed, told when to get up, bathe and sleep, and must remain silent until approached for confession. The client is able to receive but not to give, yet his or her lack of autonomy is coupled with a sense of complete safety. The image of mother that clients are guided to through Naikan is that of a self-sacrificing, caring, warm and affectionate figure.

Some scholars have speculated that a potential danger in Naikan would be the problem of how to mend the gap between the ideal mother that clients create in Naikan and the mother in reality whom they have to face following Naikan. Officially Naikan deals with only the 'facts' of the past; however, as clients progress, the very structure of the method is such that they can easily start to neglect or downplay their mothers' negative aspects and emphasize the positive. According to some, the image of the mother would then be 'unrealistic' or 'meta-realistic'. Murase's (1996: 73) suggestion that such purified images of the mother form the fundamental support sustaining Japanese notions of guilt would indicate that in this sense Naikan is serving as a tool for the social construction of conservative Japanese values.

Naikan guides are also aware that not all parents are ideal, but they still demand that clients reflect on their past to realize the debt they owe to their parents. In this process, DeVos writes, 'parental figures become symbols and fictions, not actual people. The mother is romanticized as an all-giving person, and the image is reinforced in all forms of Japanese popular culture' (DeVos 1980: 126). It has been argued that any therapy seeking to view the family critically or negatively fails in Japan (Reynolds 1980, 1983; DeVos 1980; Murase 1996). Reynolds even sees this Japanese unwillingness to view the supportive family negatively as one of the reasons for the failure of Freudian psychoanalysis in Japan (1983: 130), a point also made by several

Japanese anthropologists. Naikan is often understood as a method in which clients construct idealized mythical parents as substitutes for the actual ones, a technique some would say is common to popular Japanese culture, where the Japanese emperor was seen as the mythical father-figure of all Japanese during World War II.

However, my own interpretation of this would be different: the Naikan client is not, in fact, creating a mythical, idealized parent. The Naikan method reveals that one's view of one's parents (and others) is based on a selective reading of past events; that is to say, it includes and highlights certain events (especially times when one was hurt), and excludes countless other events (such as the times one was fed, all the times one's parents spent money on one's upbringing, or worked to earn such money, and so on). Recollecting those positive events, when one received love and affection from others, and using those events to create a new context within which one can view one's parents and others in a different light, is surely not a completely 'objective' process, but it is certainly no less objective than the client's original view of his or her parents. Arguably, it is more objective, since it includes more perspectives and more information. In any case, it is quite a different thing from creating an 'idealized' picture of one's parents. It is the client's previous negative views which are revealed to have been 'idealized' – in a negative way – because in order for such views to appear justified, reasonable and objectively 'true' to the client, they had to be based on an exclusionary principle that removed countless acts of kindness from the overall picture.

When seen in this way, the focus on the mother in Naikan may have less to do with Japanese cultural norms, conservative or otherwise, and more to do with the fact that reflecting on one's relationship with one's mother is an especially effective means for breaking down fantasized notions of self-sufficiency and independence, and bringing home the realization that one's life took shape in complete dependence on the care and support of others. The reason why the mother is the paradigmatic case for such reflection is because of the unique relationship we all have with our mothers, having been conceived in their wombs, nurtured there, born, breastfed, and countless other acts, without which we would not have been able to survive. From the Naikan perspective, even a person abandoned from birth would still have something to feel grateful for towards his or her mother, just for the fact that they were taken care of in the womb and protected until birth; for that alone, such a person would still owe a debt impossible to pay back, namely his or her life. This function that the role of mother plays in Naikan is therefore not by any means limited to Japan.

The Naikan world view

How do these factors combine for the purpose of healing in Naikan, and what kind of healing? I believe the answer lies in a world view prevalent in

Japanese society: I say world view, because while it is a system for understanding questions of health and illness, it goes beyond them to the nature of
self, society, nature and the universe. The importance of *ki* in Japan and the
results of my own research suggest that health and illness in Japan are not
individual attributes; rather, health and illness are relational.

Anyone who has gone to an acupuncturist knows that *ki* is all about alignment. According to the traditional medical systems of China, India, Tibet
and Japan, if one's *ki* is aligned properly, one is healthy and in harmony with
the universe. However, over time one's *ki* can come out of alignment, and
then it needs to be realigned, which will bring about healing. In Naikan, we
see just this practice taking place. Because one's health is relational, distor-
tions in one's relationships will bring about illness. Hence, Naikan attempts
to realign clients' relationships, starting with their most important relationship, their mother. Once these are repaired, according to the world view
implicit in Naikan, healing will occur.

When seen from this angle, it becomes very clear that each element of
Naikan is precisely aimed at bringing about this realignment. Let us take the
'tomb and womb' environment and the importance of 'death', for example.
The womb-like setting of Naikan, the dependence of the client on the
practitioner, and the emphasis on starting and ending with mother, all push
the client towards a remembrance of unity, a time when that client's *ki* was in
balance. Emphasis on death performs the same function from the opposite
pole: it impresses a sense of urgency on the client that his or her relationships
need to be aligned soon, because time is running out.

The same holds true for Naikan's three themes. They focus the rewriting
of the client's autobiography around the issue of relationships. Yet by not
allowing clients to dwell on what trouble other people caused them, Naikan's
three themes tilt the scale in favour of viewing others in a more positive light.
The client's old views gradually give way to feelings of guilt, which in turn
give way to cathartic feelings of acceptance and unity. In the process, the
client's self-victimizing autobiography, and hence misaligned 'self', comes
under critique and can be replaced by a new autobiography, and a new 'self'
that is in a more proper alignment with the universe. This aspect of Naikan
can be seen as a historiographical operation, in that it encourages clients to
re-evaluate and rewrite their autobiographies or personal histories along
prescribed lines and set values. The history of the self is constructed in a way
that places its origins in birth in the mother, and encourages clients to look
forward to death in order to test and challenge the limits of their current
understanding of the self.

Viewing what is going on in Naikan through this lens has several theoretical
implications for medical anthropology and anthropological studies of the
self. One of the strengths of medical anthropology is that the categories of
biomedicine are not accepted as natural facts but are understood as cultural
constructs, although this is not in any way to deny the reality of pain and
suffering, and the need for effective medical treatments. So, when discussing

the categories of *ki* or Western categories of depression, anxiety, etc., it is important to remember that neither are 'facts of nature' or 'truthful' insights into bodily conditions, but that both are means to label emotional states, affects and physical distress. Thus, the world view that I would argue is present in Naikan, and which is visible elsewhere in Japanese and East Asian culture, would therefore not be limited to explaining health and illness phenomena in Japan. Just as biomedicine could be used to study and attempt to explain the Naikan process, so could this cosmology and its model of relational health be used to explain experiences outside Japan.

This perspective helps to overcome the dichotomy of 'integration vs independence'. This binary model is itself a reflection of a particular intellectual framework, one that is rejected in Naikan. Instead, the Naikan world view perceives a harmony of 'integration and independence'. Indeed, one could say that to move toward such a harmony is a main objective of many religious cultivation practices in Japan and other Asian cultures. Similarly, I would suggest a move away from the dichotomy of the 'egocentric vs sociocentric' model of selfhood often used to contrast the Western self with the Japanese self. By recognizing what they have received from others and returned to others, clients come to appreciate the relational nature of their health, illness, life and self. This realignment, like the realignment of *ki*, brings about healing and hence an independence from their illness and a degree of freedom; yet it is an independence that is tied to an awareness of how inseparably integrated they are in their relationships, society, and the world at large.

Therefore, this relational healing seems to support the views of psychologists such as Markus and Kitayama (1991), who write that the Japanese have 'interdependent selves' which challenge the idea of self as being an essential unity, something internal and something apart from society. The word for self in Japanese, *jibun*, refers to 'one's share of the shared life space'. We have seen how anthropologists such as Kondo (1989, 1992), Bachnik (1992), Lebra (1992) and Rosenberger (1992b, 1992c) also discuss that Japanese self is not apart from the realm of the social, but rather shifting, cultivated and fluid.

Yet while Naikan's world view supports these notions of selfhood, it also suggests more complex understandings of the self. The first is the importance of 'death' in the constitution of the self. At the border of what is understood as the self and the person, 'death' can be understood variously as the limit of the self, or religiously as a transition into a limitless self. At the other end of the autobiography of the self is birth. The study of Naikan shows that conceptions of birth and death are intricately connected with conceptions of the self. Naikan also calls attention to the embodiment of the self and the mind–body relationship in its holistic approach to healing. The Japanese word *mi*, which means both 'body' and also 'self', indicates that self is not merely mental but also physiological.

Lastly and most importantly, Naikan suggests we must be critical of theories of Japanese self that encourage the view that there is 'a Japanese self' in the singular, which can be compared and contrasted with 'a Western self'. Rather, the Japanese come to Naikan with various understandings of the self, which then come into conflict with the underlying notion of self in Naikan's world view. For 'successful Naikan' to take place, this conflict must be present, and the client's history of the self must be rewritten in a way more in concord with the Naikan view of self. If there were in fact one standard 'Japanese self' that was already inherently relationally-oriented, one could argue that the Naikan method would be ineffective or redundant.

In this chapter we explored the connection between Naikan and Shin Buddhism; however, there are certainly Naikan centres run by practitioners of other religions: the practitioner Usami is a Zen monk, Nagashima lived in a Zen temple for six years, Kimura is the founder of a religion based on yoga, one centre is run by a Shingon Buddhist monk, and some centres are run by practitioners who do not follow any religion. A recent tendency among Naikan centres has been to retain an aspect of spirituality while not tying Naikan to one religion in particular. Thus, standing in tension with Naikan's more traditional Buddhist heritage is a side of Naikan that might seem to resemble New Religious Movements and even the New Age, especially considering how Yoshimoto was himself a layman who adapted aspects of Buddhist practice and tradition. Andreasen writes:

> Of course, the great challenge to Shin Buddhism after World War II has been the New Religions of Japan. They are in many respects at the other end of the religious spectrum with belief in spirits, exorcism and a great number of rites to ensure 'this-worldly benefits' ... Perhaps the most important element of New Religions is the reliance on and important role of laymen ...
>
> (Andreasen 1998: 179)

To what extent has Naikan remained immune to this challenge? Could the recent trend in Naikan towards an emphasis on 'this-worldly benefits' such as 'healing' and 'happiness', and away from traditional other-worldly concepts such as salvation, be drawing the practice away from Yoshimoto's roots? We will turn towards these questions in Chapter 7 and situate Naikan within these broader social developments, but first we will examine the social organization of Naikan.

Plate 5.1 A Buddhist altar with a picture of Yoshimoto located in the middle of one of the rooms for doing Naikan at Yoshimoto's centre.

Plate 5.2 A print of Nigabyakudō, a famous Shin Buddhist painting and a favourite of Yoshimoto's. This painting hangs on the inside of a screen at Yoshimoto's centre, so a client would see the image while doing Naikan. This was the only time I saw anything on the inside of a screen.

6 The social organization of Naikan

The history of Naikan organization

Inspired by his own spiritual practices and reflections, in 1953, at the age of thirty-eight, Yoshimoto Ishin decided to retire from his career as a business-man (in which he had been very successful) and devote himself full time to developing and establishing his new method of 'Naikan', or 'inner-reflection'. He founded the first Naikan centre at Nara, the ancient former capital close to modern Kyoto and still a city of temples and shrines as well as being the home of one of Japan's biggest New Religions, Tenrikyō. In the following year he was able to persuade the penal authorities to allow him to introduce his method to the inmates in Nara Prison, with substantial positive effect on their morale and the rate and permanency of rehabilitation. He also began to accept, without any fee, clients who wished individually to try the method, and his fame began to spread by word of mouth in addition to the publicity that his success in the prison had begun to attract. It is reported (Nagashima 1991: 74) that until 1961, when the number of clients began to become substantial, Yoshimoto not only did not charge fees, but even on occasions paid the travel costs and lost wages for individuals who were strongly motivated to try Naikan, but who could not afford to lose income by stopping work for one week.

Also, by 1965 Naikan had started to attract the attention of specialists working both in psychology and psychiatry. In particular, medical practi-tioners in mental hospitals were beginning to recognize that the method could prove useful as an adjunct to conventional psychiatric and drug-based interventions (Takemoto 1981a: 3). Yoshimoto called the late 1960s the 'golden age' of Naikan as recognition spread, the flow of clients increased, former clients began to express a wish to practise and promote Naikan, hospitals and prisons began to seriously recognize the possibilities of Naikan, and Naikan's three themes were established.

At the same time, Yoshimoto recognized the need to remove Naikan's Buddhist overtones in order to make the method acceptable at the prison, as it is unconstitutional in Japan for any public institution to propagate a religion. Yoshimoto avoided terms he had previously employed, such as 'the Buddha's mercy' or 'salvation', and emphasized that Naikan had no doctrines, that the practitioner was not a guru, and that no mediumship or shamanism (often associated with the New Religions) was involved. As the language of religion dropped away, the language of psychiatry began to spread (though not by Yoshimoto himself). Below I devote a section to the process of the medicalization and psychologization of Naikan that has taken place since it began to be adopted by medical, penal, business and educational institutions (Miyazaki 1992: 6).

A substantial step forward was made in 1975 when a private hospital, the Takemoto Hospital in Kagoshima, became the first multi-purpose medical facility to set aside a specific space for Naikan practice (Takemoto 1981a: 3), and from 1976 the method was introduced for the treatment of alcoholics at the hospital. The hospital's founder, Dr Takemoto Takahiro, had experienced Naikan and subsequently sent the medical staff to experience Naikan at the hospital's expense.

Today Takemoto is one of the leading and most influential medical figures in the Naikan community. At the Takemoto Hospital alcoholic patients do Naikan two months after the start of their treatment, this being deemed to be the point at which they are psychologically and physically ready for it. Given the special nature of their needs, Naikan is introduced slowly, beginning with attendance at *danshukai*, which is a kind of Alcoholics Anonymous-type setting in which other people (mostly more 'senior' patients) who have experienced Naikan talk about this experience. This is followed by starting Naikan, initially for one hour each day in order to build motivation progressively (Miki 1993: 3).

Through the late 1970s and 1980s there was a rapid spread of Naikan, both in Japan and overseas (Table 6.1). At the same time as this formal inventory of events was unfolding, the number of Naikan centres in Japan was steadily expanding, from Yoshimoto's original one to a current total of over forty centres and twenty-eight hospital locations internationally.

Naikan associations

In Yoshimoto's view, religions that become institutionalized, such as Japanese Buddhism, lose their essence by becoming overly concerned with matters such as the collection of alms. Yet, as with the continued development of any movement, religion or practice, such ideals always come into conflict with sociological and practical pressures for organization, efficiency, regulation and control. Thus, when the first annual Naikan conference was organized in 1978, Yoshimoto announced that he was pleased to see so many people from all over Japan, but he would have been even more pleased to see them spending their time doing Naikan instead of wasting it at a conference, showing again his preference for personal experience over intellectual understanding. It is an episode well known in Naikan circles, and it illustrates the tension between the ideal of no organization and the practical issues that make some degree of organization necessary for Naikan to survive.

Table 6.1 Chronology of the spread of Naikan

1972	First Naikan retreat in Europe led by Franz Ritter.
1978	Japan Naikan Association (JNA) is established on the initiative of Dr Takemoto for the purpose of establishing Naikan on a firm basis independent of Yoshimoto's control[1] and for advancing the theorization and spread of Naikan as a serious therapeutic method.[2]
1980	Naikan introduced in Europe (Austria) by Professor Ishii Akira.
1981	Naikan introduced in the USA by Dr David K. Reynolds.
1985	*Naikan Konwakai* or Study Group of Naikan Practitioners in Japan is established, which later becomes the Association of Naikan Centres (ANC). Naikan is introduced in Italy.
1986	The first Naikan centre in Europe is founded by Franz Ritter in Austria (*Neue Welt Institut*). Naikan is introduced at the Drug Rehabilitation Centre in North Italy.[3]
1987	The second Naikan centre in Europe is established by Gerald Steinke near Bremen.
1988	The third Naikan centre in Europe is founded by Holst Kern near Munich. Death of Yoshimoto Ishin.
1989	Naikan is introduced in China.[4]
1990	Naikan centre founded in Salzburg by Roland Dick. Motoyama Yōichi founds the Association of Self-Discovery (ASD).
1991	Naikan centre established in Vienna by Josef Hartl. The First International Naikan Conference is convened in Tokyo at Aoyama Gakuen University.
1994	The second International Naikan Conference in Vienna. The Association of Naikan Centres (ANC) established.
1997	The third International Naikan Conference in north Italy.
2000	The fourth International Naikan Conference in Tokyo. Death of Yoshimoto Kinuko and Yanagita Kakusei.

1 See Murase (1981a: 11).
2 See Takemoto (1990: 27).
3 See Ritter (1989: 62).
4 See Oh (1996: 6).

Regardless of whether Yoshimoto would have been pleased about it or not, there are currently three nation-wide Naikan organizations and several regional ones. The first is the *Nihon Naikan Gakkai*, or Japan Naikan Association (JNA), which organizes the national annual Naikan conference and is research-oriented, especially towards psychological and medical research. The second is the *Naikan Kenshūsho Kyōkai*, or Association of Naikan Centres (ANC), which serves to legitimize practitioners, as I explain below, and which is the most selective of the Naikan organizations. (What information I did receive came through insider contacts, such as Yoshimoto's son, Yoshimoto Masanobu, and a few practitioners, and materials published by the association.) The third is the *Jiko Hakken Kai*, or Association of Self-Discovery (ASD), which publishes a monthly journal on Naikan that provides information on periodical meetings for those who have experienced Naikan. Such meetings are also organized by regional associations such as The Association of Happiness, The Swan Association and The Bamboo Shoot Association.

There is no registration process for opening a Naikan centre, no official training or certification, and no official requirements or standards. Since anyone can practice Naikan, the ANC plays an interesting role through its selective membership and its recognition of only 'recommended' Naikan practitioners. A practitioner seeking recognition submits an application and current members decide whether he or she is an 'appropriate' Naikan practitioner or not. It seems that practitioners who join the association are then generally recognized through various channels as authentic Naikan practitioners. This might indicate a hierarchy in Naikan's organization with a select group of first-generation Naikan practitioners (those who were guided by Yoshimoto) that decides what forms of Naikan deviate from Yoshimoto's style, creating a certain tension between efforts at improving Naikan for the future and an inherent conservatism.

Figure 6.1 illustrates how the three national Naikan organizations can be seen as focused on different levels. The JNA organizes the National Annual Conference; the ANC is primarily for practitioners and legitimizes them; and the ASD is concerned primarily with those who have experienced Naikan and may wish to pursue further Naikan, for example by meeting in post-Naikan groups. What is important to note about the organization of Naikan is its fluidity and lack of any centralized authority. The Naikan conferences have no control over what happens in individual Naikan centres, and practitioners choose whether to attend them.

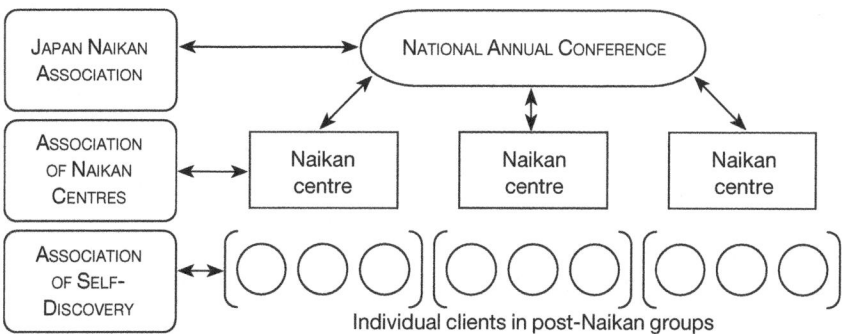

Figure 6.1 Levels of Naikan organization.

The ANC, while it can 'recognize' centres as operating on Yoshimoto's principles, cannot prevent any individual from founding and running a centre based on unauthorized modifications of these principles. The structure is a voluntary one in which most practitioners, as well as many medical doctors, interested academics and laypeople actively participate. The Naikan association publishes a journal and the annual conference's proceedings, and most practitioners and other followers subscribe to these, but they are not obliged to take cognizance of their contents. Nevertheless it does create a sense of community, a sense of participation in a common cause and a means of communication and information-sharing among those who have had the experience of Naikan.

The demographics of Naikan centres

Over forty Naikan centres are scattered across Japan, although the ANC recognizes only thirty of these, and of these only ten to thirteen are publicly recommended by the ASD in its publications. In addition, Naikan is used in some twenty-eight hospitals in Japan alone. Although the late 1980s saw the end of Naikan's dramatic rise in levels of attendance within Japan, which has in fact been decreasing since Yoshimoto's illness and death in 1987, new centres continue to be founded and Naikan's popularity continues to grow abroad. Significantly, a 2004 issue of the popular American Buddhist magazine *Tricycle* (Kain 2004: 58–61, 116–17) featured an article on Naikan at the ToDo Institute in Vermont, USA.

The popular Naikan centres can attract 300–400 clients each year, but the majority of centres attract less than fifty. The total number of clients per year for all centres seems to be around 2,000. Unfortunately, it is almost impossible to collect accurate statistics on the number of clients per year, or even on the existing number of Naikan centres, because there is no registration system for founding a Naikan centre. The Japan Naikan Association (JNA) is aware of over thirty Naikan centres, but in the absence of any official certification, there are no restrictions on anyone founding a Naikan centre or claiming to be a Naikan practitioner. Yoshimoto himself never established any guidelines or standards for being a practitioner, saying rather that anyone who had experienced Naikan could be a practitioner. Nevertheless, the desire to maintain Yoshimoto's authentic style since his death has led practitioners to praise certain methods and criticize others as deviant.

Thus, a newly opened centre might apply for recognition from the ANC only to be rejected. Such was the case for a centre in Tokyo that remains unrecognized, even though its practitioner attends the annual conference and has given presentations there. When I was looking for a centre in Tokyo at which to do my own initial Naikan, for example, I was told by people in the local community (scholars and members of the post-Naikan group there) that the nearest Naikan centre was in Tochigi, a three-hour train ride north of Tokyo in the countryside. The Naikan centre in Tokyo was not mentioned to me. Instead, it was viewed as deviant, because it combined the standard one-week Naikan session with a session on past lives. Currently, however, there is the *Shiroganedai* Naikan centre in Tokyo, which did not exist in 1997 when I started my research. The *Shiroganedai* Naikan centre is recognized by the ANC, and the Naikan journal *Yasuragi* includes it in their list of centres.

The names of the ten most 'established' centres were constantly mentioned to me by members of the core community, and the Naikan journal *Yasuragi* always advertises the list of recommended centres in every issue. Some centres that I knew existed disappeared from the list. One of the editors of *Yasuragi* explained to me that the journal is only willing to recommend centres that the Association of Self-Discovery are certain practice the classical Naikan method.

Lack of recognition can be a significant factor for a struggling Naikan centre, since from the numbers it is clear that Naikan is not yet a large-scale practice in Japan. The peak of Naikan, in terms of attracting clients, was the period 1976–1984, ending shortly before Yoshimoto's death in 1987 (see Figure 6.3). During this period, Yoshimoto's Naikan centre in Nara attracted over 1,000 clients per year. As well as leading Naikan, Yoshimoto was engaged in giving lectures and took part in several documentaries for NHK, Japan's national broadcasting company.

Figure 6.2 illustrates, how since Yoshimoto's death, the most popular Naikan centre has been Yanagita's *Meisō no Mori* in Tochigi (now run by Shimizu alone since Yanagita's death in 2000), whose attendance rose steadily throughout the 1990s. At the same time, Yoshimoto's own centre in Nara has been in decline.[5] Figure 6.2 also indicates the total number of clients in the mid-1990s at all Naikan centres that report their statistics to the ANC, showing a sharp decline of almost 20 per cent in 1995, when the Tokyo subway gas attack by the AUM Shinrikyō group occurred.

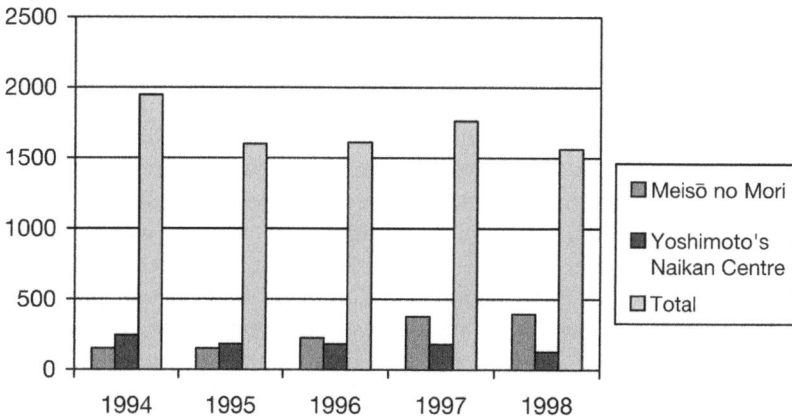

Figure 6.2 Number of clients at Naikan centres, 1994–1998.

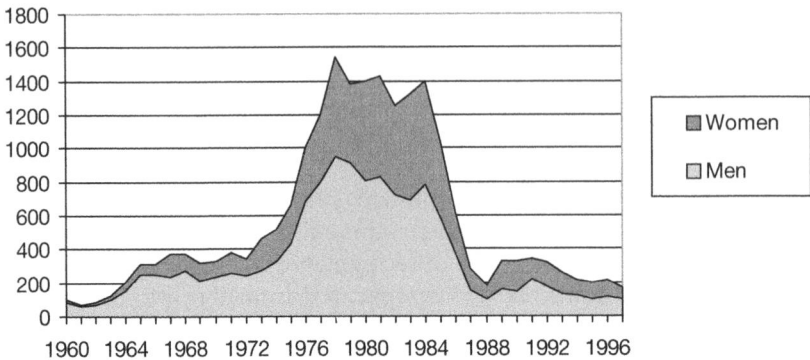

Figure 6.3 Number of clients at Yoshimoto's Naikan centre.

Statistics from 1960 to 1984 come from Yoshimoto (1997: 198). Statistics from 1985 to 1997 were compiled by myself at Yoshimoto's Naikan centre in Nara.

A further problem that has arisen since Yoshimoto's death has been that of finding practitioners to carry on Naikan for future generations. Under Yoshimoto's guidance, a second generation of Naikan practitioners emerged, including individuals such as Yanagita. However, these practitioners are now in their late fifties to early seventies; some, such as Yanagita, have died already. They are having difficulty in finding and training a third generation of Naikan practitioners, who will be willing to take on the Naikan way of life. Practitioners have told me of the difficulty in finding anyone willing to make the commitment of sharing his life with Naikan clients, with a wife who is ready to prepare meals for ten to twenty people, three times a day, all year round and rise before 5.00 a.m. every day with no weekend breaks. Only *Meisō no Mori* has found successors after Yanagita in the couple of Shimizu Yasuhiko and Shimizu Yoshie, who are willing to accept such conditions. As Mr Shimizu's mother, Shimizu Shizue, also assists in Naikan quite regularly, there are effectively three practitioners at *Meisō no Mori*.

During my year of fieldwork in 1997–1998, these urgent issues became even more serious through the loss of Yoshimoto Kinuko as a Naikan practitioner. After Yoshimoto Ishin's death in 1987, his wife Kinuko took over his position at the centre until sickness prevented her in January 1998. Like Yoshimoto, Kinuko achieved enlightenment through *mishirabe*, and Yoshimoto used to say that it would have been impossible to run the Naikan centre without her. Before dying he told others that Kinuko would inherit his Naikan spirit and there was therefore nothing to worry about; thereafter, she has been highly respected among Naikan practitioners. Now there is a fear among practitioners that Naikan's 'essence' may not be maintained and passed on to future generations. As a result, conflict continues among Naikan practitioners over what is authentic Naikan, what kinds of variations are acceptable and whether Naikan is psychotherapy, self-cultivation, religious practice or non-religious.

Part of the problem is undoubtedly the unprofitability of running a Naikan centre. Yoshimoto frequently stated that he did not want to use Naikan as a tool for moneymaking or to regard it as a business. To do so, he thought, would be immoral, as it would be making money from religion, something considered very improper in Buddhism. Today, Naikan centres do charge for their services, but the fees are low considering the high cost of living in Japan. On average, a seven-day Naikan session costs ¥60,000–70,000 (£400–500 sterling or US $600–700), which is not a significant sum considering one receives a bed and three meals a day – a typical hotel in Japan would be more expensive. If understood as a mere occupation rather than as a religious practice or way of life, Naikan hardly seems a good economic proposition for its practitioners. In fact, many cannot survive off Naikan practice alone and have other jobs as well, while those centres in the countryside grow as much of their own food as possible. Although the situation has in some ways improved as Naikan has become better known to the general public, the number of clients has not been rapidly increasing, creating great economic insecurity.

While economic and ideological pressures produce certain kinds of tensions, in other respects the situation has opened out. In 1987 Takemoto (1987: 35) suggested that the fundamental problem was that very few people still knew about Naikan. In that year the JNA had only 200 members, and Takemoto's survey suggested that only 18.7 per cent of doctors in university hospitals and 8.8 per cent of the directors of private hospitals knew about Naikan. Since then Naikan has become much better known. NHK has broadcast programmes about Naikan, books are widely available in shops, magazine articles have been published in mass circulation publications, and there is widening knowledge and interest in medical circles. Some bookshops include books on Naikan in their psychology sections, others now have small special sections usually adjacent to psychology devoted to Naikan and some of its main alternatives, in particular the probably better-known Morita therapy (Reynolds 1976; Iwai 1986; Ohara 1997; Hasegawa *et al.* 1991; Kōra 2000).

The demographics of Naikan have also changed. At the time Yoshimoto started the first centre in his own house, most of his relatively few clients were adults; in the Nara Juvenile Prison they were adolescents. Since those early days, and with the expansion of the movement, the age and social ranges have broadened. Today there is no one age group that dominates. Clients range in age from ten to eighty years old (Figure 6.4). Occupations include students, teachers, homemakers, business people, bureaucrats, shopkeepers, manual workers, nurses, medical personnel and many others. Some companies now send their staff for company-sponsored (and paid) Naikan. Those hospitals that include Naikan in their programmes routinely send their staff to particpate.

Reynolds (1979: 6) reports that in the 1970s centres tended to attract lower and middle class clients. In the last decade this has changed and larger

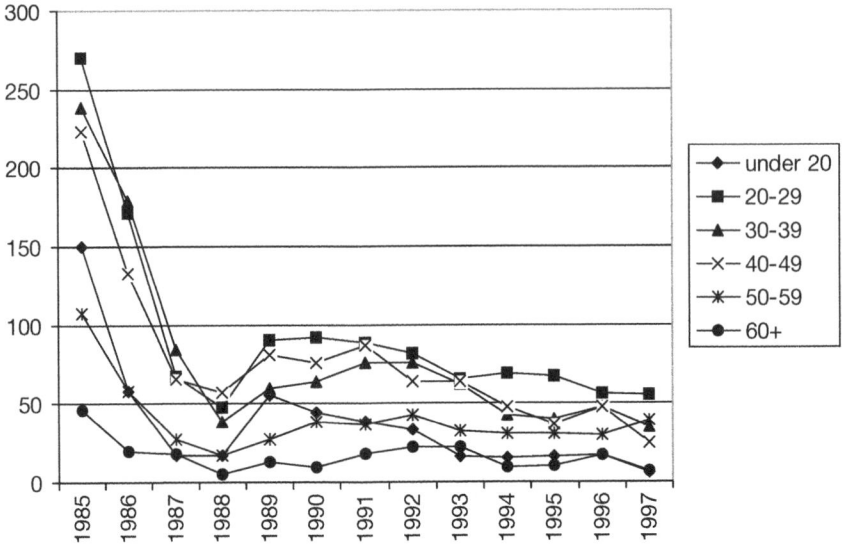

Figure 6.4 Clients by age group at Yoshimoto's Naikan centre.

Statistics compiled by myself at Yoshimoto's Naikan centre in Nara.

numbers of intellectuals – university students, university teachers (especially psychologists), doctors, writers and musicians – have been appearing. Yanagita commented on the rise of young people with high educational backgrounds in the last decade at *Meisō no Mori*. Among his clients have been the writer Kamiwatari Ryōhei and the journalist Yanagita Kunio (no relation), both of whom have written and lectured about their experiences and have commented on it in magazine interviews. The demographics of Naikan centres abroad reflects this diversity as well. In general, statistics for the five years preceding 1997 suggest that the sex ratio is about balanced (Miki 1997: 112).

Currently, there are also twenty-eight hospitals within Japan that apply Naikan as part of treatment for various symptoms. In particular, the intro-duction of Naikan at the Tottori University Hospital was seen as a watershed by the medical doctors in the Naikan community, as it was the first state university hospital to do so. (The status of state universities is in general higher than that of private universities in Japan.) It was discovered early on that Naikan proves effective for alcohol and drug dependency (Takemoto 1981a, 1981b, 1984a, 1984b). It also proved effective for psychosomatic illnesses, such as eating disorders, school rejectory syndrome, fevers and psychogenic pain (Ikemi 1963, 1973). It has even be applied for more serious conditions, such as neurosis, depression and schizophrenia (Kawahara 1996).

What are the primary reasons that people come to do Naikan? Here again, one runs into the problem that reliable statistics are unavailable, and many practitioners purposefully refrain from asking their clients the reason for their visit. From the information that is available, however, it seems that clients fall into three categories in this regard. The first group consists of those seeking self-improvement, self-realization, self-understanding or a step towards spiritual awakening. The second group are those seeking help with substance abuse, eating disorders, psychosomatic illnesses, and so on. The third group are those who have problems in life, work, study, human relations and marriage. Of course, these groups are very general and cannot be delineated strictly: an alcoholic with work-related problems seeking self-improvement would obviously fit into all three.

One may also wonder to what extent such problems are 'solved'. Already in Chapter 4 we have discussed the ways in which these problems are engaged and dealt with in Naikan, and in Chapter 3 we examined recorded confessions. The latter show that Naikan is certainly perceived as efficacious by some clients, but these cannot give an overall impression since they are pre-selected by practitioners as models of successful Naikan. Statistical information on the extent to which clients perceive an efficacious result from Naikan would be interesting, yet it is lacking.

In its absence, I can only say from my own ethnographic work that results are various. Certainly there are those who feel that Naikan has had a profound impact on their lives, such as the various practitioners like Yanagita, who gave up their jobs to do Naikan and share it with others full-time. Then there are those who feel that Naikan had little or no effect on them. One young woman I spoke with, for example, said that the recorded confessions at a centre with strong Buddhist overtones actually gave her nightmares, with their images of sinfulness and going to hell. A large number of clients, however, have an experience which we saw in Yanagita's confession in Chapter 3: that Naikan had a significant impact on them, but that this impact wore off gradually over time. Others may experience the opposite: that they only came to realize the impact it had on them much later.

The shift in the social background of clients is certainly related to the publicity factor. In something of a self-fulfilling prophecy, a local newspaper (*Toyama Shinbun* 1994) reported that the Hokuriku Naikan centre had been attracting young women in their twenties in the previous two or three years. The article suggested that these women, materially well-off and socially independent though they were, nevertheless still found life empty, and their search for fulfilment led them to Naikan. While the traditional core of clients remains much unchanged – alcoholics, children suffering from 'school rejection' syndrome (*hikikomori*), and adults facing family disorder and life crises – one distinct shift has been towards these younger, better-educated and often female clients, and another has been the appearance of clients suffering from malignant and terminal cancers (*Asahi Shinbun* 1994).

Another factor is that the hospice movement is still poorly developed in Japan. Information given to terminally-ill patients in hospitals is sparse, and many patients die not knowing – or at least not until it was too late to make serious spiritual and other preparations – the severity or nature of their illnesses. Slowly mounting pressure from patients and relatives to force hospitals to make more honest disclosures is creating more awareness in Japan of 'deathing' or preparation for death. The problem is that there is a very underdeveloped infrastructure and few resources to which terminal patients can turn. Naikan, with its emphasis on the resolution of conflicts and coming to terms with relationships, has been proposed (e.g. by Nagashima 1993: 135–7) as a possible approach to terminal care, and an increasing number of clients in this category seem to have discovered Naikan for themselves.

Certain social trends have benefited Naikan, such as the expansion of interest in psychosomatic medicine (*shinshin igaku*). Quite early in the development of Naikan, Dr Ikemo Yūjirō, a leading figure in psychosomatic medicine in Japan, came to hear of Naikan and invited Yoshimoto to give lectures at the conferences and public meetings that he organized. In 1977 Naikan was represented at the International Psychosomatic Medical Conference and was reported on extensively again in a major national newspaper, *Yomiuri Shinbun*, on 13 August 1997. In this conference Naikan featured along with a spectrum of 'Japanese' therapies, including Morita, Zen Therapy, Fasting Therapy and incense treatment (*Monko*). Partly as a result of this exposure, Naikan was then represented in a number of technical and popular encyclopaedias published in great numbers in Japan, including ones on educational psychology, emotional disorders, behavioural reform and children's clinical psychology (Naikan Kenkyūsho 1980: 28–31).

By the same token, however, Naikan has been affected negatively by certain other events in Japanese society. Most noteworthy of these was the sarin gas attack in 1995 on the Tokyo subway system by members of the AUM Shinrikyō new religion and the subsequent disclosures of bizarre apocalyptic plans which included the abduction and murder of critics. AUM emphasized yoga-like body practices, some requiring total isolation, and Naikan of course has some formal resemblance to this. This forced Naikan to distinguish itself from such cults, especially as the aftermath of the AUM events brought about a precipitous decline in the number of new Naikan clients (Miki 1997: 112) (see Figure 6.2).

Out of such concerns, at the annual Naikan conference in 1997, which I attended, the question of the appearance and physical self-presentation of Naikan practitioners was raised. Some Naikan practitioners are Buddhist priests, and others who are not may still adopt the shaved head and the wearing of *samue*, the traditional Japanese working clothes that look rather like a monk's outfit, especially to those unfamiliar with it. This emphasis on separation from religion has had one very visible effect to which we will return: the movement of some sections of the Naikan community towards a 'scientific' representation of Naikan, a pressure which crucially raises the question of what is 'authentic' Naikan in the first place.

'Authentic Naikan' and Naikan variants

A major conflict within the Naikan community is the question of what constitutes 'authentic' Naikan practice. Even though Yoshimoto started his Naikan centre in 1953, it took him until 1968 to establish the 'three themes' that form the basis of the current Naikan method. Yoshimoto was always eager to hear his clients' comments and suggestions. He frequently repeated his opinion that 'There is no one absolute method. Each person is free to try the method he or she feels is right, for what is most important is to help people' (Miyazaki 1992: 6).

This liberal attitude has been interpreted in various ways. Some practitioners see Yoshimoto's method as the archetype and attempt to maintain it without modification or innovation. Others, particularly doctors who apply Naikan in hospital settings, have modified Naikan to suit their needs and institutional constraints. Most practitioners, however, agree on the importance of two principles: making Naikan more efficacious will expand its reach and appeal, and maintaining Yoshimoto's basic style will preserve its uniqueness and integrity. Nevertheless, those committed to maintaining a rigid style tend to judge innovations as deviations that jeopardize Naikan's original essence.

This can be illustrated with the example of the recollection of past experiences. Recalling one's deeds and attitudes in relation to significant others is the root of the Naikan method. However, interpretations of exactly what this means vary among practitioners. Yoshimoto used to ask his clients to start towards the beginning of elementary school, although he never justified this particular starting point in any theoretical manner. Some practitioners, however, set the starting point earlier. For example, when undergoing my own Naikan at *Meisō no Mori*, I was asked to start from the time I was born, or at least from my very earliest memories. It was explained to me that people who had lost a parent, especially their mother, early in life or even at birth, could feel a reassuring sense of their mother's affection with the thought that the very fact that they were now alive means that they were protected and fed by their mother in the womb for nine months.

Iwamoto Naomi, who conducts Naikan in a hospital setting, also suggests that active recall of the past for adults should start before their elementary school age (Iwamoto 1991: 5). Upon hearing this, however, another practitioner, Motoyama, argued that in his experience it is better if clients start with the lower elementary school years, not because he denied the therapeutic effect of recalling very early memories, but rather because Naikan sets for itself certain goals and limits, the most important of which is 'Seeing the facts as they are and knowing one's true self' (Motoyama 1990: 5). To this Iwamoto in turn responded by questioning what is meant by the terms 'fact' and 'as it is' (Iwamoto 1991: 5) on the basis that it is impossible to establish that anyone's memory of the past is 'correct', since it is inevitably edited and undergoes retrospective modification. Such correspondence points to the relative openness in Naikan interpretation.

In light of such disagreements, the term 'variations' (*henpō*) was introduced by Sugita (1994: 82–5) as a more neutral alternative to sectarian terms such as 'deviations'. He suggests that 'original' Naikan has twelve defining characteristics:

1. sensory deprivation;
2. fixed periods of meditation, each one focused on a particular significant other;
3. adherence to the three themes;
4. regular two-hourly visits by the practitioner;
5. accommodation of clients in the practitioner's house;
6. a session lasting one full week;
7. a regime of sixteen hours of meditation per day (from 5.00 a.m. to 9.00 p.m.);
8. the broadcasting of recorded confessions during meals and periods away from formal meditation;
9. formality and politeness during *mensetsu*, including *gasshō*, pressing one's palms together and bowing;
10. the provision of home-cooked meals;
11. a clear explanation of Naikan at the beginning of the week;
12. a group discussion at the end of the week to share experiences and provide collective feedback.

Sugita suggests that any method which is lacking any of these items can be called a 'variation', although it is the first four which are primary, and any method which fulfils them qualifies as Naikan to some degree.

Given the lack of regulations, such a strict identification of 'authentic Naikan' would yield a host of variations. Kusunoki has categorized these variations into eight main types (1997: 6):

1. Short Naikan, whereby one conducts Naikan by oneself in a room at home or at school and keeps a diary rather than interacting with a practitioner. For example, such a method is used in schools in which teachers require students to do ten to fifteen minutes of Naikan each morning and to keep a Naikan diary.
2. Counselling Naikan, an 'emergency' form used by some practitioners for clients who have difficulties in completing the full one-week Naikan and attempt to withdraw part-way through.
3. Naikan used in medical settings, such as the case of medically referred clients who may also be on medication, or the transposition of Naikan methods to hospital settings where patients may spend shorter periods on a daily basis or over longer stretches of time undertaking Naikan.

4   Naikan combined with a course of Eastern medicine such as *kanpō* (Chinese medicine).
5   Psycho-spiritual Naikan, a method that combines Naikan with past-life therapy.
6   Behavioural Naikan, a three-day Naikan for busy people, especially businessmen, which is only represented so far by a single practitioner with a centre in Tokyo. The practitioner takes a much more active role than in traditional Naikan, and clients are required to reflect not only on significant others, but also on their relationship to their own body and mind.
7   Vision Planning Naikan, whereby the individual aims at clearly grasping his or her personality in order to actualize the life he or she wishes. Naikan here plays one part in the process of the person coming to understand his or her personality.
8   Naikan Role Playing, which, although identified as a variation by Kusunoki, is virtually unknown.

A reasoned reaction to these variations was voiced by the late Murase Takao, who until his death in 1998 was probably the leading intellectual in Naikan circles. He suggested that there are many Naikan variants in Japan as well as abroad. Although these variants may be meaningful, it is important to confirm what original Naikan is, and how it differs from such variants (Murase 1996: 94–125).

According to Kusunoki, it is Behavioural Naikan that has attracted the most criticism from traditionalists as being too short, too activist and too different from classical introspection to qualify as the real thing. But there are other variants that have received approval, including some not mentioned by Kusunoki, such as the Ishida method, which is a combination of Naikan, hypnosis and autonomous training (*jiritsukunrenhō*). The Toyotama Citizens Hospital method is a combination of a day of Naikan practice once a week (from 8.30 a.m. to 5.00 p.m.), brief daily Naikan and the keeping of a Naikan diary (Yasuoka 1991: 78). The combination of fasting and Naikan is seen as a variant, but is really a method closer to *mishirabe*, the Buddhist deprivation technique that inspired Yoshimoto to develop Naikan (Kikuike 1991: 128). Yasuoka suggests that all these variants could be useful as preparations, but judges them less effective than the original.

Each Naikan centre also has its own particular flavour. The centres publish brochures, revealing their emphases as well as practical information on prices and transportation. Many centres avoid mentioning Naikan's roots in Shin Buddhist self-cultivation practice. The Hokuriku Naikan centre, for example, prefaces its brochure with a quotation from the writings of Murase Takao together with his title as professor at Gakushūin University. The Tōyoko Inn Naikan centre, started by a businessman on the top floor of one of his hotels in a Tokyo suburb, employs quotations from Plato: 'Know Thyself' and 'What is the ultimate philosophy? Knowing how to prepare for death'. The centre's brochure also uses quotations from the *Tenseijingo*, one of the most prestigious columns in the major daily news-paper *Asahi Shinbun*, which reported on Naikan in both July and August 1991 (Takemoto 1991: 1). A few Naikan centres are indeed located in Buddhist temples. The rest, for the most part, are very hesitant to represent themselves as in any way religious, but rather stress the secular, 'scientific' and academically acknowledged aspects of the practice. Those located outside of the cities may extol their peaceful surroundings.

A few examples may better illustrate this variation among centres. *Gasshōen* is a well-respected Naikan centre located in a temple in Mie Prefecture. It was founded by the Buddhist monk Mizuno Shūhō, who in his advanced years experienced Naikan and returned to practise it himself at his temple until his recent death, whereupon it passed on to his son. A meeting with Nishida Tenkō, the founder of *Ittōen*, a Buddhist-based new religion, greatly influenced his way of life (Inoue 1977), and he subsequently adopted the principle that 'We have been given life and therefore we work not for a living, but to return the gift to those who gave it to us'. Naikan at *Gasshōen* takes place in a strongly Buddhist atmosphere, and during his life Mizuno refused to accept as clients those who did not accept his basic philosophy of life. The food supplied to clients is extremely simple, brown rice-based vegetarian dishes.

Igarashi, the practitioner at the Sapporo Naikan Zen Temple in Hokkaido combines Naikan with *zazen* meditation, breathing technique, yoga and hypnotism. He argues that breathing and posture are important during Naikan, since mind and body constitute a single entity, and he suggests that one can only have effective Naikan if one adjusts both mental and physical habits (Igarashi 1978: 74, 1991: 66). He also pays close attention to diet and serves his clients only two brown rice meals a day.

A perceived danger is that without a central authority, there is no limit on variants or on the use, and even improper use, of 'Naikan'. In 1991 such misuse of the term caused considerable damage to Naikan when two teenagers in a private reformatory in Hiroshima died in a sealed container called the 'Naikan Room'. The principal of the institution applied the term 'Naikan' (inner-looking or introspection) to solitary punishment, although this had little or nothing to do with the Naikan practice. As Naikan becomes more recognized, the risk of such abuse also grows.

Spirituality and science: the medicalization of Naikan

Yoshimoto originally saw Naikan as a method appropriate to seekers after truth, a kind of enlightenment technique, and not a means for curing illness (Nagashima 1991: 72). When it was suggested to him that his approach limited Naikan's potential scope, he agreed and progressively widened the range of applications of his method. The Japan Naikan Association is now the forum in which this widening primarily takes place within approved channels.

This widening has come principally from the fact that the JNA has adopted a scientific stance towards the explanation of Naikan's efficacy. Kusunoki has undertaken a survey of the themes of the JNA's annual conferences during its first decade. He categorized these into the following seven areas of research:

1   'Model Naikan clients' (usually by using psychological tests).
2   Levels of meaning in Naikan, including the religious approach, the philosophical approach and the psychological approach.
3   The efficacy of Naikan, including the evaluation of clients' behaviour and writing before and after Naikan, evaluation of physiological indicators such as blood pressure, brain waves and pulse during Naikan and the application of some forms of psychological evaluation tests.
4   Symptoms of Naikan clients.
5   Failure in Naikan.
6   Naikan variants.
7   Correct introduction and orientation to Naikan to ensure that clients have 'deep' Naikan (Kusunoki 1987: 3).

Kusunoki comments that the JNA has had a tendency to emphasize scientific approaches, which has had the unfortunate result of weakening research on Naikan in relation to religion, its point of origin. This shift in emphasis is evident if one examines the JNA's research reports over the last twenty-two years. Discussion of Naikan in relation to religion was more evident in the first four or five years, but has been decreasing since then. At the same time interest in 'variants' has intensified. As a result, practitioners interested in religion have increasingly dropped away from this forum.

One example is the Zen Buddhist, Usami, who practices Naikan at his temple (*Senkōbō*) in Mie Prefecture. The depth of Usami's Naikan so impressed Yoshimoto that he asked Usami to start a centre. Since then, he has been respected in the Naikan community for the depth of his Naikan and the report that he attained enlightenment through its practice. In 1980 he made a presentation on his Naikan experience and the realization of ultimate selflessness that it contained, and on the parallels between Naikan and Zen (Usami 1980: 84). Yet after a few years he stopped attending the annual conference. As Kusunoki points out, people like Usami who approach Naikan from a spiritual standpoint soon come to feel that they have no contribution to make in the heavily science-oriented JNA.

The 1980 conference was something of a watershed, as at the same meeting Yanagita (1980: 71–81) also presented a paper approaching Naikan from religious point of view by comparing Yoshimoto's words with Buddha's teaching. He examined Yoshimoto's attitude towards reincarnation, his use of fundamental questions such as 'Where do we go if we die now?' and 'Why were we born into this world?' and argued that Naikan contains something mystical that is beyond conventional psychotherapy, since the ultimate goal of Naikan is to achieve emancipation or enlightenment. As he has said later, Yanagita understands Naikan as a 'pre-stage' of religious experience (1997:111).

Since 1980 the number of such 'religious' presentations has decreased drastically as the medicalization and psychologizing of Naikan has increased. In the late 1980s, with the basic themes of Naikan well established, the questions of its 'spread' and 'efficiency' became the major preoccupations according to Takemoto (1987: 25), who argued that Naikan's main weaknesses were its lack of a theoretical foundation, and the difficulty of conducting it in hospital settings. He suggested that it was necessary to adapt to the times, including avoiding the use of particularly gloomy or tearful confession tapes and replacing them with 'light and joyful' ones. As early as 1981 Takemoto has been arguing, as a pioneer of its use in hospitals, that there are problems with its introduction into medicalized settings, including the physical restrictions that it places on clients and, from the point of view of medical practitioners, its lack of any clear symptomology or indicators of success.

The theme of the thirteenth annual conference in 1990 was 'Does Naikan need Theory?' At that meeting, Takemoto (1990: 26) admitted that the theorization of Naikan had not seen much progress since the beginning. The problem was seen as residing in the fact that Naikan was neither a psychology nor a therapy, but had arisen in a completely different context. Its origins were in religious self-cultivation and although Naikan itself represents a substantial modification of this, it fundamentally shares the same goal. Yoshimoto hoped that his method would bring about positive changes in personality. Although he provided explanations of why Naikan is effective, these explanations were highly religious in nature and lacked any sense of theory. Indeed, Yoshimoto resisted theorization, arguing simply that 'Naikan is Naikan'. As it began to appear to some practitioners that Naikan could be more than simply a method of self-cultivation and self-improvement, and in fact could be represented as a psychotherapy, the need for more thorough theorization became increasingly important. Its popularization and respectability were seen as dependent on research and theory, not only in presenting itself to the public, but also in recommending itself to the medical profession. Takemoto suggested that this process is necessary to spread Naikan in the medical field, to get Naikan accepted as an acceptable treatment under the national health insurance scheme (which would be of immense economic benefit), and to establish indicators (*tekiōshō*) (Takemoto 1990: 27).

The annual conference of 1983 discussed in particular the structural modification of Naikan in medical settings and suggested the overcoming of its religious overtones by avoiding terms such as 'confession', 'indebtedness' and 'sacred space', and by stressing that Naikan releases one's self rather than restrains it. One participant in a later conference suggested that the term 'Naikan Method' (*Naikan Hō*) is better than 'Naikan Therapy' (*Naikan*

Ryōhō) on the basis that counselling has two different approaches, one therapeutic and the other developmental, and that Naikan falls into the second category. Others have attempted to solve the problem by calling Naikan 'meditation therapy' because of its requirement to 'sit' for one week (Yanagita 1986: 55). Whatever the precise terminology, it is evident that the fault line lies between the majority in the JNA who seek greater theorization and are pushing Naikan towards medicalization and recognition as a psychotherapy, and the minority who wish to retain its religious roots, its self-cultivation aspects and its role in leading to the ultimate state of enlightenment.

Always in the background are the admonitions of Yoshimoto himself. According to the founder, the goal of Naikan is to reach the state of mind in which one can live in joy and happiness under any adverse circumstances and painful situations (Yoshimoto 1981: 153). He used to describe the process of Naikan as digging in the ground searching for a buried treasure: the treasure is the 'true self', and there is no salvation without this digging.

These struggles in the Naikan community reveal Naikan's complex and ambiguous nature. Yoshimoto's belief that Naikan is the purpose of life for which we are all born, as it has to do with the process of revealing our 'true selves' (Miyazaki 1989: 2), has been very much played down by those interested in psychologizing Naikan. Yoshimoto's own statement that there is no one absolute method, but that the salvation of people is the final end (Miyazaki 1992: 6) of course leaves the field open to contention, but also to modification in the context of social and cultural changes. As early as 1979, Reynolds noted that Naikan had been shifting from an emphasis on guilt and compensation to an emphasis on love and happiness (Reynolds 1979: 7). In my own field work in 1997–1998, it was apparent to me that discourse on Naikan has been continuing to move towards terms such as 'happiness' and 'spirituality'. I deal with this trend in the next chapter, when I look at Naikan in relation to New Age and New Spirituality Movements.

A natural tendency has also been to compare Naikan with other established therapeutic practices, and in particular psychoanalysis. Takino (1979: 15), for example, suggests that both Naikan and psychoanalysis share an emphasis on a 'form' that the client must follow, but that in Naikan these forms are derived from traditional Japanese practices. One practising psychoanalyst has taken an interest in Naikan and has tried to theorize Naikan by way of an analysis of clients' dreams (Kitami 1981, 1983). Ohta (1991: 23–31) observes that both Naikan and psychoanalysis are accompanied by strong emotional experiences as clients recall and recover their pasts, while Oda (1992) suggests that while Naikan is formally similar to psychoanalysis in its method, which centres on the client's relation to his or her mother and on recalling the past, Naikan differs from psychoanalysis in its humanism, since its goal is to get the client to realize his or her indebtedness to life. Oda also detects parallels between Naikan and Morita Therapy, on the one hand, and Frankl's Logotherapy and Paradoxical Psychotherapy on the other. But, on the whole, attempts to deepen the theorization of Naikan through comparison with other 'systems' have not been particularly insightful or revealing.

More necessary would be a comparison with other forms of therapy within Japan and indigenous to Japan. Morita Therapy is one of the better-known Japanese psychotherapeutic methods. It was established by a psychiatrist Morita Shōma in the 1920s. Although he never emphasized the direct influence of Buddhism on his therapy, it is well-known that Morita himself was greatly influenced by Zen Buddhism. He started Morita practice while he was working at the Jikei Medical University, and this university hospital still has a Morita Therapy section. Since almost all Morita practitioners are medical doctors, Morita Therapy is widely practised at hospitals and has the tendency of being highly medically theorized and institutionalized. Like Naikan, Morita has its origins in Buddhism and places bodily engagement at the core of its therapeutic techniques (Reynolds 1980, 1983). While both have a session lasting one week, Naikan requires that the client sit, while Morita requires a week of compulsory rest in bed. Yet the recollection of past memories is absent in Morita.

In particular, non-verbal therapies tend to be popular among Japanese. Along with meditation therapy like Zen, Jungian therapies are especially popular in contrast to the unpopularity of Freudian psychoanalysis. Sand-play Therapy, for example, which was introduced in Japan by Kawai Hayao, a leading Jungian clinical psychologist, has become especially popular. The presence of Naikan in Japan is therefore not in a context of Western psycho-therapies, but rather indigenous Japanese psychotherapies or particular therapeutic methods that have been taken from the West and modified for use in Japan. This is, however, obviously not the case for the practice of Naikan outside of Japan.

The expansion of Naikan abroad

Naikan's spread overseas has been another source of innovation and development. As indicated in the chronology above (Table 6.1), Naikan has been known in Europe since 1972, when the first Naikan retreat was held in Europe by Franz Ritter (Ritter 1989: 62), and in 1980 Ishii conducted the first formal Naikan in Austria. Since then, Naikan has spread in a very modest way in Europe and in the United States, although interestingly not yet in the rest of Asia. The spread of Naikan abroad can be discussed under three rubrics: its institutional diversification, the felt need for certification and its impact on theorization.

The chronology above outlines Naikan's expansion outside Japan. The details are more complex and a range of centres have sprung up, largely in German-speaking countries. Some of these are 'pure' Naikan centres (for example, Neue Welt Institut, Zentrum Salzburg and Naikido Zentrum Wien Haus Ötscherland), others reflect the rather widespread European problem of drug addiction and are essentially centres using Naikan for rehabilitation of former addicts (for example, the Drug Rehabilitation Centre, see Ritter 1989: 64), while a third group employ Naikan in the setting of Western Buddhist centres. An interesting spiritual movement in the West has been not simply the adoption but the adaptation to Western conditions of Buddhism of a number of schools – Tibetan and Theravadan 'insight meditation' (Kulananda 1997) in particular. Examples of such centres and monasteries now abound and those that utilize Naikan include Scheibbs Buddhist Centre, Maetori Centre (Buddhism Psychology) and Geiya House Meditation Centre (Ritter 1989: 64).

In North America a rather different pattern has emerged and has been institutionalized primarily in the form of the Constructive Living Method started and still run by David Reynolds, the first foreign scholar to make a serious study of Naikan in Japan (Reynolds 1976, 1980, 1983). In addition to his earlier scholarly work from the perspective of medical anthropology and comparative psychology, Reynolds has also produced a stream of popular books in which he adapts Naikan to North American conditions (e.g. Reynolds 1984). The Constructive Living Movement is considered by many Japanese practitioners to be a distinct 'variation', or even as not really Naikan but rather a new technique developed by Reynolds. It is of substantial interest, however, because of what it reveals about the potential adaptability of Naikan.

The second major innovation has been in certification. Many European countries require that practitioners of any therapeutic techniques who practise professionally, i.e. charge fees, must be licensed. Pressure to adopt a similar system is beginning to arise in Japan and may bring with it a similar formalization of Naikan methodology. The certification system evolving in German-speaking countries involves three steps:

1   one year must elapse between personal experience of Naikan and permission to begin practice as an assistant under an established practitioner;
2   establishment of the independent practice under the guidance of the established practitioner; and
3   establishment of the independent Naikan centre (Ritter 1989: 64).

The third issue has been the impact of globalization on Naikan's theoretical basis. This has been stimulated partly by the spread of Naikan, but also by the interest internationally in indigenous psychotherapies, an interest reflected in the growing anthropological literature on the subject (e.g. Heelas and Lock 1981) and by a growing 'nationalism' in Japanese psychological circles, no doubt as a result of Japan's larger world role economically and politically. In 1986, for example, Professor Takuma Taketoshi gave a lecture at the 35th Congress der Deutschen Gesellshaft für Psychologie at Heidelberg in which he argued that Japanese psychology had been dominated by the influence of

German and American psychology since the Meiji period, when Japan opened to the West and was totally dominated by American psychology after World War II. But by the 1980s Western psychologists were beginning to show greater interest in indigenous Asian psychologies (Takuma 1987).

Similarly, in 1989 Ishii and Yanagita attended the Seventh Biennial Conference of the Association of Psychological and Educational Counselors, which met on that occasion in Bangkok and at which the overall theme was indigenous psychotherapies. Ishii suggested there that only Japan and India have produced truly indigenous systems, of which Naikan is a leading example, and that there is an urgent need for more such indigenization as American-style psychotherapies are culturally difficult to adapt to Asian needs and assumptions (Ishii 1989: 2). This question of adaptability, of course, also applies to Naikan itself.

At the 1978 Naikan conference, Dr Takino Isao, the pioneer in attempting to introduce Naikan into France, discussed the problems that he had encountered (Takino 1978: 139–50). In France, Naikan was perceived as a method of re-education rather than as a psychotherapy, and was treated with some suspicion because of the fear that it was a method that prevented free expression for the sake of respecting other people. French individualism and Japanese 'groupism' or relationalism clearly clashed on this point. Takino suggested to the French that Naikan shares the traditional Japanese technique of *michi* or the learning of 'form' (*kata*), and that this *michi* suggests a way of life rather than simply the adoption of new methods or techniques. To his French dialogue partners, this suggested Catholic meditation and as a result they tended to identify Naikan with religion rather than with psychotherapy (Takino 1978: 141). Similar comments were made by German psychologists when Ishii discussed Naikan with them, and in particular they found the notions of guilt and indebtedness to be uniquely Japanese. This led Ishii (personal communication) to suggest that such words should be avoided to prevent people from misidentifying Naikan as religion.

Ishii has played an important personal role in the spread of Naikan in Europe, partly because of his command of the German language. It was also he who influenced Franz Ritter, now the leading German commentator on Naikan as well as a practitioner. Ritter had for some time been interested in the relationship between meditation and psychology and was on his way to Nara to visit a Zen temple when he encountered Ishii. Ishii's explanation of Zen interested Ritter and he went instead to experience Naikan at *Senkōbō*, the Zen Temple in Mie mentioned earlier.

Ritter later talked about his understanding of the relationship between meditation and psychotherapy in Naikan at one of the annual conferences (Ritter 1986). He had formerly been a staffer at the Buddhist Centre in Scheibbs, Austria (Buddhistisches Zentrum Scheibbs), and was familiar with a range of Asian therapies, since that centre had been eclectic in its introduction of new forms. But among all the therapies that he had experienced, Ritter found Naikan to be the most fascinating. This led him to leave the Buddhist Centre and to establish the first Naikan centre in Europe in 1986. Ishii, on his frequent visits to Europe, suggested to me that Naikan clients there tend to be intellectuals or otherwise highly educated people, many of whom are also interested in so-called New Age or New Spirituality Movements and who find the 'oriental' aspects of Naikan congenial. This attraction has overcome to some extent the perception by some foreign scholars of comparative psychotherapies that Naikan is a self-punitive method and too uniquely Japanese to be effective for non-Japanese (Murase 1999: 16–17).

As we have seen, Naikan is not yet practised on a large scale, yet it continues to develop and is steadily establishing itself outside of Japan. Naikan's expansion abroad and its medicalization raise a number of questions, which we will address in the next chapters as we continue our investigation of Naikan in its broader contexts. We will now turn to Naikan's future, comparing it to New Age and New Spirituality Movements, and evaluating its current trend towards a language of 'healing', 'spirituality' and 'happiness'.

7 Healing and spirituality
The new face of Naikan

In the last few years, a curious shift has been taking place with regard to Naikan's image. Books on Naikan are increasingly appearing with titles speaking of 'exploring one's happiness' and 'healing'. In articles written by Naikan practitioners, at the Naikan annual conference and even in Naikan centres outside of Japan, the themes of 'spirituality', 'happiness' and 'healing' are becoming increasingly prominent. Gone, it seems, is Yoshimoto's emphasis on traditional Buddhist religious themes, such as the need to recognize one's own indebtedness or sinfulness in order to experience salvation. Also ebbing away is the presentation of Naikan as a form of scientifically based psychotherapy. Instead, Naikan is being increasingly presented as somehow akin to the New Age movement, New Spirituality Movements or 'New New Religions' in Japan.

This recent development raises a host of questions. A shift in language is definitely taking place, but to what extent does this represent a deeper shift within the Naikan community away from its traditional roots in Buddhism? In other words, is this change merely on the level of Naikan's presentation (a more effective way of marketing Naikan), or does it reflect a change within the Naikan community, or in the use of the Naikan method itself? And to what extent can terms such as 'radical', 'counter-cultural' or 'New Age' be used to describe Naikan's current trend, or do they need to be rethought in the Japanese context?

These issues need to be addressed at two levels: change within the Naikan community, and Naikan's relationship with broader national and international social change. Thus, the first part of this chapter looks at the most prominent Naikan practitioners, starting with Yoshimoto himself, to see how they stand with regard to the question of spirituality, and how these stances have changed over time. The second part of the chapter asks to what extent this recent portrayal of Naikan reflects broader trends in Japan and internationally. I will start with some preliminary remarks on the so-called 'Healing Boom' in Japan, then move on to how scholars have viewed the New Age Movement, New Spirituality Movements and New New Religions. Along the way I will question the meaning and applicability of some of these terms with regard to the Japanese context and Naikan in particular. I will seek to determine to what extent Naikan's recent shift can be understood as participating in these movements, reacting to them, or presaging them. All this will serve to answer the question of how Naikan has changed in recent years and why. It will also shed light on broader questions, such as to what extent such movements can rightly be called 'counter-cultural' in the Japanese context.

My own assessment is that Naikan has passed through four stages and is now entering a fifth, namely that of 'spirituality' and 'healing'. As discussed earlier, Naikan began in 1942 as a religious practice for self-cultivation, essentially a form of *mishirabe* adapted to enable any person to practise it. By introducing Naikan to prisons as a reform treatment in 1954 and removing some of its religious vesture, Yoshimoto moved Naikan into its second stage, during which it flourished, especially in the 1960s. The third stage came in the 1960s and 1970s, when Naikan became popular in schools for treating disaffected students.

There followed the medicalization of Naikan and its use in hospitals as a form of psychotherapy, which has been the fourth and still continuing stage. In 1965 the psychologist Ishida Rokurō reported his research on Naikan, which provided the stepping stone for Naikan's recognition as a psychotherapy. In 1972 two influential books were published by psychologists: *Zenteki Ryōhō: Naikan-hō* (Zen-like Therapy: Naikan Method) by Sato and *Naikan Ryōhō* (Naikan Therapy) by Okumura. Yoshimoto himself published a small book, entitled *Naikan to Seishi Eisei* (Naikan and Psychological Health) in 1978 (Yoshimoto 1978a), which seems to be influenced by these psychological tones even though the content of the book is not so different from other writings of Yoshimoto. Now, however, it seems that Naikan is entering a fifth stage, a 'spiritual phase' at odds with the scientific grounding of the medicalization stage. If this is indeed the case, this recent trend invites us to examine the history of spirituality in Naikan.

'From salvation to healing'

A glance at recent publications by Naikan practitioners illustrates the new focus on 'healing', 'happiness' and 'spirituality'. A prime example is a book written in 1998 by psychologists and Naikan practitioners Miki Yoshihiko and Miki Junko, entitled 'Naikan Work: Becoming Happy by Healing the Heart's Anxiety' (*Naikan Work: kokoro no fuan wo iyashite shiawase ni naru*), and subtitled 'For people who feel like they have a hole in their heart: a workbook for exploring happiness' (Miki and Miki 1998). In this book they explain that 'Naikan is a journey to encounter the real self', and also 'Naikan is a heart's journey to explore happiness'. Instead of tying these phrases to 'self-realization', they relate them to an emerging spirituality, a spirituality that can be accessed by disciplined Naikan practice. Other recent titles follow this trend as well, including: *Isshūkan de jiko kaikaku* (Self-Revolution in a Week) (Ishii 1999), *Naikan: Kokoro wa gekiteki ni kaerareru* (The Mind

Can Be Changed Dramatically) (Yokoyama and Nagashima 1997), *Kokoro to seimei ga yomigaeru: Naikan ryōhō to kanpō* (Bringing the Mind and Life Back to Life: Naikan Therapy and Chinese Medicine) (Kitamura 1998). One wonders: has the presentation of Naikan changed in an effort to jump on the bandwagon of the 'Healing Boom' in Japan? Or is it rather that the Healing Boom is now promoting features that have always been present in Naikan?

Fundamentally, these questions regard the relationship between the recent shift in Naikan's presentation and a larger shift taking place in Japan, one that religious studies scholar Shimazono has called 'From Salvation to Healing' (1995b: 263–70). In popular understanding, 'salvation' tends to connote a specifically religious process, such as recovery from illness or disaster due to God's intervention. On the other hand, 'healing' indicates a recovery without any necessary relation to God. When we delve into the etymology of these words, we find that in several cases these words can be used interchangeably; the distinction is not as clear as we might initially assume. The *Oxford English Dictionary* defines salvation as:

1   The saving of the soul; the deliverance from sin and its consequences, and admission to eternal bliss, wrought for man by the atonement of Christ.
2   Preservation from destruction, ruin, loss, or calamity. In mod. use chiefly with more or less allusion to sense 1.

(Oxford English Dictionary 1961, v. 9: 69)

It likewise defines healing as:

1   The action of the vb. heal; restoration to health; recovery from sickness; curing, cure.
2   Mending, reparation; restoration of wholeness, well-being, safety, or prosperity; spiritual restoration, salvation.

(Oxford English Dictionary 1961, v. 5: 163)

Thus, although there is an obvious semantic overlap between the two terms, the emphasis of salvation is on the preventative, whereas for healing the emphasis is on the restorative, with a stronger connection to the health of the body and mind. Whereas salvation conjures up the grim alternative (of damnation, for example), healing leaves this question open. Lastly, whereas healing points to the here and now, salvation tends to point to the hereafter.

The close connection between the two terms is evident in the notion of 'religious healing', now immensely popular not only among new religions, but also in mainstream ones (especially in Christianity, most prominently in its Pentecostal branch, but also increasingly in Judaism). It is also reflected in the sudden popularity of the term 'spirituality' rather than 'religion' as an ecumenical, non-sectarian and inclusive term more in keeping with universalist sentiments. While New Age has certainly done much to popularize the term, it is not restricted to such new religious movements, but has in my view become one of the most important operational concepts linking and indeed merging salvific and healing processes into a single holistic understanding of people's relationship to the non-mundane realm.

Yoshimoto: founder and adapter of Naikan

The reasons for the shift from language with specific religious connotations to the language of a broader, ecumenical 'spirituality' may be elucidated by examining how the presentation of Naikan and the method itself has changed under its founder, Yoshimoto, and his successors and disciples. As discussed in Chapter 6, Naikan's worldview was originally that of Shin Buddhism. The moment he achieved enlightenment after his several trials of *mishirabe*, Yoshimoto was struck by a powerful sense that he had a mission to make this method known to as many people as possible and share this 'joy' (1997: 101). He said, 'I realized that I am such a sinful person, that I would be the last person to achieve salvation, even after everyone else, and at that very moment I realized that I was already always saved' (1997: 97–9). Such a statement is completely in line with the philosophy of Shin Buddhism. It echoes Shinran's saying that 'Even the good man can achieve salvation, let alone the sinner'.

At the time of its founding, then, Naikan was deeply religious, in the sense that its Buddhist heritage was explicitly retained in its presentation. For Yoshimoto, Naikan was a way of 'seeking salvation through the recognition of one's own sin'. Even though he did not use terms such as Buddha or Buddhism, his questions often reflected his belief in Buddhism. He often asked questions such as 'Where are you going if you die at this moment?', 'Do you think you are a good person or a bad person?' and 'Concentrate on Naikan as if you were going to hell otherwise.' This could be startling to someone from a different background. Reynolds, for example, admits to having felt uncomfortable with Yoshimoto's questions; he felt they presented things in too much of a black-and-white way, and seemed to be forcing him to admit that he was a bad person (1983: 26). Most likely Yoshimoto used such questions to impress on clients a sense of impermanence and reflexivity regarding their self-evaluations, and for older generations, such questions might even have sounded non-religious or secular. However, in the view of several Western academics, such questions seem to have resulted in a view that Naikan focuses heavily on guilt and rejects a positive evaluation of the self, and hence is effective only for the Japanese.

Yoshimoto's desire to continue to make Naikan more accessible led him to increasingly distance it from such Shin Buddhist language. As mentioned earlier, in order to introduce Naikan to prisons, he had to prove that it was not a religious practice. He stopped wearing his Buddhist monk's stole, and no longer spoke of salvation. He presented Naikan not as a religion, but rather as a way of life, and pointed out that:

1   Naikan contains hardly any talk about the Buddha's mercy and salvation;
2   it has no particular sutra or doctrine;
3   it does not deal with the supernatural, nor does it rely on the oracle of a particular spiritualistic medium;
4   it requires merely the skill to practise self-examination, and makes no condition of joining a certain religion after participation (Yoshimoto 1997: 188).

It continued to be taught in Naikan, however, that each person has a 'Buddha nature' within him- or herself.

Although Naikan achieved success in prisons, especially in the 1960s, Yoshimoto saw a problem in that each time the head of the prison changed, the whole prison policy would change as well, requiring the painstaking effort of reintroducing Naikan each time. Instead, Yoshimoto decided to introduce Naikan to schools, so that children could encounter Naikan at an early age, before they ended up in prison. He sent Naikan confessional tapes to many schools, and eventually some schools started introducing Naikan, and teachers began to recommend that disaffected students attend a Naikan centre. Many schools began introducing short Naikan-like self-reflection times either at the beginning of the day or during the moral education class.

Soon medical doctors and psychologists realized Naikan was effective for alcoholism and psychosomatic illnesses, prompting them to research the method and theorize its efficacy as a psychotherapy. Throughout its transitions from religious practice to prison reform to educational method to psychotherapy, Yoshimoto himself continued to say that 'Naikan is Naikan'. Nevertheless, he was happy that Naikan was becoming widely practised. After Takemoto wrote a book entitled 'Naikan and Medicine' (1978), Yoshimoto even started giving lectures in which he claimed that Naikan was medicine. However, this is also in line with a common metaphor used in Buddhist writings, whereby the Buddha is referred to as a doctor, his teachings or Dharma as medicine, and ordinary suffering beings as the patients.

Yanagita: bringing in mysticism

After Yoshimoto's death, some Naikan practitioners adhered very closely to their mentor's style, hesitant to make changes for fear of being diverted from or losing the 'essence' of Naikan. Quite different, however, was Yanagita Kakusei, whom we have already encountered, and whose Naikan confession we examined in Chapter 3. While seeking to remain true to Yoshimoto's Naikan philosophy, Yanagita also showed his mentor's flexibility, modifying his style to best suit his clients. Hence, since its founding in 1981, *Meisō no Mori* has been the most popular and influential Naikan centre in Japan.

Yanagita's childhood was a difficult one. He was born in Akita Prefecture, a northern part of Japan in 1930. He lost seven brothers while he was still young. Then he lost his mother when he was eleven years old and his father when he was sixteen. Throughout his life, he suffered from various illnesses; nor was he able to enjoy a good education. Yet despite all these obstacles, Yanagita managed to become successful in a trading business and eventually became the president of a company.

Yanagita's interest in alternative health and meditation started long before his encounter with Naikan. Then he experienced Naikan under Yoshimoto's guidance in 1976, an event that changed his life. In 1977, he started *kibō club* (the Hope Club), in Tokyo, which met two Sundays a month for yoga, other meditations and one-day Naikan sessions. Reynolds describes the majority of members as working males in their thirties and forties (1983: 47). In 1981 Yanagita decided to retire early at the age of 50 and bought a large piece of land in Tochigi Prefecture. There he founded *Meisō no Mori*, or 'Meditational Forest'. He did not see it as merely a place to do Naikan, but rather as a 'space' where people could heal themselves. He continued to actively practise meditational methods.

Yanagita inherited all of Yoshimoto's methods, but he shifted their emphasis and rephrased them, speaking of 'happiness' and 'healing' instead of 'salvation'. He emphasized the importance of acknowledging the love one received from others. Once a person recognized all the love he or she had received, that person could experience 'happiness'. In his publications, Yanagita did not hesitate to include his mystical experiences or those of his clients, some of which we explored in Chapters 3 and 4. The broadcasts at *Meisō no Mori* include confessional tapes of clients who relate such mystical experiences.

Some Naikan practitioners think that because of Yanagita's openness about his mystical experiences, people at his centre start having similar experiences due to the power of suggestion. In my view, because Yanagita did not hesitate to talk about his experiences, other Naikan clients may have felt comfortable sharing their own experiences. Yoshimoto himself had mystical experiences, but he never emphasized them, seeing them as mere passing sensations that should not distract one from focusing on Naikan's three themes.

Yanagita boldly states that Naikan is the pre-stage to religious experience (1997: 111). Unlike some Naikan practitioners and doctors who are more hesitant to state any relation to religion, he concludes that the purpose of Naikan is to achieve *gedatsu*, or emancipation from one's desires. The popularity of *Meisō no Mori* indicates that he succeeded in crafting an idiom for Naikan that made it more accessible and appealing to people, while retaining a Naikan philosophy that was in its fundamentals the same as Yoshimoto's.

Ishii: expansion of Naikan abroad

Another influential figure in the Naikan community, a professor of law at Aoyama University in Tokyo, is Ishii Akira, most known for being the first to introduce Naikan abroad. He himself underwent Naikan many times under Yoshimoto's guidance, and has experienced Naikan more than thirty times over the past thirty years. Though not a regular Naikan practitioner, Ishii conducts Naikan occasionally, and there are always those who are eager to receive his sessions.

Ishii was a serious student of Zen meditation when he was a student at Tokyo University. He was seeking enlightenment through Zen, so rather than attend university lectures, he chose to live in a temple for most of his university years. Several years later, he was introduced to Naikan by one of his university friends, and after experiencing it he realized it was what he needed. In his earlier attempts to achieve enlightenment, he claims, he was trying to achieve the state of 'egolessness', but this only flared up his own ego. He realized this problem while examining himself in relation to his mother, father and other close people during Naikan.

Ishii's approach to Naikan is quite liberal, and he frequently says that 'Naikan is a way to happiness'. It is important to note that both Yanagita and Ishii were interested in meditation methods like yoga and Zen before they encountered Naikan. They noticed some similarities between Naikan and other meditational techniques, but they both chose Naikan as their lifetime practice. Therefore, they had no hesitation in emphasizing the meditative aspects of Naikan or even adding things such as breathing techniques if they judged they could be effective for some clients to get into Naikan fully.

It is in Ishii's work in spreading Naikan abroad that we see a clear move towards presenting Naikan as akin to New Age. As noted, Franz Ritter, the founder of the first Naikan centre outside of Japan, met Ishii on his way to a Japanese Zen temple in 1970. Interested by Ishii's enthusiastic descriptions of Naikan, Ritter later tried it out and, like Ishii and Yanagita, he found Naikan to be the best for him after experiencing various meditation methods over the years. He returned to Austria and founded the Naikan New World Institute, now located some sixty kilometres south of Vienna.

Pamphlets promoting Ritter's institute might appear rich in New Age language, speaking of the 'Naikan Network' (*Naikan Netzwerk*). Interestingly, Naikan is presented as combining both an Eastern/New Age outlook and a scientific one. According to one such pamphlet, prepared by Helga and Josef Yoko Hartl and written in German, Naikan has 'two roots' (*zwei Wurzeln*), namely a 'meditational approach', which involves 'inner observation' and is described as 'a way of achieving solutions that are beyond our western-rationalistic way of seeing things and contains more than a thousand years of experience'; and a 'therapeutic approach', which attributes present neurotic behaviour and pain to past learned behaviour. Naikan 'liberates' and leads one 'to a higher spiritual plane', resulting in 'a deep love for existence, extensive insight into what is most deeply human in us, and the ability to accept what is'.

Meals at these Naikan centres abroad tend to be vegetarian and, in contrast to Japan, Naikan's Buddhist connection is strongly emphasized. In a conversation with me, Ishii explained that most people who attend Naikan sessions in Europe tend to be relatively young, highly educated and are seeking to explore and investigate themselves.

Nagashima and Motoyama: spirituality-talk becomes acceptable

We saw at the beginning of this chapter how recent book titles indicate a shift in Naikan's public representation, and now we have seen how this shift was to some extent prepared by Yoshimoto and furthered by Yanagita at his *Meisō no Mori* centre and by Ishii in his promotion of Naikan abroad. Another indicator of this recent shift in Naikan's public representation is the millennium special edition on spirituality of *Yasuragi*, the most widely recognized magazine within the Naikan community (Ichikawa *et al.* 2000). I would like to look specifically at two articles in this issue on Naikan and spirituality, written by the prominent Naikan practitioners Nagashima Masahiro and Motoyama Yōichi.

Nagashima Masahiro was born in 1948 in Toyama Prefecture in northern Japan. Since he was a teenager, he says he was pressed by the questions 'Why are we alive? What do we live for?' He spent a long time living at a Zen temple while trying to achieve enlightenment, but after years without progress, he felt like a failure at self-cultivation. Having heard about Naikan, he decided to visit Yoshimoto. The subsequent self-realization brought to him through Naikan was the most powerful experience he had had, and he begged Yoshimoto to be his master. He started living at Yoshimoto's Naikan centre in Nara and helped out by tending the garden and similar activities. After staying there for nine years, he decided to go back to Toyama and open his own Naikan centre. For Nagashima, Yoshimoto was like a father as well as being a great master, and he has been recognized as the Naikan practitioner to most closely inherit the spirit and method of Yoshimoto. Even the layout of Nagashima's Naikan centre follows closely that of Yoshimoto's centre. Modest about himself and always paying respect to Yoshimoto, Nagashima sees his role as maintaining the 'archetype of Yoshimoto Naikan', so that it can be preserved and passed on to future generations.

Motoyama Yōichi likewise says that he was troubled and distressed by many things from an early age. As a high-school student he began to read books on spirituality in order to find a solution to his problems. Eventually he understood in his head what he needed to do to be happy, but he could still not bring himself to that state. After trying various methods of self-alteration in vain, he encountered Naikan at the age of twenty-eight on the recommendation of his wife. He recalls that he was so moved that his whole body was filled with joy and peace, such as he had never felt in his whole life. He, too, thought that Naikan was what he had been looking for all these years.

Since then, his life became Naikan-oriented and he repeated Naikan practice whenever time allowed. However, each time he did Naikan, he could maintain a good state of mind only for a short while before his 'ego' reasserted itself. Eventually he came to the conclusion that somebody like him would not be 'saved' unless he led a life in which he could be in the Naikan environment for twenty-four hours a day. Fortunately his wife and Yoshimoto supported him, and he started his Naikan centre in Saitama Prefecture, near Tokyo, when he was thirty-two years old. Later, he moved to Tokyo after being appointed as director of a new Naikan centre there, *Shiroganedai*. He stands close to Nagashima's position in that he also feels the strong need to maintain Yoshimoto's Naikan style and spirit so that the Naikan world will not lose its original method in the context of the medicalization of Naikan as a psychotherapy.

In the millenium special edition of *Yasuragi*, both Nagashima's and Motoyama's articles make reference to the World Health Organization's (WHO) suggestion for a revised new definition of health, which includes 'spiritual' health alongside 'physical, mental and social' health. (It is to be noted that the WHO's revised definition has not taken place at this stage, but it was reported in some countries, including Japan, as if it were already definitive, and *Yasuragi* reported it as a decision that had already been made.) The WHO's suggested new definition seems to have validated the concept of spirituality for those Naikan practitioners who had been wary about Naikan being mistaken for a New Religion.

In his article, Nagashima points to the WHO's suggested new definition to argue that 'spiritual' includes meanings that cannot be covered by the word 'mental'. The millennium, he writes, has been called the era of the heart (*kokoro*), during which the importance of mental health has been emphasized. However, he believes it is also important to think seriously about how to maintain spiritual health. Spiritual health to him means maintenance of the 'heart', which can perceive the fact that we are not self-made individuals, but have been supported by all existing things, especially the people around us, and which can therefore feel grateful. This is, in his view, nothing but Naikan's philosophy itself. Therefore, he concludes, 'The 21st century is really the era of Naikan' (2000: 2–3).

Motoyama also begins by addressing the WHO's definition, and says that 'spiritual' refers to that which exists behind the empirically and materially existing things in the world. He suggests that the key words in understanding 'spirituality' are 'gratitude, bonds, death, universality, acceptance of facts, objectivity, love, consideration (or compassion) and sympathy', since they positively express existence beyond ourselves. Hence people who can perceive things beyond mere empirical and material existence are 'spiritual' people. On the contrary, the key words to describe 'unspiritual' people are 'self-centredness, superiority, inferiority, solitude, suffering, anxiety, fear, discrimination, laziness', i.e. those things by which people only look inwardly to themselves (2000: 4–5).

Motoyama directly relates Naikan to spirituality. Real happiness can be obtained only by realizing spiritual things, because the essence of the human being is a spiritual being (2000: 5). Naikan makes people happy because doing Naikan means touching the spirituality of one's significant others, even if they themselves are unaware of their own spirituality (2000: 5–6). Thus, spiritual people feel oneness with other people and other things in joy and peace, whereas unspiritual people experience alienation from other people and other things in solitude, emptiness, discontent and tension (2000: 5).

By looking at Yoshimoto and four of his most prominent followers, and their attitudes towards spirituality, we gain the impression that there has indeed been a shift towards presenting Naikan as having a strong connection with spirituality, and towards using the language of 'healing' and 'health' instead of 'sin' and 'salvation'. However, we also see that the shift is taking place across the board – both with practitioners who are more liberal in adapting Yoshimoto's techniques and philosophy, such as Ishii and Yanagita, and with those who are more conservative in their efforts at preserving Naikan, such as Nagashima. This would seem to indicate that it is more a shift in emphasis, seen to be in keeping with Yoshimoto's original vision for Naikan, rather than a fundamental change or redirection of Naikan. To examine this question further, it will be necessary to look at the broader national and international scene.

The healing boom

A visitor to any major bookstore in Japan will be guaranteed to find a section called 'Spiritual World' (*seishin sekai*). In that section, our visitor will encounter titles such as 'Healing Power', 'How to Heal Your Soul' and 'Spiritual Healing'. Indeed, he or she will soon discover the words 'spirituality' and 'healing' are often used in close connection. This has been the case, at least, since the so-called 'Healing Boom' in Japan.

Many scholars suggest that this Healing Boom started quite recently (Ueda 1994, 1997; Shimazono 1995a, 1996). The medical anthropologist Ueda has been among the first to address the Healing Boom in Japan and to note that the word 'healing' (*iyashi*) as a noun started appearing frequently in mass media only recently, although the verb 'to heal' (*iyasu*) has always been in common usage (1997: 211). He introduces the work done by Yumiyama, a religious studies scholar, who reports that the word 'healing' appeared in the mass media in the late 1980s (Ueda 1997: 211–12). After searching through major Japanese newspapers, Ueda found that the word 'healing' as a noun appeared for the first time in 1988 in two major Japanese newspapers *Mainichi Shinbun* and *Yomiuri Shinbun*, and even after that, the word did not appear frequently in newspapers until late 1994 (1997: 212).

The disastrous earthquake in Kobe on 17 January 1995 likely also contributed to the rise of the Healing Boom, which soon spread widely beyond the fields of medicine and clinical psychology, where it had originated, into literature, art and commercial enterprise. Thus, Ueda defines healing as including, but also going beyond, medicine. For him, healing exists in the image of 'relatedness'. What is unique in healing is that there is no healing by oneself; instead, healing is always 'healing each other', through which people recover their sense of relatedness (1990: 231).

Connected with 'healing' has been the rise of holistic medicine, which began in the USA in the 1970s as a reaction against the separation in modern Western medicine of body and mind, and the treating of the body as distinct parts rather than as a whole. The Japan Holistic Medical Association was established in 1987, and now has many medical doctors of both Western and Eastern medicine as well as lay members. Holistic medicine is especially concerned with the concept of healing, as opposed to the mere treatment of a localized illness, injury or disease (Ueda 1997: 223; Obitsu and Tsumura 1996).

Ueda also compares healing with medical treatment. Even though treatment is the act of treating either body or mind, healing has the connotation of working on both mind and body (1997: 215). The background for the successful spread of healing is the popular interest in 'healing without relying on religion'. Meditation, Eastern body techniques and 'healing goods' such as crystals are receiving more popular acceptance, since people wary of religion do not perceive these things as threatening. Thus, the Healing Boom is partially supported by people who have a strong negative reaction to religion, but are still interested in healing (1997: 213–14).

Shimazono also tries to define the word 'healing'. He links healing with the notions of reconciliation (*wakai*), sacredness and wholeness. Shimazono gives the definition of *iyashi* or healing in the encyclopaedia as 'to heal mind, body and hunger' (1995a: 4) which is a synonym for salvation with a different nuance. The function of healing in New Religions is to get rid of the conflict arising from the family through self-examination and forgiving each other (1995a: 4). He suggests understanding healing as a new concept that includes both 'treatment' and 'salvation', and is linked to 'reconciliation' (1995a: 5).

The major power of healing is to enable a change in the attitude people have toward their illness and difficulties. Members of new religions, Shimazono notes, may relate things such as: 'I found the meaning of life through my illness', 'I was led to recognize my faults' and 'I can accept this illness as a challenge from God' (1995a: 8). Segments of life previously seen as unrelated suddenly appear as parts of one consistent story with an underlying meaning. Once this happens, a person can start to feel less worthless about his or her existence and can begin to appreciate who he or she is (1995a: 8).

It is clear that the above ways of seeing 'healing' as it appears in the Healing Boom are very close to Naikan's world view and practices. In its emphasis on the recovery of memory in relation to significant others, Naikan promotes a reconstruction of one's understanding of oneself based on a restoration of one's relationships with others. As we saw when examining the ways in which perception is altered through Naikan (in Chapter 3), the healing of oneself cannot happen by remaining focused on the self as removed from others, as if constructing a solipsistic autobiography, but only through reconciliation between oneself and others by focusing on relationships. It seems then, that Naikan was influenced by the Healing Boom towards emphasizing terms such as 'happiness' and 'true healing', since this trend has only occurred in the last few years, but the Healing Boom also reflects a philosophy that has always been at the core of Naikan.

New Age and Naikan

The 'New Age' is by now a well-recognized term, associated with practices and beliefs regarding spiritual phenomena and drawn from Eastern traditions or Western ones outside the Judeo-Christian mainstream, such as Celtic mythology, runes and Druidism. Despite some general consensus that New Age involves concepts such as reincarnation, mystical experience, mind expansion, meditation, spirituality, inner self and healing, scholars disagree as to how to classify New Age. However, it seems that a main shared interest is changing one's current situation or reality through working on the self, and a notion of healing. York, for example, describes the characteristics of the New Age as follows:

> Another important area within New Age – one that relates to a preponderance of cultic effort in general – is that of healing. Much of the New Age and human potential effort is concerned less with global ecological concerns than it is with personal health. In this connection, it is worth mentioning the emphasis on self-healing (Bernie S. Siegel, Norman Cousins, Meir Schneider, Onslow H. Wilson, Kenneth R. Pelletier, Louise L. Hay, and the magazine *Medical Self Care*, etc.) as well as such therapy techniques as acupuncture (shiatsu), biofeedback, body cleansing, bodywork, chiropractic therapy, flower essence therapy, reiki, rolfing, visualization and imagery, and yoga.
>
> (York 1995: 37)

In the West, New Age is typically seen as counter-cultural. York cites as his reason for examining New Age the fact that it represents 'a theological perspective with particular sociological consequences, which has been largely absent from or ignored in the Judeo-Christian hegemony dominating the West' (1995: 2). He sees New Age as the 1980s replacement of counter-cultural movements of the 1960s (1995: 21–2). In fact, he goes so far as to see it as a new religious movement (NRM), following the recognized historical trend that a religion arises in one place and then spreads by diffusion to other areas (1995: 2).

Yet to see New Age as a single movement is misleading, since it lacks clearly shaped doctrines and organization, and is rather an assembly of amorphous movements and 'networks'. Indeed, as York himself recognizes, New Agers tend to avoid fixed frameworks in order not to annul each individual's participation, perceptions and experiences, and to prevent New Age from fossilizing into a religion (1995: 1–2).

Might Naikan fit into the general trend of New Age? It may be helpful to look at two characterizations of New Age by Shimazono (1996) and Heelas (1996). Shimazono (1996: 31–4) lists 19 major tenets of New Age, of which these five are closely shared with Naikan:

1   Self-realization through self-alteration or self-awakening.
2   Recognition of the unity of the sacredness of the cosmos, nature and the essential self. High levels of essential reality are immanent in the cosmos and nature.
3   Self-alteration brings healing and changes the environment. The individual's spiritual-awakening and self-alteration contributes to the coordination of nature and other people, and brings healing both for the individual's mind and body and for the greater environment, including the social one.
4   Thought changes reality. Positive thinking brings successful reality and negative thinking brings failure and unhappiness. A person's fate is the outcome of his/her thought.
5   Belief in the 'transmigration of the soul' and karma.

All of these tenets are present at some level in the aspects of Naikan we have explored up till now. The first, 'self-realization through self-alteration or self-awakening', clearly lies at the core of Naikan practice. A recognition of the unity of the sacredness of the cosmos, nature and the essential self is also experienced by some Naikan clients, as we have seen, especially in looking at mystical experience. The centrality of self-alteration in the process of healing (point 3) and of thought changing reality (point 4) emerged in our discussions in Chapters 3 and 4, where I showed the four ways in which the perception of Naikan clients is altered, and how a reconstruction of autobiography plays a role in healing. Lastly, we have seen how belief in transmigration of the soul (or consciousness) is not overtly expressed in Naikan, but that it was a central belief of Yoshimoto and continues to influence much Naikan practice today.

Heelas provides an analysis of New Age that focuses on the way the self is conceptualized, and how New Age might be a reaction against modernity. The key for him is that 'New Agers make the monistic assumption that the self itself is sacred' (1996: 2). I summarize his points as follows:

1   '[New Age] has to do with a way of life, a set of values, which apparently rupture or transcend what modernity has to offer' (1996: 3).
2   'To experience the "Self" itself is to experience "God", the "Goddess", the "Source", "Christ Consciousness", the "inner child", the "way of the heart", or, most simply and, I think, most frequently, "inner spirituality"' (1996: 19).

3   Whereas the Christian seeks 'salvation through worship, prayer, obedience and discipline, all in connection with that which is infinitely higher than him or herself; the New Ager seeks actualisation through context – setting and "work" – working on ego-attachments, typically in a setting orchestrated by those who mastered what it is to go within' (1996: 37).

4   The New Age movement is largely a middle and upper-middle class phenomenon sociologically.

5   '[T]here is little indigenization. Although there are signs of New Age teachings fusing with local cultural formations ... the overall picture is very much one of homogeneity' (1996: 121).

With the spread of international communication networks and globalization, New Age has spread rapidly and innovations within it are rapidly disseminated. For Heelas, New Agers are precisely those who do not want to be identified with the project of modernity and its underlying capitalist system (1996: 138). In other words, New Age is pursued as an antidote to the 'homelessness' of the modern man, as discussed by Berger, who is 'ever in search of himself' (Berger *et al.* 1973: 94). Modernity, in giving a tremendous amount of freedom and emphasizing individual autonomy, has resulted in alienation and identity crisis as well. This has consequences for religion, as Berger *et al.* write:

> The 'homelessness' of modern social life has found its most devastating expression in the area of religion. The general uncertainty, both cognitive and normative, brought about by the pluralization of everyday life and of biography in modern society, has brought religion into a serious crisis of plausibility.
>
> (Berger *et al.* 1973: 184)

Naikan seems to fit well within many of the characteristics Shimazono and Heelas have attributed to New Age. Could it be, then, part of a reaction to the 'alternative' modernity of Japan? It is tempting to see it in this light. In taking a traditional, yet far from mainstream, Shin Buddhist practice (*mishirabe*) and modifying it for general use, even to the point of removing most of the explicitly religious elements, Yoshimoto was following a line similar to that of New Agers, who mix old and new in order to transcend institutionalized religions.

However, there are three main problems in connecting Naikan with New Age. First, 'New Age' is not a well-recognized term in Japan; instead, 'Spiritual World' (*seishin sekai*) is the phrase Japanese are familiar with. This is an obstacle that can be dealt with; Shimazono sees Spiritual World and New Age as equivalents (1996: 23). Second, New Age is generally understood as originating in the United States, although Shimazono (1996: 20, 46–71) and Heelas (1996) both believe it should be understood as a global phenomenon and plural movements rather than a single one. Lastly, as we have seen, there is a tendency to see New Age as counter-cultural in the West (Nelson 1989; York 1995), or as evidence of 'Easternization'. It is hard to see how this could be applied to the Japanese context, since Naikan is not counter-cultural; nor does the term 'Easternization' make much sense. This leads us to the necessity of examining New Age specifically within the Japanese context.

New Spirituality Movements: reconciling East and West

Japan has always been a country where foreign goods and concepts are not imported as-is, but indigenized to the Japanese sensibility. Thus it is hardly surprising that the term 'New Age' has never gained wide popularity in Japan. The term used in Japan, 'Spiritual World', was first used in 1977 according to Matsuzawa (1982, cited in Shimazono 1996: 13). If we accept that New Age appeared in the United States in the early 1970s, then Spiritual World may have arisen under the influence of New Age. It is in the Spiritual World section of bookstores in Japan that one finds New Age books from the United States, such as Shirley Maclaine's *Out on a Limb* (1986), alongside books by the founders of Japanese New New Religions (*shin shin shūkyō*), and books on alternative healing and Eastern medicine.

In this section, I would like to introduce Shimazino Susumu's attempt to understand the New Age and the Spiritual World in Japan as part of a global phenomenon, rather than viewing the Japanese Spiritual World as merely an import from the Western 'New Age movement'. To do this, he coined the term 'New Spirituality Movements' (*shin reisei undo*), or NSMs. His use of this term is helpful in analysing how spirituality is understood in contemporary Japan, to what extent the recent shift of Naikan reflects broader trends in Japan and internationally, whether it is a part of these movements, or a reaction to them, and whether such phenomena should be understood as counter-cultural.

Part of the impetus for coining the term 'New Spirituality Movements' was his agreement with other scholars that the term 'New Age movement' is misleading, as it gives the impression that there is a single movement with a strong emic North American connotation, whereas in reality there are a variety of movements (Shimazono 1996: 46–71). According to Shimazono, neither 'Spiritual World' nor 'New Age' constitutes an independent phenomenon; rather, they participate in a global phenomenon spreading and permeating everywhere, but especially in developed countries, attracting in particular young individuals from a higher educational background. This global phenomenon of which New Age is a part, involving common thoughts and attitudes and occurring in various separated geographical and cultural areas around the same time, may take on various forms, but each occurs autonomously, although they are mutually influenced by media and electronic communication networks (Shimazono 1995a, 1996: 48). Better would be to formulate a concept that is inclusive of those who think they belong to North American and European New Age, Japanese who are familiar with 'Spiritual World', and people who are not conscious of being belonging to those movements, but who share similar thought patterns and ways of life.

New Spirituality Movements, according to Shimazono, are characterized by the unity of science and religion, the overcoming of the mind/body distinction and the creation of a new spiritually-based cosmology drawing on existing indigenous traditions. Haga and Kisala write:

> Despite their lack of such structural elements, however, such movements do promote a worldview or way of thought that can be called religious. They often constitute an amorphous gathering of those who share the same interests, as indicated by reading the same books or participating in the same activities; occasionally a more formal, although small, association is formed. However, they do not encourage the development of either rites or doctrine, and leadership is often unclear.
>
> (Haga and Kisala 1995: 239)

They define the five characteristics of these movements as follows (Haga and Kisala 1995: 239):

1 Stress is placed on a transformation of consciousness. Through the use of meditation or other, often psychological, techniques a higher level of consciousness is sought, leading to the development of psychic powers or the ability to perceive mysterious phenomena.
2 A spiritual existence is believed to permeate the universe and be tangible to us on an intimate level. It is the deepening of intercourse with this spiritual existence that is both the means and the goal of the transformation of consciousness.
3 It is believed that a spiritual transformation of humanity is in the offing, and that the spiritual enlightenment of each individual contributes to this advancement.
4 It is further believed that individuals have within themselves the power to arrive at this spiritual enlightenment, and that there is no need to rely on external powers or rituals. Traditional religion, which teachers such reliance, has only served to stifle the individual's enlightenment.
5 It is maintained that there is no opposition between religion and science, that the two are in fact one. However, there is a need to overcome the false dualism found in modern science, which only serves to separate human beings from nature.

One notes an interesting usage of the terms 'spirituality' and 'religion', which are far from coterminous. Indeed, one of the distinctive characteristics of NSMs is the idea that a new era of 'spirituality' is dawning after a long period of 'religion' (Shimazono 1996: 50). In some cases this may result in a simplistic dichotomy of viewing religion as rigid, external and imposed, whereas spirituality is fluid, internal and individually explored. Thus, NSMs have network-oriented cooperation among themselves rather than hierarchical control mechanisms characteristic of formal religious organizations (Shimazono 1996: 50).

The history of NSMs in the United States and Europe differs somewhat from that in Japan. In the United States they have their roots in the counterculture of the 1960s, something without clear parallel in Japan, and they inherited occult traditions which have always existed, but which were suppressed under Christianity. In Japan, however, the 'spiritual succession' was not, of course, from pre-Christian traditions, but rather from animism and folk Shinto, from Buddhism, especially esoteric Buddhism and Zen Buddhism, and from the East Asian tradition of *ki* which has its origin in China (Shimazono 1996: 61–3).

On the whole, NSMs try to respect individual autonomy and avoid restrictions on that autonomy by groups or organizations. Thus, there is a close connection between the world view and organizational form of these movements: people who support NSMs do not form long-term religious bodies, but rather small-scale loosely organized communities, sometimes called 'networks'. In this respect NSMs may resemble Thomas Luckman's (1967) idea of 'invisible religion', which does not create any formal religious structures, but which is nevertheless practised in private or with friends outside of rigid organizational settings (Shimazono 1995b: 239). However, we must remember that in reality mass media, contemporary social organizations and systems have important functions in connecting people who share similar thoughts and attitudes (1995b: 238).

The counter-cultural connotations of New Age may be perceived as too radical in Japan. NSMs, on the other hand, have close connections not with foreign religious ideas, but with traditional Japanese religious culture. In several cases NSMs and Japanese New Religions have been supported by older Japanese religious traditions, such as folk Shinto, animism and Japanese Buddhism, whereas one does not see a corresponding support for New Age in the West from Christian churches. In Japan, New Religions developed widely, whereas the major monotheistic religions (Judaism, Christianity and Islam) have not taken root. This stands in stark contrast to Europe, where New Religions in the Japanese sense have not appeared spontaneously.

The classification of New Spirituality Movements is insightful and useful as an attempt to grasp New Age and Spiritual World as reflecting a global phenomenon rather any single movement. However, there are also problems in this portrayal. It is slightly one-sided to view New Age as purely 'counter-cultural', reacting against the traditional moralities and values supported by historic religions such as Christianity. New Age does not neglect tradition, but on the contrary, draws on old traditions. As Heelas writes:

New Agers can ignore apparently significant differences between religious traditions, dismissing them as due to historical contingencies and ego-operations. But they do have faith in that wisdom which is experienced as lying at the heart of the religious domain as a whole.

(Heelas 1996: 27)

One must therefore be slightly more critical than Shimazono in using the term 'counter-cultural'. If 'counter-cultural' is to be understood as something against the Western Judeo-Christian traditions, then there cannot be any counter-culture in countries like Japan. But if counter-culture is more naturally understood as something against the dominant cultural and social traditions, then it is untrue that NSMs are not counter-cultural by nature as Shimazono claims (1996). Since the Meiji Era, a dominant aspect of Japanese culture has been the importation of Western values and ideas. Therefore, a re-evaluation of traditional Japanese cultural values in the form of 'Spiritual World' may in fact be part of a counter-cultural reaction among the Japanese – a return to tradition, albeit in a different form.

There is, furthermore, one additional twist to understanding the background of NSMs in Japan. Most people who were introduced to the Spiritual World are people who read books by Westerners devoted to Eastern meditation and Buddhist practices, including Japanese traditional values such as animism and Zen Buddhism. What is ironic here is the fact that these counter-cultural Japanese, who reacted against the dominant Western culture and re-evaluated Japanese traditions, did so under the influence of Westerners. It is often said that Japanese cultural values can be appreciated once they have been transported to the West and then re-imported back to Japan. *Reiki* is especially a good example of this as more Europeans and North Americans are familiar with this practice than Japanese. Due to the wide spread of 'alterative healing' in the West, through transpersonal psychology, Japanese are now beginning to accept *Reiki*. In a similar way, the acceptance and popularity of Naikan abroad may become a factor in the continued growth of Naikan within its country of origin.

New New Religions and psycho-religious movements

Japan is rich soil for new religions. Compared with the small number of Christians, estimated at less than 1 per cent of the population, there is a vast number of 'New Religions' and 'New New Religions' that have their roots in Shinto, Buddhism and some eclectic systems of thought. In general, the large number of religious movements that began in the early nineteenth century are understood as 'New Religions', of which *Nyorai kyō* and *Kurozumi kyō* are the oldest (Yumiyama 1995: 88). Such New Religions reached their peak in the 1950s and 1960s. Generally, they can be divided into those of Buddhist origin and those of Shinto origin, although in practice most are syncretic. A well-known example of the former is *Sōka Gakkai*, a lay Buddhist movement arising from the Nichiren school of Buddhism, while an example of a Shinto-based New Religion is *Tenrikyō*. Collectively the New Religions claim a membership of millions, and taken together they constitute the single biggest form of social movement in modern and contemporary Japan. They tend to have a belief system that includes salvation brought by either the founder of the religion or Buddha, and are today demographically dominated by middle-aged housewives.

'New New Religion' (*shin shin shūkyō*), on the other hand, is a term coined by Nishiyama Shigeru in 1988 as a subset that has developed since the 1970s. Shimazono (1995b: 223–34) defines the characteristics of New New Religions and what differentiates them from the (old) New Religions as follows:

1   Decreased interest in the practical difficulties in life such as illness and poverty. Instead, increased interest in solitude and the social pressure which restricts the freedom of the individual.
2   Increased interest in controlling the condition of the body and mind through the practice of meditation and other practices (breathing methods, relaxation, body work and other psychotherapeutic techniques).

Increasingly, however, as well recognized by scholars on religion, it is becoming difficult to classify phenomena as strictly religious or non-religious.

It is clear that Naikan shares some characteristics of the New New Religions. Considering the fact that Naikan was established in the early 1940s, Yoshimoto succeeded in eliminating much of the religious tone of Naikan to ensure that it would not be confused with a New Religion. However, his attempt to decrease its religious tone actually resulted in its acquiring some of the tone and characteristics of future New New Religions.

More specifically, however, Naikan can be seen as a 'psycho-religious movement', a term coined by Shimazono to describe movements that focus on healing but hover between psychotherapy and religion (1995b: 269). The categories of psycho-religious movement and New New Religion are overlapping, with some movements being both at once, but all of these are subsumed under his umbrella term of NSMs. *Seichō no Ie* and *Hito no Michi* are two major psycho-religious movements focusing on 'thought conversion'. Such beliefs are an interesting replacement of the traditional focus on the intervention of a supernatural power (such as God) and may be part of a more general trend towards the psychologization of religion in modern societies.

This is a thought already anticipated by Gehen, who wrote in 1957 that 'we now live in the era of psychology' due to the process of the modernity which transformed the condition of humans:

> Over the last century the infinite diversity of individual particularities has attracted and rewarded the interests of psychologists, both in the arts

and in science. Nor should one forget that even at the level of the larger society an emphasis on the lived immediacy of the personality has come to constitute a principle for the creation of persistent relations and reciprocities.

(Gehen 1980: 159)

Along similar lines as Berger, Gehen saw that the institution had lost its power and became unstable in modernity, allowing and indeed forcing us to emphasize the autonomous individual. Once religion had lost its plausibility, people were left with a multitude of 'free choices', encouraging intellectualization and subjectivization.

In my view Naikan and Morita Therapy are good examples of this 'psychologization of the religion'. Both have roots in Buddhism – Naikan in Shin and Morita in Zen – and both have attempted to remove the religious colouration of their original forms of practices and establish themselves as psychotherapy. Clearly, the medicalization of Naikan is the main means by which this process is occurring, and with the spread of Naikan abroad, especially to the United States, one might expect intensified pressures in this direction. In reality, as we have seen, Naikan abroad has presented both of the 'two roots' of Naikan in meditation and psychotherapy, seeming to support the claim that Naikan is indeed a psycho-religious movement.

It is often said that a 'return to religion' (*shūkyō kaiki genshō*) has occurred in developed countries (Yuasa 1989: 26). Yuasa reports that the number of small-scale communities, such as New New Religions, has been increasing in Japan (1989: 26). He understands that these 'cults', as he calls them, take fluid, only lightly restricted forms, and emphasize practical activities for the attainment of mystical experiences by oneself, rather than the spreading of the doctrines of their 'communities'. Paralleling Shimazono's argument of the psychologization of religion, Yuasa interprets the interest of individuals in ideologies and practices, which are not part of a religion but rather similar to Jungian psychology, as answering an interest in the spiritual world. He sees this as a search for religiosity, but from different angles than the usual fixed forms of religion (Yuasa 1989: 26). Thus, like the ecological and alternative healing movements (which are largely based on non-Western modes of thought), psycho-religious movements such as Naikan can be understood as attempts to overcome the dichotomy of science and religion and therefore as seeking 'alternative knowledge'.

In its fundamental practice and worldview, the change in Naikan has been slight, and more in its representation than actual practice. Most recently, Naikan has been increasingly represented as a healing method capable of overcoming the scientific/religious dichotomy and taking part in the Healing Boom. In this latest guise Naikan, without any special effort to represent itself as scientific, is now being successfully accepted by the public. In fact, this may be the most likely trend at the beginning of the twenty-first century.

As in the broader phenomenon of New Spirituality Movements, healing and salvation are closely connected in Naikan. Rather than understanding this shift as 'from salvation to healing', it might better be understood in Naikan's case as 'healing *through* salvation'. Not many people nowadays will be tempted to use the term 'salvation' due to its heavily religious connotations, but this formulation is more accurate in that it shows how Naikan's initial impulse has not changed despite changes in the language in which it is presented. In Naikan, most clients experience some degree of self-realization the moment they recognize the love they have received from others and their own imperfections, guilt or 'sinful nature', at which they are shocked but despite which they are accepted. After such realizations, many clients feel that not only are they now saved, but they have been always saved, a feeling that brings them healing. Though salvation is a strong word, it may remain the best way of describing such experiences, especially since these experiences themselves do not appear to have changed over the course of Naikan's history, despite changes in Naikan's representation.

Although Naikan is certainly taking part in the Healing Boom and shares much with NSMs, this is not due to fundamental shifts in Naikan. On the contrary, the fundamental shifts were made by Yoshimoto himself, primarily in his modification of *mishirabe* to create Naikan. Yoshimoto established Naikan before New New Religions thrived in the place of 'old' New Religions in Japan, and long before the rise of New Age in the United States and Spiritual World in Japan. One might suppose, actually, that Yoshimoto was ahead of his time in creating Naikan, and that historical development caught up with him eventually. When this happened, it is unsurprising that other Naikan practitioners used this as an opportunity to promote Naikan in a new national and international scene.

My final understanding of Naikan is that this is a practice which is religious, educational, spiritual and psychotherapeutic all at once. In my view this rich combination of resources has allowed Naikan to represent itself in various ways over the years. Certainly this representation has varied, primarily due to external factors. Thus, the AUM gas attack in 1995 had a strong negative impact on portraying Naikan as religious, whereas the Healing Boom has influenced Naikan towards a language of 'spirituality' and 'healing'. This will likely be the niche in which Naikan will situate itself as it moves into the twenty-first century – a comfortable public space that allows it to retain its religious heritage in a limited and non-threatening way while avoiding an over-medicalization and theorization of itself as a scientific practice.

Epilogue

Naikan offers us a mirror in which we can find reflected several intriguing and interrelated issues regarding both Japanese society in particular and medical anthropology in general. Typically, Naikan has been understood as a fascinating case study of a therapeutic system within a single, limited culture, and in general an easy tendency for anthropologists has been to consider that different cultures have different healing systems that are actually culturally specific belief systems not necessarily grounded in, or applicable for, more universal human experience. Although critical medical anthropologists investigate the cultural situatedness of even biomedicine, it is more common to believe that biomedicine (and a range of other Western fields of knowledge, including theoretical knowledge) is not susceptible to this critique, as it is based on scientific knowledge that is universally applicable and not 'culture-bound', even if it may be differently coloured depending on specific cultural difference. This privilege is rarely accorded to non-Western indigenous bodies of knowledge.

Against this common conception, I have tried to demonstrate in this book that Naikan is more than a culturally specific therapeutic method, in part because it is grounded on aspects of human experience and the human mind and body that are far more universal in nature than specifically Japanese – for example, everyone has or has had a mother, has been helped by others, will die, faces suffering, wishes for happiness and so on. That is not to deny its very specific Japanese character or the history of its origins and development. It is merely to say that, like many other practices, techniques, technologies and bodies of knowledge that have traversed cultural lines and have thereby been altered, while retaining their essence and usefulness, Naikan may certainly have a validity that extends beyond the borders of Japan. This seems to accord with the experiences of those few individuals who have set up Naikan centres in Austria, Germany and elsewhere, and who have modified certain aspects of the Naikan practice while retaining its key components.

The tendency in scholarship may still be to gravitate to the extremes of total cultural relativism or a culturally unaware universalism, but the insufficiencies of such extremes should be apparent to all, and Naikan seems a good example to illustrate this. My own impression is that such practices are neither universal nor culturally specific; rather, the matter is much more complex and intricate than what such an easy dichotomy allows room for. For example, various meditation practices, yoga and other techniques have been becoming increasingly popular in the West, where they are often removed to a greater or lesser degree from their original cultural context. How this changes them, however, is a complex and interesting question. Similarly, Buddhist thought is clearly not specific to one culture; nevertheless, having entered Japan, it naturally mixed with Japanese culture. These questions challenge us to think beyond the limited either/or possibilities still predominating in much of social theory.

Thus, it is my hope that this ethnography of Naikan can help to challenge some of our own assumptions about how we understand health, illness and the interaction between thoughts, memories, emotions and attitudes, and both physical and mental well-being. A further direction for medical anthropology would be to explore how globalization affects cultural understandings of health and illness by bringing different systems together, thereby allowing individuals to participate in an eclectic range of medical practices. For example, Austrians who are dissatisfied with biomedicine may turn to alternative therapies like Naikan, or use such therapies as supplements to the dominant medical system. On a larger scale, however, how are medical systems themselves changing and adapting as a result of globalization? For example, biomedicine has been becoming more sensitive to differences across ethnic and other groups, but this is in many ways quite a different issue, as individuals seeking alternative health care do not necessarily do so along lines of 'ethnic group' or 'cultural differences'. Thus, increasing demand by individuals in North America and Europe has been pushing governments, hospitals and public health agencies to make room for, and investigate, alternative healing practices. By offering detailed studies into different systems for understanding health and illness, medical anthropologists can benefit public health through this on-going process.

As many anthropologists experience, I came to find that several of the theoretical questions I set out with at the outset of my research proved less appropriate as I learned more. First of all, I realized the term 'Naikan psychotherapy' is not entirely appropriate in describing Naikan. Many Naikan practitioners see Naikan more as a way of life, and the kind of transformation many clients show seems distinctive from that encountered in traditional therapeutic treatments. Naikan aims at having clients achieve a state of true and lasting happiness, a joyous and serene mind, which seems beyond the task of merely bringing abnormal neurosis to a state of normal neurosis, as in the classical Freudian perspective. Of course, there may be an increasing number of psychotherapeutic approaches practised in the West (some drawing from Asian philosophies and practices) that may share this bolder aim.

Secondly, I came to realize that the very question of why psychotherapies are not popular in Japan is itself a question based on certain assumptions that may be inadequate. This question is similar to one which I received so many times whenever I presented Naikan at the conferences: 'how do you evaluate Naikan's efficacy as a therapy?' Even though contemporary anthropologists are very sensitive and self-critical about the imposition of the Western frame-work onto the research subjects, it is still prevalent in my opinion. Being interested in the cross-cultural understanding of health and illness, there are some obvious questions that I have been struggling with. First of all, what is health and what is illness? How do we define them?

Medical anthropology has been very innovative in its attempts to under-stand various forms of illness and disease including the concept of culture-bound syndromes, but most of the work tends to focus on 'illness', not on 'health'. Compared to the attention given to illness, disease and the eradi-cation of disease, for example, there is virtually no consideration being paid to what 'health' actually constitutes, beyond the mere absence of disease, which is a most inadequate definition. Critical medical anthropologists do critique the notion that the biomedical framework is culture-free, yet they also often restrict their focus to cultural differences regarding the concept of illness, while still ignoring the notion of health, in which case they would also succumb to a function-oriented biomedical view of health, that is to say, health as merely freedom from infection or malfunction and as something that is achieved after eliminating such ailments. One could say this definition is a bit like running a virus-checking programme on one's computer, and finding that if there are no viruses present, the computer is fully operational and healthy. The inadequacy of this model is that human beings are quite different from computers in their capacity for self-development. When seen from a perspective that acknowledges a tremendous potential to human development, physically, emotionally and mentally, such as that presented in Naikan, this negative definition of health is severely limited in that it com-pletely neglects the possibility of such growth and development. Considering the sophisticated evaluation methods for judging *how sick* people are, it is surprising that there is no equivalence in judging *how healthy* people are, both physically and mentally, using a positive scale and not merely a negative one. When it comes to mental health, the situation is even more com-plicated.

In great part due to Kleinman's major work on depression and neur-asthenia in China (1986, 1988, 1991; Kleinman and Good 1985), we are now more aware of the problem of the universalization of the biomedical framework when it comes to diagnosis. However, such critical sensitivity is often lacking when it comes to judging the efficacy of psychotherapies. The very question of failure indicates that success and failure should be easily measurable in the case of therapies. However, in the case of Naikan, practitioners often take a very long-term view in judging Naikan's effect.

'Planting a seed' might be a more appropriate way to describe how practitioners view Naikan. For example, there are occasionally a few clients who cannot bear it and leave the centre after the second or third day. In a way, it seems to make most sense to categorize these cases as 'Naikan failures'. However, many such individuals often come back to do Naikan again in a few years' time; therefore, practitioners tend to avoid judging right away that Naikan was not suitable for these clients. Yanagita considered that clients are all at different stages in their lives, thus it is difficult to standardize any evaluation of Naikan's effectiveness. Those with no psychological hang-ups can follow Naikan's three themes and attain visible progress at the end of one week. Those with a great deal of past trauma, however, often have intense aversion towards someone close to them, and therefore have difficulty following the themes; therefore, it might take many days for such people to even start following the Naikan method. At the same time, such people are often those who have very powerful transformational experiences.

The popular question of why Western psychotherapies are not popular in Japan may not be the best epistemological orientation to understand cross-cultural dialogue about mental health, illness and therapies. Biomedicine is widespread and has been the legitimate and dominant form of treatment in Japan, so it may be natural to wonder why psychotherapies did not gain a similar kind of status in Japan. However, it might also be an unnecessary presumption at some level. As such psychotherapies are a Western invention, it is not necessarily relevant to wonder why this form of therapy never became popular in Japan. In a way, it is as potentially loaded a question as asking why Christianity did not become more popular in Japan, or why Buddhism has not become more popular in the West.

It is clear that the very concept of psychotherapy is based on the famous Cartesian dichotomy of body and mind. Even those who recognize that one's mental condition affects one's physical condition, and vice versa, still hold the view that body and mind remain principally independent of each other. This sharp division of the human person into body and mind is, in fact, a relatively new concept and was not always the way they were viewed, even in the West (Kabat-Zinn 1990; Ozawa-de Silva 2002). It is important to know that such a view, which is the basis of biomedicine, has not been predominant historically or geographically. Because of the worldwide domination of bio-medicine, however, it is common for people nowadays to view the separation of body and mind as a fact, rather than a construction. Seen from this angle, psychotherapy is actually a unique way of approaching our psychological problems, and its domination for half a century is an interesting topic for investigation.

It is difficult to estimate whether Naikan's influence in Japan will increase or decrease in the coming years, especially in the midst of the turmoil of losing several of its influential figures in the last few years. Yoshimoto's death had a great impact on Naikan, but those who received training under his guidance were determined to maintain it by running their centres, doing research to contribute to the theorization of Naikan, and vigorously promoting it. However, the scenery of the Naikan community has been changing since 1997 when I started conducting my fieldwork in Japan. Professor Murase, who was the most respected scholar in the Naikan community, as well as a clinical psychologist, died in 1998. Then, both Yoshimoto Kinuko and Yanagita Kakusei died in early 2000.

Naikan abroad is very much an on-going process and it will not be affected adversely by the loss of leading figures in Japan. It has the potential to expand in the coming decade, since there are many who will find this Eastern method appealing, with its combination of Buddhist and more modern techniques. The prospects for Naikan abroad seem to be more positive than in its country of origin.

In Japan, the generation of Naikan practitioners and scholars who had direct contact with Yoshimoto are ageing. Unless they attract members of the next generation who are willing to dedicate themselves to Naikan practice, the continuation of Naikan centres may become a critical issue. I speculate that the increase in centres and the lack of centralized regulation will lead to an increase in variations of Naikan, and that new centres will deviate from Yoshimoto's style. As Yoshimoto Masanobu, Yoshimoto Ishin's son, told me, each practitioner has been revealing his own preference and style more strongly since Yoshimoto's death. For him, this shift has been negative, since it threatens to distort his father's established method. During the time of Yoshimoto, people could ask him for advice, while Yoshimoto himself was regarded as the personified validation of Naikan, sometimes regardless of his own wishes. Since his death, the aim of the whole Naikan community has been to define what the essence of Naikan is. It is rather ironic that Yoshimoto's flexible attitude in not restricting Naikan to one set method and his willingness to modify and adapt it during his lifetime has been transformed into a rigidity within the Naikan community following his death, largely out of respect for him.

This lack of doctrine and definition has been causing tension within the community and also some competition as to whose opinions should be respected. This exclusiveness may be detrimental to the expansion and development of Naikan in Japan. It is also possible that next generation practitioners may become independent of the current Naikan organization and even start their practice without relying on the term 'Naikan'. To some extent, Reynolds himself has been practising in this way. Even though he makes references to Naikan and Morita Therapy, he named his practice the 'Constructive Living Method' (CLM), since he conducts sessions both in the United States and in Japan. By doing so, one can escape from the criticism of the Association of Naikan Centres or individual practitioners. What Yoshimoto began, by distancing Naikan from its association with Shin Buddhism and by naming his modified method 'Naikan', is now possibly moving in the direction of removing even the name 'Naikan'.

Yoshimoto said 'Naikan is Naikan', and as we discovered, Naikan can be used as psychotherapy, self-cultivation, the treatment of alcoholics at hospitals, a healing technique, a religious practice, an educational non-religious training method and reform treatment for prisoners. The Naikan done at Naikan centres will remain a 'Naikan' which cannot be covered by any one specific category, but increasingly some centres will emphasize certain aspects of Naikan over others. Naikan will assume various forms according to the prevailing trends, especially due to the continuing process of globalization. The question remains open as to which group of practitioners are most faithfully keeping alive the spirit of Yoshimoto and Naikan: those who have formed organizations in order to keep pure the final method he developed, or those who (in keeping with his advice) do not meet or conduct research, but have instead continued the adaptation of Naikan into its numerous variations. In this, Naikan faces a familiar challenge well known in the history of religious and cultural developments: a tension between the 'orthodox' and 'heterodox', and the pressure towards the institutionalization of a revered founder's inherently anti-institutional thought and ideals.

Notes

1 Introduction

1 Later, when Yoshimoto registered his temple, he listed it as part of the smaller Kibe sect, one of the ten sects of Shin Buddhism, and closest to the Honganji sect.

2 According to Kinuko Yoshimoto, *byōnin* refers to those who suffer from worrying about the world hereafter; she also said that, as far as she knows, *mishirabe* is no longer practiced (Takemoto 1989: 32).

3 In their comments during the discussion session of the 1979 annual conference of the JNA, *Nihon Naikan Gakkai Taikai Ronbunshū*, vol. 3, 1979, p. 23.

4 When I revisited the *Meisō no Mori* for the second time in 2003, I felt immediately comfortable, as if I had come back to my favourite place, so it was a quite different experience from my first visit. However, it still took a good three days to have any experience such as a sudden flow of past memories.

2 Enclosed silence, sacred space: death, meditation and confession in the Naikan environment

1 On the issue of near-death experience see Kübler-Ross (1982, 1983, 1986, 1989, 1997).

2 In *Cratylus* (Plato 1997: 118).

3 Descartes' philosophical position is often described as dualism of the subjectivity and objectivity, dualism of the mind and the body, reductionism and positivism, but it may be worth commenting that Descartes himself did admit that there is an ambiguous but very close interaction between the body and mind. It is mentioned by Merleau-Ponty that 'a famous letter of his to Elizabeth draws the distinction between the body as it is conceived through use in living and the body as it is conceived by the understanding' (1978: 199). Despite Descartes' shift of position in later life, Cartesianism has been interpreted as a reductionistic dualism and until recently has been the most influential philosophical foundation for natural and social science.

4 This topic is discussed in greater detail in my article on alternative sociologies of the body (Ozawa-de Silva 2002).

5 *Dōjō* literally means 'training hall', and is commonly used for Japanese martial arts such as *aikidō, jūdō* and *karate*, which combine mental and bodily training.

6 Ihara had already experienced Naikan when he gave this explanation at the

Department of Shinryō Naika at Kyūshū University (*shinryō* = psychological treatment, *naika* = internal medicine), which was recorded as a part of his confession tape.

7 Shinryō Naika (*shinryō* is psychological treatment and *naika* is internal medicine) is a common form of Japanese-style biomedicine, which does not aim at psychological illness as such, but operates from the assumption that psychological states arise from diseases that are basically physiological in nature (Ikemi 1963, 1973; Ohnuki-Tierney 1984).

3 Naikan confessions

1 Personal communication with Ishii. He also gave a lecture on Naikan, entitled 'A Way to Happiness', which was recorded.

2 Since the earlier cases are taken from Yoshimoto's Naikan centre in Nara and the later cases from *Meisō no Mori*, it would be hasty to draw out conclusions regarding the development of Naikan over time from these cases alone. Naikan has developed over time, of course, and I handle this issue in Chapters 5–7.

3 In Japanese: *Kochira ni korareta mokuteki to dōki ni tsuite otazune shitai no desu ga.*

4 Nagayama is a psychiatrist who has written several articles on Naikan (e.g. Nagayama 1998).

5 Personal conversation with Ishii. On the issue of Yoshimoto's farting, see also Sone (1989: 94).

6 In some cases the precise times of the *mensetsu* sessions must be guessed, since they are not always given on the tape. This can be done with some confidence, since *mensetsu* is usually conducted regularly at intervals of two hours or, as in this case, 90 minutes.

7 Or 'that kind of spirit'.

8 That is, after Hiroshi's first Naikan session a year prior.

9 *Obon* is a week-long national holiday in Japan, during which people normally return to their homes to venerate the family ancestors.

10 Usually clients begin their week of Naikan on a Sunday. However, I started Naikan in the middle of the week with another woman in her mid-thirties who started on the same day. Sometimes we were called into a separate room so that we could listen to certain tapes on our third day or fifth day, while the other clients were listening to other tapes, since they were at different points in their Naikan.

11 On these experiences, see also Yanagita (1982: 47–8).

4 Embodied memory and the reconstruction of autobiography in Naikan

1 Schacter writes:

> Halbwachs believed that social groups exert a profound influence on the content of individual memories, and help to create various illusions, condensations, and distortions. Although Halbwachs's views are extreme in a number of respects – he believed that all memories are in some sense collective rather than individual – his ideas are important because they represent a first attempt to systematically discuss sociocultural factors as a source of memory distortion.
>
> (Schacter 1997a: 12)

2 Ross writes, for example:

> A better bet for the future formulation of novel ideas might be those studies that deal with memory contexts in social frameworks – for example, sociology, anthropology, and folklore – which have been only fringe contributors to memory theory up to now. My sampling of theoretical concepts thus draws from those disciplines that concern themselves with the preservation of the temporal integrity of society as well as those that emphasize the continuity of the individual.
>
> (Ross 1991: ix)

3 Rubin (1996a), Ross (1991), Barclay (1996), Hirst and Manier (1996), Bruner and Feldman (1996), Fivush *et al.* (1996), Robinson (1996), Fitzgerald (1996), Tonkin (1992), Connerton (1995) and Csordas (1994).

4 Schacter writes:

> memories are not simply 'awakened' from storage by a retrieval cue; rather, information in the retrieval environment contributes to, and is often part of, the subjective experience of remembering. Therefore, the retrieval environment probably plays a role in distorted remembering ... Tulving went on to hypothesize that 'memory distortions, rememberers "remembering" things that did not occur, could be attributed to the constructive role of retrieval information'.
>
> (Schacter 1997b: 16)

5 This is not to deny the phenomenon of 'false memory', but to say that this is not a useful way of approaching narratives of autobiographical memory or illness narratives. The powers of the imagination in the issue of false memory have been much studied by doctors, psychologists and neurologists. Daniel Schacter's *Memory Distortion* (1997a) is one such example. The psychologist Elizabeth Loftus wrote that 'A growing number of investigations demonstrate that under the right circumstances false memories can be instilled rather easily in some people' (1997: 71), as shown by an experiment in which she gave volunteers a list of childhood events and asked them to imagine such events as having occurred. Her results led her to conclude that an act of imagination might remind some people of a real experience, but she believes a more likely explanation is that imagining the event simply made it more familiar and that familiarity was mistakenly related to childhood memories. False memory has also been studied in the context of child abuse, pointing to the impressionability of patients under encouragement or suggestions from their therapist (e.g. Pendergrast 1996), something that has led in some cases to families being ruined.

6 Csordas writes of a woman who experienced Charismatic healing:

> Her relationship with her mother remained the central issue, with maternal imagery recurring frequently. Another important sequence of embodied imagery occurred during her retreat, in which she 'connected' with the presence of a mother and grandparents who were 'pouring out love.' As she thanked her mother for her attempts to love, she 'felt embraced by Jesus'.
>
> (Csordas 1994: 124)

7 Thus Csordas (1994), in understanding healing as a self-process, describes the body as the existential ground of self. In his observation of imagination in Catholic

Charismatic healing, he emphasizes the importance of the postural model as: (1) product of the gestalt creative powers of our psyche, (2) in perpetual inner self-construction and self-destruction (1994: 66). For him, 'The postural model is a function of self precisely as a preobjective capacity for orientation in the world' (1994: 65).

8 For this reason Douglas (1973) argues that the Protestant project to abolish ritual is misguided, since it neglects the importance of ritual practice for the imagination and hence religious experience. Of course, the importance of religious experience in Pietism and liberal Protestantism since Schleiermacher is not common to all forms of Protestantism, and the case of the Quakers indicates that even minimalist ritualistic forms can be closely tied to religious experience. The latter seems to come closer to Naikan practice.

9 The case of this man, called KC, has also been described in Hayman *et al.* (1993) and Tulving *et al.* (1988).

10 Yanagita writes of a different experience as well:

> The morning sunshine wrapped my whole body ... as if a golden magnetic wave was pouring over me. I felt that my body was gone, or that it was very light and floating on air as if walking in a wondrous dream ... I wondered: There is nothing wrong with my body and no tension in it – is this being healthy? Is the truly healthy body like this? This was a moment of happiness the likes of which I had not felt in forty years.
>
> (Yanagita 1982: 45)

> He goes on to speak of sensations of lying peacefully beneath water, happiness, visions of Amida Buddha, feelings of gratitude and graciousness, complete health, the desire to thank his body and even feelings of divinity. In various ways this imagery is shared by other Naikan clients, especially those who achieve deep Naikan.

11 Yanagita (1997: 126).

5 Interdependent selfhood, Buddhism and the role of mother

1 Geertz's famous statement about selfhood is that it is:

> a bounded, unique, more or less integrated motivational and cognitive universe, a dynamic center of awareness, emotion, judgement, and action organized into a distinctive whole and set contrastively both against other such wholes and against a social and natural background.
>
> (Geertz 1975: 48)

2 In asserting this, Kondo links herself directly with the emerging perception of the significance of the creation of narratives in the social sciences, in the sociology of story telling (Plummer 1995), of the role of rhetorical devices in the construction of both personal narratives of identity and of social science narratives about narratives.

3 They further write:

> Autobiographical memory is a constructive process: evidence for its creative nature comes from a variety of sources ... people also revise their own personal histories. Long-term recollections are often constructions that reflect the

impact of people's beliefs, knowledge, and goals at the time of retrieval, in addition to stored memories.

(Ross and Wilson 2000: 232-3)

Just as individuals sometimes exaggerate their stability, they may also over-estimate the degree to which they have changed. Retrospective overestimation of change is likely when people experience a circumstance that they expect to produce change, but that in reality has minimal impact. Self-help programs are a context in which people's expectancies and hopes of change are likely to be disappointed ... More generally, a tendency to revise the past in order to claim personal improvement may explain why many individuals report that they benefit from ineffective pop therapies and self-improvement programs.

(Ross and Wilson 2000: 236)

This problem is, however, in a sense anticipated in Naikan through the recording of confessions, whereby clients do not need to rely upon their memory of previous feelings and problems, but can listen for themselves to how they described them on their first few days of Naikan.

4 The North American authors base their theories on what they call 'the well-validated premise that people in our culture are motivated to think highly of themselves' (Ross and Wilson 2000: 239), and admit that the situation may be significantly different in 'collectivist cultures', in which Japan would presumably be included. Their view is questionable, however, that 'Because group member-ship is salient to them, individuals from collectivist cultures may use the same social comparisons when evaluating themselves or other people. As a conse-quence, their judgments of themselves would parallel their evaluations of other people'.

5 Although there are obviously significant differences between Japanese and Tibetan schools of Buddhism in terms of culture and practice, both countries follow the Mahayana or 'Great Vehicle' tradition of Buddhism, and their teachings on the fundamental topics such as the Four Noble Truths are the same. My reason for including an oral teaching here, rather than the more conventional method of summarizing or quoting from a book, is that the Buddhist tradition is primarily an orally-transmitted one and places great value on oral means of presentation.

6 This section on the Four Noble Truths is an edited version of an oral teaching by Geshe Lobsang Tenzin at the Drepung Loseling Institute, Atlanta, Georgia, on 9 August 2005, which happened to be *Chokhor Duchen* (Tibetan), the anniversary of the Buddha's first teaching, and is included here with his permission. It was edited both from notes and from a live recording by Brendan Ozawa-de Silva, who apologizes for any mistakes or omissions.

7 John Pettit translates this well-known verse as: 'Profound, peaceful, immaculate, luminous, and unfabricated: / Such an ambrosial Dharma have I found! / If I try to teach it, nobody will understand, / So not speaking, I shall stay in the forest' (1999: 42).

8

Faith, according to Shinran, means not doubting the Buddha's wisdom or his compassionate vow to save all sentient beings. Where faith exists, so does the realization that the power of salvation lies with Amida. Hence, no calculated attempts to win salvation is needed. The *nembutsu* spoken at this stage is not a personal act but the act of Amida bestowed on the believer. It is inextricably linked to faith as the true cause of birth in Pure Land. Through faith, one is born in Amida's Pure Land, not in the expedient realm. Because salvation occurs through his unfathomable (*fukashigi*) vow, Shinran called it birth in Pure Land that is difficult to fathom (*nanjigiōjō*).

(Dobbins 1989: 29)

9 Williams writes:

The most widespread of the cults devoted to Buddhas is that of Amitābha or Amitāyus. In contemporary Japanese Buddhism it accounts for more practitioners than any other Buddhist tradition, and in these forms in practice it most nearly approaches a devotional monotheism, no matter how inadequate such terms may ultimately turn out to be.

(Williams 1989: 251)

10 Dobbins provides the following quote attributed to Shinran:

Here you have come crossing the borders of more than ten provinces, unconcerned about [any risk to] your own lives. And what is it your wish to ask? Solely about the path leading to birth in Pure Land. But you are gravely mistaken if you presume that I know of any path to Pure Land outside of the *nembutsu* or that I am aware of other scriptures [indicating one]. If that is what you desire, there are many learned priests in Nara and on Mt. Hiei; you should go and ask them what is required for birth in Pure Land. As for me, Shinran, I have received and put my faith in the words of the good man [Hōnen]: 'Simply utter the *nembutsu* and you will be saved by Amida.' Apart from this, I have nothing else to point out.

Is the *nembutsu* truly the key to birth in Pure Land? Or is it an act that will lead me to hell? Frankly, I do not know. But even if I have been deceived by Hōnen so that the *nembutsu* leads me to hell, I have no regrets. The reason is this. If I were capable of achieving Buddhahood by exerting myself in other religious practices and yet said the *nembutsu* and fell into hell, then there would be reason to regret being deceived. But since all other practices are beyond my reach, hell is where I am bound to reside anyway. If, however, the vow of Amida is true, then the teachings of Sākyamuni cannot be false. And if the Buddha's teachings are true, then, the interpretations of Shan-tao cannot be false. And if Shan-tao's interpretations are true, then how can Hōnen's words be lies? And if Hōnen's words are true, then how can the things I say be in vain?

This, in short, is my humble faith. Over and above this, it is up to each of you individually to take up the *nembutsu* in faith or to reject it.

(Dobbins 1989: 41)

11 Yoshimoto started his speech at the first Naikan annual conference in 1978 with this statement.
12 Nakatsu continues:

The problem is the salvation of the people who are living now. The problem is how am I to understand the people who have passed away? 'The person who lives true *shinjin*, however, abides in the stage of the truly settled, for he has already been grasped, never to be abandoned. There is no need to wait in anticipation for the moment of death, no need to rely on Amida's coming. At the time *shinjin* becomes settled, birth too becomes settled.' (Shinran, *Mattosho*, first letter). The stage of the truly settled is also called 'no retrogression into present life' (*gensho-futai*). This means we don't retrogress to the life of delusion again, but 'we are assured of reaching buddhahood' (Shinran). We are emancipated from anxiety about life after death.

(Andreasen 1998: 137)

13 The 1997 edition, which I use, is newly edited and published as *Naikan Hō* (Yoshimoto 1997).
14 In short, if the Oedipus complex is the disposition of 'I want to kill my father to get my mother', in the Ajase complex it is 'I want my mother not to become female', since the child reacts negatively when he sees his mother behaving like a 'woman'.
15 Japan has often been described as a 'maternal society' (Kawai 1975), in which every woman is a mother, and every man a son. 'Mother-worship' is in fact not uncommon among Japanese, and can be linked to worship of the divine figure like Kannon, the Buddhist god/goddess of mercy, who has been compared to the Virgin Mary.
16 Later, a woman told me about an experience she had when doing Naikan for the third time. Upon sitting down behind the screen on the first day, she felt so relaxed, warm and happy that she could return to that space that she began to cry. When I told her of the 'womb environment' idea, she thought it described her situation well.

6 The social organization of Naikan

1 See Murase (1981a: 11).
2 See Takemoto (1990: 27).
3 See Ritter (1989: 62).
4 See Oh (1996: 6).
5 I was recently informed that Yoshimoto's Naikan centre now has a new resident practitioner, Dr Maeshiro, who is also a psychiatrist. As I have not had time to visit yet, I do not know whether this centre is attracting more clients since the arrival of Dr Maeshiro.
6 Statistics from 1960 to 1984 come from Yoshimoto (1997: 198). Statistics from 1985 to 1997 were compiled by myself at Yoshimoto's Naikan centre in Nara.
7 Statistics compiled by myself at the Yoshimoto's Naikan centre in Nara.

References

Amstutz, G. (1997) *Interpreting Amida: History and Orientalism in the Study of Pure Land Buddhism*, Albany, NY: State University of New York Press.

Ando, O. (1995) *Meisō no Seishin Igaku: Toransu Pāsonaru Seishin Igaku Josetsu* [*Psychiatry of Meditation: An Introduction of the Transpersonal Psychiatry*], Tokyo: Shunjūsha.

Andreasen, E. (1998) *Popular Buddhism in Japan*, Richmond, Surrey: Japan Library.

Asad, T. (1983) 'Notes on body pain and truth in medieval Christian ritual', *Economy and Society*, 12(3): 237–327.

Asahi Shinbun (1994) 'Naikan wo tsūjite jinsei mitsumenaosu: gankanja raga chūmoku' ['Looking again at oneself through Naikan: attention by cancer patients'], *Asahi Shinbun*, 14 February.

Bachnik, J. (1992) '*Kejime:* defining a shifting self in multiple organizational modes', in N. Rosenberger (ed.), *Japanese Sense of Self*, Cambridge: Cambridge University Press, pp. 105–20.

Barclay, C.R. (1996) 'Autobiographical remembering: narrative constructions on objectified selves', in D.C. Rubin (ed.), *Remembering Our Past: Studies in Autobiographical Memory*, Cambridge: Cambridge University Press, pp. 94–125.

Bartlett, F.C. (1932) *Remembering*, Cambridge: Cambridge University Press.

Ben-Ari, E. (1990) 'Many voices, partial worlds: on some conventions and innovations in the ethnographic portrayal of Japan', in E. Ben-Ari, B. Moeran and J. Valentine (eds), *Unwrapping Japan*, Manchester: Manchester University Press.

Benedict, R. (1989 [1946]) *The Chrysanthemum and the Sword: Patterns of Japanese Culture*, Boston, MA: Houghton Mifflin.

Benson, H. (1975) *Relaxation Response*, New York: Morrow.

Berger, P. (1967) *The Sacred Canopy*, New York: Doubleday.

Berger, P., Berger, B. and Kellner, H. (1973) *The Homeless Mind: Modernization and Consciousness*, New York: Random House.

Berzin, A. (1997) 'An introduction to Mahamudra and its practical application to life', in T. Gyatso [H.H. the XIV Dalai Lama] and A. Berzin, *The Gelug/Kagyu Tradition of Mahamudra*, Ithaca, NY: Snow Lion Publications, pp. 19–93.

Bloom, A. (1965) *Shinran's Gospel of Pure Grace*, Tucson, AZ: The University of Arizona Press.

Bossy, J. (1985) *Christianity in the West, 1400–1700*, Oxford: Oxford University Press.

Breuer, J. and Freud, S. (1957) *Studies on Hysteria*, J. Strachey (trans./ed.), New York: Basic Books.

Bruner, J. and Feldman, C.F. (1996) 'Group, narrative as a cultural context of autobiography', in D.C. Rubin (ed.), *Remembering Our Past: Studies in Autobiographical Memory*, Cambridge: Cambridge University Press, pp. 291–317.

Buruma, I. (1995) *A Japanese Mirror: Heroes and Villains of Japanese Culture*, London: Vintage.

Butler, T. (1989) 'Memory: a mixed blessing', in T. Butler (ed.), *Memory: History, Culture and the Mind*, Oxford: Basil Blackwell.

Cohen, A. (1994) *Self Consciousness: An Alternative Anthropology of Identity*, London: Routledge.

Connerton, P. (1995) *How Societies Remember*, Cambridge: Cambridge University Press.

Craib, I. (1994) *The Importance of Disappointment*, London: Routledge.

Crapanzano, V. (1973) *The Hamadsha: A Study in Moroccan Ethnopsychiatry*, London: University of California Press.

Csordas, T.J. (1994) *The Sacred Self: A Cultural Phenomenology of Charismatic Healing*, Berkeley, CA: University of California Press.

Dale, P.N. (1991) *The Myth of Japanese Uniqueness*, New York: Palgrave Macmillan.

Davidson, D. (1979) 'What metaphors mean', in S. Sacks (ed.), *On Metaphor*, Chicago, IL: University of Chicago Press.

DeVos, G. (1960) 'The relation of guilt toward parents to achievement and arranged marriage among the Japanese', *Psychiatry*, 23: 298–301.

DeVos, G. (1980) 'Afterword', in D.K. Reynolds, *The Quiet Therapies: Japanese Pathways to Personal Growth*, Honolulu, HI: University of Hawaii Press, pp. 113–32.

Dobbins, J.C. (1989) *Jōdo Shinshū: Shin Buddhism in Medieval Japan*, Bloomington, IN: Indiana University Press.

Doi, T. (1981) *The Anatomy of Dependence*, Tokyo: Kodansha International.

Douglas, M. (1973) *Natural Symbols: Explorations in Cosmology*, Middlesex: Penguin Books.

Encyclopedia of Eastern Philosophy and Religion: Buddhism, Taoism, Zen, Hinduism (1989) Boston, MA: Shambhala.

Fitzgerald, J. (1996) 'Intersecting meanings of reminiscence in adult development and aging', in D.C. Rubin (ed.), *Remembering Our Past: Studies in Autobiographical Memory*, Cambridge: Cambridge University Press, pp. 360–83.

Fivush, R., Haden, C. and Reese, E. (1996) 'Remembering, recounting, and reminiscing: the development of autobiographical memory in social context', in D.C. Rubin (ed.), *Remembering Our Past: Studies in Autobiographical Memory*, Cambridge: Cambridge University Press, pp. 341–59.

Foucault, M. (1967) *Madness and Civilization*, London: Routledge.

Foucault, M. (1976) *The Birth of the Clinic*, London: Routledge.

Foucault, M. (1991) *Discipline and Punish: The Birth of the Prison*, London: Penguin Books.

Freeman, M. (1993) *Rewriting the Self: History, Memory, Narrative*, London: Routledge.

Geertz, C. (1975) 'On the nature of anthropological understanding', *American Scientist*, 63: 47–53.

Gehen, A. (1980) *Man in the Age of Technology*, New York: Columbia University Press.

Goleman, D. (2003) *Destructive Emotions. How Can We Overcome Them?*, New York: Bantam Books.

Good, B.J. (1995) *Medicine, Rationality, and Experience: An Anthropological Perspective*, Cambridge: Cambridge University Press.

Haga, M. and Kisala, R.J. (1995) 'Editors' introduction: the new age in Japan', *Japanese Journal of Religious Studies*, 22: 3–4.

Hardacre, H. (1986) *Kurozumikyō and the New Religions of Japan*, Princeton, NJ: Princeton University Press.

Hasegawa, Y. *et al.* (1991) *Morita Riron de Jiko Hakken* [*Discovering Oneself through Morita Therapy*], Tokyo: Hakuyōsha.

Hayman, C.A.G., MacDonald, C.A. and Tulving, E. (1993) 'The role of repetition and associative interference in new semantic learning in amnesia', *Journal of Cognitive Neuroscience*, 5: 375–89.

Heelas, P. (1996) *The New Age Movement: The Celebration of the Self and the Sacraliation of Modernity*, Oxford: Blackwell.

Heelas, P. and Lock, A. (eds) (1981) *Indigenous Psychologies: The Anthropology of the Self*, London: Academic Press.

Hirst, W. and Manier, D. (1996) 'Remembering as communication: a family recounts its past', in D.C. Rubin (ed.), *Remembering Our Past: Studies in Autobiographical Memory*, Cambridge: Cambridge University Press, pp. 271–90.

Horii, S. (1982) 'Seishin igaku no taciba kara' [From a psychiatric perspective], *Nihon Naikan Gakkai Taikai Ronbunshū* [*Collected Papers of the Japan Naikan Association*], 5: 17–19.

Ichikawa, H. (1991) *Seishin toshite no Shintai* [*The Body as Spirit*], Tokyo: Keisou Shobō.

Ide, N. (1999) 'Syūkyō teki shōchō to shiteno kagami no imi ni tsuite' ['On the meaning of the mirror as a religious symbol'], *Shūkyō Kenkyū* [*Journal of Religious Studies*], 72(4): 76–7.

Igarashi, K. (1978) 'Naikan sokushin shinka eizoku no kufū' ['How to develop and stabilize Naikan'], *Nihon Naikan Gakkai Taikai Ronbunshū* [*Collected Papers of the Japan Naikan Association*], 1: 73–7.

Igarashi, K. (1991) 'Naikan dōnyū no kufū to shinka sokushin' ['Devices for the introduction of Naikan and the promotion of deep Naikan'], *Nihon Naikan Gakkai Taikai Ronbunshū* [*Collected Papers of the Japan Naikan Association*], 14: 66–7.

Ikemi, Y. (1963) *Shinryō Naika* [*A Psychological Treatment of Internal Medicine*], Tokyo: Chūkō Shinsho.

Ikemi, Y. (1973) *Zoku Shinryō Naika* [*A Psychological Treatment of Internal Medicine, II*], Tokyo: Chūkō Shinsho.

Ikuta, K. (1992) *Waza kara Shiru* [*Learning from Performance*], Tokyo: Tokyo Daigaku Shuppansha.

Inoue, K. (1977) 'Shindekoi no Gasshōen shu: Mizuno Shūhō sensei' ['People at Gasshōen Temple who are asked to 'die': Shūhō Mizuno'], *Daihōrin*, April.

Ishida, R. (1984) 'Naikan Bunseki Rhōhō' ['Naikan analysis therapy'], *Gendai no Esupuri: Meisō no Seishin Rhōhō* [*Esprit of the Present: Meditational Psychotherapies*], 202: 112–25.

Ishii, A. (1979) 'Naikan-hō no PR' [Naikan PR], *Nihon Naikan Gakkai Taikai Ronbunshū* [*Collected Papers of the Japan Naikan Association*], 3: 27–8.

Ishii, A. (1989) 'Asia Shinri Ryōhō-sha Kaigi ni Shusseki shite' ['Attending the 7th Biennial Conference – Workshop of Association of Psychological and Educational Counsellors of Asia'], *Naikan News*, 5: 2–3.

Ishii, A. (1999) *Isshūkan de Jiko Kaikaku: Naikan-hō no kyōi* [*Self-Revolution in a Week: The Miracle of Naikan*], Tokyo: Kōdansha Sophia Book.

Iwai, H. (1986) *Morita Ryōhō* [*Morita Therapy*], Tokyo: Kōdan-sha Gendai Shinsho.

Iwamoto, N. (1991) 'Naikanhō niokeru Shokikensakunenrei ni tsuite' [The Naikan Method of examining one's life from an early age], *Naikan News*, 10: 5.

Jackson, M. (1983) 'Knowledge of the body', *Man, n.s.*, 18: 327–45.

James, W. (1999) *The Varieties of Religious Experience*, New York: The Modern Library.

Kabat-Zinn, J. (1990) *Full Catastrophe Living*, New York: Deltra Trade Paperbacks.

Kain, J. (2004) 'The beautiful trap', *Tricycle*, 8(3): 58–61, 116–17.

Kapferer, B. (1983) *Celebration of Demons: Exorcism and the Aesthetics of Healing in Sri Lanka*, Bloomington, IN: Indiana University Press.

Kawahara, R. (1996) *Naikanryōhō* [*Naikan Therapy*], Tokyo: Shinkouigaku-shuppan.

Kawai, H. (1975) *Boseishakai Nihon no Byōri* [*The Sickness of Japanese Maternal Society*], Tokyo: Chūō Kōdansha.

Kikuike, K. (1991) 'Naikan Heiyō Zesshoku Ryōhō ni okeru Naikan no Hataraki ni tsuite', [How Naikan functions when accompanied by fasting], *Nihon Naikan Gakkai Taikai Ronbunshū* [*Collected Papers of the Japan Naikan Association*], 14: 125–8.

Kitami, K. (1981) 'Yumebunseki kara mita Naikankatei ni tsuiteno Ichikōsatsu (1)' ['One consideration of Naikan from the perspective of dream analysis (1)'], *Nihon Naikan Gakkai Taikai Ronbunshū* [*Collected Papers of the Japan Naikan Association*], 4: 60–1.

Kitami, K. (1983) 'Yumebunseki kara mita Naikankatei ni tsuiteno Ichikōsatsu (2)' ['One consideration of Naikan from the perspective of dream analysis (2)'], *Nihon Naikan Gakkai Taikai Ronbunshū* [*Collected Papers of the Japan Naikan Association*], 6: 62–4.

Kitamura, I. (1998) *Kokoro to seimei ga yomigaeru: Naikan ryōhō to kanpō* [*Bringing the Mind and Life Back to Life: Naikan Therapy and Chinese Medicine*], Tokyo: Sōgensha.

Kleinman, A. (1986) *Social Origins of Distress and Disease: Depression, Neurathenia and Pain in Modern China*, New Haven, CT: Yale University Press.

Kleinman, A. (1988) *The Illness Narratives: Suffering, Healing and the Human Condition*, New York: Basic Books.

Kleinman, A. (1991) *Rethinking Psychiatry: From Cultural Category to Personal Experience*, New York: The Free Press.

Kleinman, A. and Good, B. (1985) *Culture and Depression: Studies in the Anthropology and Cross-Cultural Psychiatry of Affect and Disorder*, Berkeley, CA: University of California Press.

Kondo, D. (1989) *Crafting Selves*, Chicago, IL: University of Chicago Press.

Kondo, R. (1992) 'Multiple selves: the aesthetics and politics of artisanal identities', in N. Rosenberger (ed.), *Japanese Sense of Self*, Cambridge: Cambridge University Press, pp. 40–66.

Kōra, T. (2000) *Morita Rhōhō no Susume* [*On Morita Therapy*], Tokyo: Hakuyōsha.

Kratz, C. (1991) 'Amusement and absolution: transforming narratives during confession of social debts', *American Anthropologist*, 93(4): 826–51.

Kübler-Ross, E. (1982) *Living with Death and Dying*, London: Souvenir Press.

Kübler-Ross, E. (1983) *On Children and Death*, New York: Macmillan.

Kübler-Ross, E. (1986) *Death: The Final Stage of Growth*, New York: Simon & Schuster.

Kübler-Ross, E. (1989) *On Death and Dying*, London: Routledge.

Kübler-Ross, E. (1997) *Death is of Vital Importance* (1995), translated by A. Suzuki, *Shinu Shunkan to Rinshi Taiken*, Tokyo: Yomiuri Shinbynsha.

Kulananda (1997) *Western Buddhism*, London: Thorsons.

Kusunoki, S. (1979) 'Naikan hō no Gihō ni tsuite Kangaeru' ['Thinking about the Naikan Method'], *Nihon Naikai Gakkai Taikai Ronbunshū*, 3: 23–4.

Kusunoki, S. (1987) 'Naikan Kenkyū Jūnen wo furikaeru' ['Looking back on the last ten years' study on Naikan'], *Naikan News*, 2: 3–4.

Kusunoki, S. (1997) 'Naikan-hō no Ōyo' ['Application of Naikan method'], *Nihon Naikan Gakkai Taikai Ronbunshū* [*Collected Papers of the Japan Naikan Association*], 20: 6–11.

LaFleur, W. (1992) *Liquid Life: Abortion and Buddhism in Japan*, Princeton, NJ: Princeton University Press.

Lakoff, G. and Johnson, M. (1980) *Metaphors We Live By*, Chicago, IL: University of Chicago Press.

Lakoff, G. and Johnson, M. (1999) *Philosophy in the Flesh*, New York: Basic Books.

Lebra, T.S. (1982) *Japanese Patterns of Behavior*, Honolulu, HI: University of Hawaii Press.

Lebra, T.S. (1992) 'Self in Japanese culture', in N. Rosenberger (ed.), *Japanese Sense of Self*, Cambridge: Cambridge University Press, pp. 105–20.

Linde, C. (1993) *Life Stories: The Creation of Coherence I*, Oxford: Oxford University Press.

Littlewood, R. (1980) 'Anthropology and psychiatry – an alternative approach', *British Journal of Medical Psychiatry*, 53: 213–25.

Littlewood, R. and Dein, S. (1995) 'The effectiveness of words: religion and healing among the Lubavitch of Stamford Hill', *Culture, Medicine and Psychiatry*, 19(3): 339–69.

Littlewood, R. and Lipsedge, M. (1997) *Aliens and Alienists: Ethnic Minorities and Psychiatry*, 3rd edn, Middlesex: Penguin Books.

Lock, M. (1980) *East Asian Medicine in Urban Japan*, Berkeley, CA: University of California Press.

Lock, M. (2001) *Twice Dead*, Berkeley, CA: University of California Press.

Loftus, E.F. (1997) 'Creating false memories', *Scientific American*, 277(September): 70–5.

Lowenthal, D. (1997) *The Past is a Foreign Country*, Cambridge: Cambridge University Press.

Luckmann, T. (1967) *The Invisible Religion: The Problem of Religion*, New York: The Macmillan Company.

Maclaine, S. (1986) *Out on a Limb*, New York: Bantam.

Markus, H.R. and Kitayama, S. (1991) 'Culture and the self: implications for cognition, emotion and motivation', *Psychological Review*, 98: 224–53.

Merleau-Ponty, M. (1964) 'Eye and mind', in J.M. Edie (ed.), *The Primacy of Perception and Other Essays*, Evanston, IL: Northewestern University Press.

Merleau-Ponty, M. (1978) *Phenomenology of Perception*, London: Routledge & Kegan Paul.

Miki, Y. (1993) 'Nangogu ni Hanahiraku Naikan' ['Naikan blooming in the Southern Country'], *Naikan News*, 14: 3.

Miki, Y. (1997) 'Nara Naikan Kenshusho ni okeru Saikin 5 nenkan no Tōkeiteki Kenkyu' ['Statistical research at Nara Naikan Centre for the last five years'], *Nihon Naikan Gakkai Taikai Ronbunshū* [*Collected Papers of the Japan Naikan Association*], 20: 112–13.

Miki, Y. and Kuroki, K. (eds) (1998) *Nihon no Shinriryōhō* [*Japanese Psychotherapies*], Osaka: Tokishobō.

Miki, Y. and Miki, J. (1998) *Naikan Work: kokoro no fuan wo iyashite shiawase ni naru* [*Naikan Work: Becoming Happy by Healing the Mind's Anxiety*], Tokyo: Futami Shobō.

Miyazaki, T. (1989) 'Naikan ni tsuiteno Oboegaki' ['A memo on Naikan'], *Naikan News*, 5: 2–3.

Miyazaki, T. (1992) 'Naikan no Genpō towa nanika' ['What is the Naikan Original Method?'], *Naikan News*, 12: 6–7.

Moran, R. (1997) 'Metaphor', in B. Hale and C. Wright (eds), *A Companion to the Philosophy of Language*, Oxford: Blackwell, pp. 248–68.

Morris, B. (1994) *Anthropology of the Self: The Individual in Cultural Perspective*, London: Pluto Press.

Motoyama, Y. (1990) 'Naikan Genpō to sono Ohyō nitsuite' [The original Naikan Method and its application], *Naikan News*, 8: 5.

Motoyama, Y. (2000) 'Reiteki to iukoto' ['Being spiritual'], *Yasuragi*, 59: 4–7.

Murase, K. (1999) 'Tougōsei wo motometeno Tabi' ['A journey for searching unity'], *The Japanese Journal of Naikan Association*, 5(1): 11–18.

Murase, T. (1981a) 'Naikan-hō ni okeru Kaizenkisei' ['Regulation of Naikan method'], *Nihon Naikan Gakkai Taikai Ronbunshū* [*Collected Papers of the Japan Naikan Association*], 4: 11–20.

Murase, T. (1981b) 'Tsumi Ishiki to Naikan-ryōhou' ['Guilt consciousness and Naikan therapy'], in T. Takemoto (ed.), *Gendai no Esupuri: Meisou no Seishin Rhōhō* [*Meditational Psychotherapy: Naikan Method's Theory and Practice*], 202: 22–34.

Murase, T. (1982) 'Sunao: a central value in Japanese psychotherapy', in A.J. Marsella and G.M. White (eds), *Cultural Conceptions of Mental Health and Therapy*, Dordrecht: D. Reidel, pp. 317–29.

Murase, T. (1996) *Naikan Riron to Bunka Kanreisei* [*Naikan Theory and its Relation to Culture*], Tokyo: Seishin Shobo.

Murata, T. (1991) 'Naikan: Jibun-shi no Ginmi, Deai to Kaishin' ['Naikan: a close examination of self-history, an encounter and enlightenment'], *Nihon Naikan Gakkai Taikai Ronbunshū* [*Collected Papers of the Japan Naikan Association*], 14: 3–5.

Murphy, R.F. (1987) *The Body Silent*, London: Phoenix House.

Nagashima, M. (1991) 'Genpo kara mita Henpō' ['Variation from the viewpoint of the original method'], *Nihon Naikan Gakkai Taikai Ronbunshū* [*Collected Papers of the Japan Naikan Association*], 14: 72–75.

Nagashima, M. (1993) 'Atama no sagaru koto' ['Things that make your head go down'], *Nihon Naikan Gakkai Taikai Ronbunshū* [*Collected Papers of the Japan Naikan Association*], 16: 135–37.

Nagashima, M. (2000) 'Naikan no Jidai' ['The era of Naikan'], *Yasuragi*, 59: 2–3.

Nagayama, K. (1998) 'Naikan Ryōhou ni okeru Byōbu no Imi: Morita Rhōhōto Seishin Bunseki no Riron to Rinshō kara' ['The meaning of the screen in Naikan therapy: from the perspectives of Morita therapy, psychoanalysis and clinical practice'], *Nihon Naikan Gakkai Taikai Ronbunshū* [*Collected Papers of the Japan Naikan Association*], 21: 90–1.

Naikan Kenshūsho (1980) *Naikan 25nen no Ayumi* [*Twenty-five Years of Naikan Steps*], Nara: Naikan Kenshūsho.

Namihira, E. (1993) *Yamai to Shi no Bunka: Gendai Iryo no Jinruigaku* [*Sickness, Death and Culture: Anthropology of Contemporary Medicine*], Tokyo: Asahi Sensho.

Nelson, E. (1989) *The British Counter-Culture*, Basingstoke: Macmillan.

Obitsu, R. and Tsumura, T. (1996) *Tamashii ga iyasarerutoki: kikō, holistic igaku, gan chiryō wo meguru taiwa* [*When the Soul is Healed: A Dialogue on Mind, Holistic Medicine and Cancer Treatment*], Tokyo: Sōgensha.

Oda, A. (1992) 'Shūkyō to Seishin-ryōho' ['Religion and psychotherapy'], *Naikan News*, 12: 1.

Oh, S. (1996) 'Chūgoku Seishinka Rinshō ni okeru Naikan Ryōho no kokoromi' ['Trying Naikan therapy in Chinese clinical psychology'], *Naikan News*, 19: 6.

Ohara, Kenshiro (1997) *Aruga mama ni Ikiru* [*Living as it is*]. Tokyo: Kōdansha Plus Alpha Shinsho.

Ohnuki-Tierney, E. (1984) *Illness and Culture in Contemporary Japan*, Cambridge: Cambridge University Press.

Ohnuki-Tierney, E. (1994) 'Brain death and organ transportation', *Current Anthropology*, 35(3): 233–42.

Ohta, K. (1991) 'Naikan Ryōhō no Sohkoukijo' ['Effective technique in Naikan therapy'], *Nihon Naikan Gakkai Taikai Ronbunshū* [*Collected Papers of the Japan Naikan Association*], 14: 21–38.

Okonogi, Keigo (1982) *Nihonjin no Ajase Konpurekkusu* [*Japanese Ajase Complex*], Tokyo: Chūō Kōron-sha.

Okonogi, Keigo (1991) *Edipusu to Ajase* [*Oedipus and Ajase*], Tokyo: Seido-sha.

Okonogi, Keigo (2001) *Ajase Conpurekkusu* [*Ajase Complex*], Tokyo: Sōgen-sha.

Okumura, N., Sato, K. and Yamamoto, H. (eds) (1972) *Naikan Ryōhō* [*Naikan Therapy*], Tokyo: Igaku Shoin.

Oxford English Dictionary (1961) London: Oxford University Press.

Ozawa-de Silva, C. (2002) 'Beyond the body/mind? Japanese contemporary thinkers on alternative sociologies of the body', *Body & Society*, 8(2): 21–38.

Pendergrast, M. (1996) *Victims of Memory: Incest Accusations and Shattered Lives, The Courage to Heal*, Hinesburg, VT: Upper Access.

Petitt, J.W. (1999) *Mipham's Beacon of Certainty. Illuminating the View of Dzogchen The Great Perfection*, Boston, MA: Wisdom Publications.

Plato (1997) *Complete Works*, J. Cooper (ed.), Indianapolis: Hackett.

Plummer, K. (1995) *Telling Sexual Stories: Power, Change and Social Worlds*, London: Routledge.

Reynolds, D. (1976) *Morita Psychotherapy*, Berkeley, CA: University of California Press.

Reynolds, D. (1979) 'Naikan ni tsuiteno Hikaku Chōsa' ['A comparative examination on Naikan'], *Nihon Naikan Gakkai Taikai Ronbunshū* [*Collected Papers of the Japan Naikan Association*], 2: 6–8.

Reynolds, D. (1980) *The Quiet Therapies: Japanese Pathways to Personal Growth*, Honolulu, HI: University of Hawaii Press.

Reynolds, D. (1983) *Naikan Psychotherapy: Meditation for Self-Development*, Chicago, IL: University of Chicago Press.

Reynolds, D. (1984) *Constructive Living*, Honolulu, HI: University of Hawaii.

Reynolds, D. (1989) *Flowing Bridges, Quiet Waters. Japanese Psychotherapies, Morita and Naikan*, New York: State University of New York Press.

Ritter, F. (1986) 'Europe ni okeru Naikan no Tenkai' ['The development of Naikan in Europe'], *Nihon Naikan Gakkai Taikai Ronbunshū* [*Collected Papers of the Japan Naikan Association*], 9: 9–14.

Ritter, F. (1989) 'Europe no Naikan' ['Naikan in Europe'], *Nihon Naikan Gakkai Taikai Ronbunshū* [*Collected Papers of the Japan Naikan Association*], 12: 62–72.

Robinson, J.A. (1996) 'Perspective, meaning, and remembering', in D.C. Rubim (ed.), *Remembering Our Past: Studies in Autobiographical Memory*, Cambridge: Cambridge University Press, pp. 199–217.

Roland, R. (1991) *In Search of Self in India and Japan: Toward a Cross-Cultural Psychology*, Princeton, NJ: Princeton University Press.

Rosenberger, N. (ed.) (1992a) *Japanese Sense of Self*, Cambridge: Cambridge University Press.

Rosenberger, N. (1992b) 'Introduction', in N. Rosenberger (ed.), *Japanese Sense of Self*, Cambridge: Cambridge University Press, pp. 1–20.

Rosenberger, N. (1992c) 'Tree in summer, tree in winter: movement of self in Japan', in N. Rosenberger (ed.), *Japanese Sense of Self*, Cambridge: Cambridge University Press, pp. 67–92.

Ross, B.M. (1991) *Remembering the Personal Past: Descriptions of Autobiographical Memory*, Oxford: Oxford University Press.

Ross, M. and Wilson, A.E. (2000) 'Constructing and appraising past selves', in D. Schacter and E. Scarry (eds), *Memory, Brain, and Belief*, Cambridge, MA: Harvard University Press, pp. 231–58.

Rubin, D.C. (ed.) (1986) *Autobiographical Memory*, Cambridge: Cambridge University Press.

Rubin, D.C. (ed.) (1996a) *Remembering Our Past: Studies in Autobiographical Memory*, Cambridge: Cambridge University Press.

Rubin, D.C. (1996b) 'Introduction', in D.C. Rubin, *Remembering Our Past*, Cambridge: Cambridge University Press, pp. 1–15.

Sansom, B. (1982) 'The sick who do not speak', in D. Parkin (ed.), *Semantic Anthropology*, London: Academic Press.

Sartre, J.-P. (1964) *Being and Nothingness*, New York: Citadel Press.

Sato, K. (ed.) (1972) *Zen-teki Ryōhō: Naikan-hō* [*Zen-like Therapy: Naikan Method*], Tokyo: Bunkōdō.

Sato, K. (1973) 'Reisei no Kaihatsu to shite no Naikan' ['Naikan as spiritual development'], in K. Sato (ed.), *Naikan-ryōhō* [*Naikan Therapy*], Tokyo: Igakushobō, pp. 2–3.

Schacter, D. (ed.) (1997a) *Memory Distortion: How Minds, Brain, and Societies Reconstruct the Past*, Cambridge, MA: Harvard University Press.

Schacter, D. (1997b) 'Memory distortion: history and current status', in D. Schacter (ed.), *Memory Distortion: How Minds, Brain, and Societies Reconstruct the Past*, Cambridge, MA: Harvard University Press, pp. 1–43.

Schacter, D. and Scarry, E. (eds) (2000) *Memory, Brain, and Belief*, Cambridge, MA: Harvard University Press.

Schudson, M. (1997) 'Dynamics of distortion in collective memory', in D. Schacter (ed.), *Memory Distortion: How Minds, Brain, and Societies Reconstruct the Past*, Cambridge, MA: Harvard University Press, pp. 346–64.

Searle, J. (1969) *Speech Acts*, Cambridge: Cambridge University Press.

Searle, J. (1979) *Expression and Meaning*, Cambridge: Cambridge University Press.

Seki, H. (1998) 'Preface to the first edition', in D.T. Suzuki, *Buddha of Infinite Light*, Boston: Shambhala, pp. 9–10.

Shimazono, S. (1995a) 'Introduction', in S. Araya, S. Tanabe, S. Shimazono and T. Yumiyama (eds), *Iyashi to Wakai: Genndai ni okeru Care no Shosō* [*Healing and Reconciliation: Some Aspects of the Care System in the Present Age*], Tokyo: Hābesutosha, pp. 1–14.

Shimazono, S. (1995b) 'Sukui kara Iyashi he' ['From salvation to healing'], in S. Araya, S. Tanabe, S. Shimazono and T. Yumiyama (eds), *Iyashi to Wakai: Genndai ni okeru Care no Shosō* [*Healing and Reconciliation: Some Aspects of the Care System in the Present Age*], Tokyo: Hābesutosha, pp. 263–82.

Shimazono, S. (1996) *Seishin Sekai no Yukue* [*The Direction of the Spiritual World*], Tokyo: Tokyodō Shuppan.

Sone, M. (1989) 'Yoshimoto Ishin Sensei' [Yoshimoto Ishin Teacher], in Nihon Naikan Gakkai (ed.), *Naikan Itosuji: Yoshimoto Ishin no Shōgai* [*Devoted to Naikan: The Life of Yoshimoto Ishin*], Kagoshima: Nihon Naikan Gakkai, pp. 91–110.

Sontag, S. (1977) *Illness as Metaphor*, New York: Farrar, Straus and Giroux.

Sontag, S. (1989) *AIDS and Its Metaphors*, New York: Farrar, Straus and Giroux.

Soya, M. (1989) 'Yoshimoto Ishin Sensei', in Nihon Naikan Gakkai (ed.), *Yoshimoto Ishin no Shōgai* [*The Life of Yoshimoto Ishin*], Tokyo: Nihon Naikan Gakkai, pp. 100–1.

Sugita, K. (1994) 'Naikan-hō ni okeru Yōgo no Saikentō' ['Reconsidering terms in the Naikan method'], *Nihon Naikan Gakkai Taikai Ronbunshū* [*Collected Papers of the Japan Naikan Association*], 17: 82–5.

Suzuki, D.T. (1998) *Buddha of Infinite Light*, Boston, MA: Shambhala Publications.

Synnott, A. (1993) *The Body Social: Symbolism, Self and Society*, London: Routledge.

Takemoto, T. (1978) 'Naikan to Igaku' ['Naikan and medicine'] in I. Yoshimoto (ed.), *Naikan to Seishi Eisei* [*Naikan and Mental Health*], Nara: Naikan Ken-shūsho.

Takemoto, T. (1981a) 'Byōin ni okeru Naikan' ['Naikan at the hospital'], *Nihon Naikan Gakkai Taikai Ronbunshū* [*Collected Papers of the Japan Naikan Association*], 4: 3–10.

Takemoto, T. (1981b) 'Naikan Ryōhou no Arukōru shō ni taisuru Chiyukisei ni kansuru Kōsatsu' ['A study of Naikan therapy for alcoholism'], *Nihon Naikan Gakkai Taikai Ronbunshū* [*Collected Papers of the Japan Naikan Association*], 4: 13–15.

Takemoto, T. (ed.) (1984a) *Gendai no Esupuri: Meisou no Seishinryohou: Naikan-ryohou no Riron to Jissai* [*Meditational Psychotherapy: The Naikan Method's Theory and Practice*], 202.

Takemoto, T. (1984b) 'Arukōru Kanja ni taisuru Naikan Ryōhou no Yūkōsei' ['The efficacy of Naikan for treating alcoholism'], in *Gendai no Esupuri: Meisou no Seishinryohou: Naikanryohou no Riron to Jissai* [*Meditational Psychotherapy: The Naikan Method's Theory and Practice*], 202: 75–85.

Takemoto, T. (1987) 'Naikan Gakkai 10 nen no Ayumi to Kongo no Kadai' ['The steps of the Naikan Association over the last ten years and subjects for the future'], *Nihon Naikan Gakkai Taikai Ronbunshū* [*Collected Papers of the Japan Naikan Association*], 10: 23–6.

Takemoto, T. (1989) 'Naikan-hō no Naritachi' ['The development of the Naikan method'], *Nihon Naikan Gakkai Taikai Ronbunshū* [*Collected Papers of the Japan Naikan Association*], 12: 32–4.

Takemoto, T. (1990) 'Naikan Ryōhō ni Riron ha hitsuyōka: Seishinkai no tachiba kara' ['Are theories necessary for Naikan therapy? From the standpoint of a psychiatrist'], *Nihon Naikan Gakkai Taikai Ronbunshū* [*Collected Papers of the Japan Naikan Association*], 13: 26–7.

Takemoto, T. (1991) 'Naikan: Saikin no Wadai' ['Naikan: recent topics'], *Naikan News*, 10: 1.

Takeuchi, T. (1997) 'Naikan towa nani ka' ['What is Naikan?'], in I. Yoshimoto, *Naikan hō* [*Naikan Method*], Tokyo: Shunjūsha, pp. 1–24.

Takino, I. (1978) 'France de Naikan-hō wo kokoromite' ['Trying Naikan in France'], *Nihon Naikan Gakkai Taikai Ronbunshū* [*Collected Papers of the Japan Naikan Association*], 1: 139–45.

Takino, I. (1979) 'Naikan Ryōhō to Seishinbunseki no Hōhōjō no Hikakukentou' ['A comparative examination of the methods of Naikan therapy and psychoanalysis'], *Nihon Naikan Gakkai Taikai Ronbunshū* [*Collected Papers of the Japan Naikan Association*], 2: 14–15.

Takino, I. (1980) 'Mo no Itonami to shiteno Naikan' ['Naikan as a mourning ritual'], *Nihon Naikan Gakkai Taikai Ronbunshū* [*Collected Papers of the Japan Naikan Association*], 3: 58–9.

Takino, I. (1981) 'Seishin Bunseki karamita Naikan-hō no kaizenkijo' ['The structural improvement which Naikan requires from the perspective of psychoanalysis'], *Nihon Naikan Gakkai Taikai Ronbunshū* [*Collected Papers of the Japan Naikan Association*], 4: 17–19.

Takino, I. (1994) 'Naikan Rhōhou to wa nanika? Ta no Shinri Rhōhou tono Taihi kara' ['What is Naikan therapy? A comparison with other psychotherapies'], *Teikyō Joshi Tanki Daigaku Kiyō* [*Teikyō Women's College Bulletin*], 14: 95–117.

Takuma, T. (1987) 'Doitsu Shinrigakkai ni Shusseki shite' ['Attending the German Conference of Psychology'], *Naikan News*, 2: 1.

Tonkin, E. (1992) *Narrating Our Pasts: The Social Construction of Oral History*, Cambridge: Cambridge University Press.

Toyama Shinbun (1994) 'Naikan Ryōhō: wakai Josei no Hōmon fueru' ['Naikan therapy: an increase in young women's attendance'], *Toyama Shinbun*, 23 June.

Tulving, E. and Lepage, M. (2000) 'Where in the brain is the awareness of one's past?', in D. Schacter (ed.), *Memory, Brain, and Belief*, Cambridge, MA: Harvard University Press, pp. 208–28.

Tulving, E., Schacter, D.L., McLachlan, D.R. and Moscovitch, M. (1988) 'Priming of semantic autobiographical knowledge: a case study of retrograde amnesia', *Brain and Cognition*, 8: 3–20.

Turner, B. (1992) *Regulating Bodies: Essays in Medical Sociology*, London: Routledge.

Turner, V. (1969) *The Ritual Process: Structure and Anti-Structure*, Chicago, IL: Aldine.

Ueda, N. (1990) *Suri Lanka no Akuma barai:imêjî to iyashi no cosumorogî* [*Image, Healing and Cosmology in Sri Lanka*], Tokyo: Tokuma Shoten.

Ueda, N. (1994) 'Imégi no Chiyuryoku: Chiryōgishiki to Shinsou no Nettowāku' ['The power of healing in the imagination: healing rituals and the network of the "deep strata"'] in E. Namihira (ed.), *Yamu koto no Bunka: Iryou Jinruigaku no Furontia* [*The Culture of Illness: The Frontier of the Medical Anthropology*], Tokyo: Kaimeisha.

Ueda, N. (1997) 'Iyashi' ['Healing'], in T. Aoki (ed.), *Iwanami Kōza Bunka Jinruigaku Vol. 11 Shūkyō no Gendai* [*Iwanami Lecture: Cultural Anthropology Vol.11: The Present Age of Religion*], Tokyo: Iwanami Shoten, pp. 209–34.

Ueda, Y. (ed.) (1979) *Notes on 'Essentials of Faith Alone': A Translation of Shinran's Yuishinshō-mon'i*, Shin Budhism Translation Series. Kyoto: Hongwanji International Centre.

Unno, T. (1998) 'Introduction', in D.T. Suzuki, *Buddha of Infinite Light*, Boston, MA: Shambhala, pp. 11–18.

Usami, S. (1978) 'Kyōiku no Tachiba kara' ['From an educational perspective'], *Nihon Naikan Gakkai Taikai Ronbunshū* [*Collected Papers of the Japan Naikan Association*], 1: 160–5.

Usami, S. (1980) 'Totsuzen Hiraketa Fushigi na Sekai' ['A mysterious world suddenly opened'], *Nihon Naikan Gakkai Taikai Ronbunshū* [*Collected Papers of the Japan Naikan Association*], 3: 82–4.

Van Gennep, A. (1960) *The Rites of Passage*, M.B. Vizedom and G.L. Caffee (trans.), London: Routledge and Kegan Paul.

Wakayama, H. (1982) 'Chiryōkōron kara no Sekkin' ['An approach from the theory of the efficacy of the treatment'], *Nihon Naikan Gakkai Taikai Ronbunshū* [*Collected Papers of the Japan Naikan Association*], 5: 21–4.

Williams, P. (1989) *Mahayana Buddhism*, New York: Routledge.

Yanagita, K. (1979) 'Watashi no Naikan Taiken' ['My Naikan experience'], *Nihon Naikan Gakkai Taikai Ronbunshū* [*Collected Papers of the Japan Naikan Association*], 2: 30–1.

Yanagita, K. (1980) 'Gedatsu no Kōzō to Naikan' ['The structure of emancipation and Naikan'], *Nihon Naikan Gakkai Taikai Ronbunshū* [*Collected Papers of the Japan Naikan Association*], 3: 71–73.

Yanagita, K. (1982) *Gusha no Naikan* [*A Fool's Naikan*], Tochigi: Meisō no Mori Naikan Kenkyūsho.

Yanagita, K. (1986) 'Kizuki no Taiken no Katei to Tokuchō' ['Characteristics of the process of experiencing realization'], *Nihon Naikan Gakkai Taikai Ronbunshū* [*Collected Papers of the Japan Naikan Association*], 9: 50–3.

Yanagita, K. (1997) *Ai no Shinryo Naikan: Yorokobi to Yasuragi no Sekai* [*Psychotherapy of Love: The World of Joy and Calmness*], Tokyo: Inahoshobō.

Yanagita, Kunio and Kawai, H. (1998) 'Tokubetsu Taidan: Shinu Shunkan to Shigo no Sekai' ['Special Discussion: The Moment of Death and the World after Death'], *Bungei Shunjyū 5gatsugō* [*Literary Chronicle*], May issue.

Yasuoka, H. (1991) 'Chiryokozo kara mita Genpo to Henpo' ['The original method and variations from the perspective of treatment structure'], *Nihon Naikan Gakkai Taikai Ronbunshū* [*Collected Papers of the Japan Naikan Association*], 14: 76–8.

Yasuragi (2000) Special issue, 59.

Yokoyama, S. (1978) 'Shūchū Naikan Taikengo no Yogo' ['The convalescence of intensive Naikan'], *Nihon Naikan Gakkai Taikai Ronbunshū* [*Collected Papers of the Japan Naikan Association*], 1: 105–9.

Yokoyama, S. and Nagashima, M. (1997) *Naikan: Kokoro wa gekiteki ni kaerareru* [*The Mind Can be Changed Dramatically*], Tokyo: Hōken.

York, M. (1995) *The Emerging Network: A Sociology of the New Age and Neo-Pagan Movements*, London: Rowman & Littlefield.

Yoshimoto, I. (1978a) *Naikan to Seishi eisei* [*Naikan and Psychological Health*], Nara: Naikan Kenshūsho.

Yoshimoto, I. (1978b) 'Naikan hō to Watashi' ['The Naikan Method and I'], *Nihon Naikan Gakkai Taikai Ronbunshū* [*Collected Papers of the Japan Naikan Association*], 1: 1–9.

Yoshimoto, I. (1981) *Naikan no Michi* [*The Way of Naikan*], Nara: Naikan Kenshūsho.

Yoshimoto, I. (1983) *Naikan eno Shotai* [*Invitation to Naikan*], Osaka: Toki Shobou.

Yoshimoto, I. (1985) *Shinzen Shingo: Watashi no Naikan Taiken* [*Before and After Faith: My Naikan Experience*], Nara: Naikan Kenshūsho.

Yoshimoto, I. (1997) *Naikan hō* [*Naikan Method*], Tokyo: Shunjūsha.

Yuasa, Y. (1987) *The Body: Toward an Eastern Mind–Body Theory*, New York: State University of New York Press.

Yuasa, Y. (1989) *Shūkyō Keiken to Shinsō Shinri: Jiga, Kokoro, Tamashii no Ekorogî* [*Religious Experience and Depth Psychology: The Ecology of Ego, Mind and Spirit*], Tokyo: Meicho Kankōkai.

Yuasa, Y. (1993) *The Body, Self-Cultivation, and Ki-Energy*, New York: State University of New York Press.

Yumiyama, T. (1995) 'Tenri kyō kara Honbushin he' ['From Tenri-kyō to Honbushin'], in S. Araya, S. Tanabe, S. Shimazono and T. Yumiyama (eds), *Iyashi to Wakai: Genndai ni okeru Care no Shosō* [*Healing and Reconciliation: Some Aspects of the Care System in the Present Age*], Tokyo: Hābesutosha, pp. 15–32.

Zopa Rinpoche, T. [Lama Zopa Rinpoche] (2001) *Ultimate Healing. The Power of Compassion*, Boston, MA: Wisdom Publications.

Index

Lightning Source UK Ltd.
Milton Keynes UK
UKOW06f0132290116

267295UK00010B/195/P